"This volume sheds indispensable light on the recent human security policy agenda in East Asia. It offers us a cutting-edge assessment of the conceptual debates and empirical cases that the region has experienced so far. On that basis, it provides us with a balanced and realistic framework that we need in overcoming the ongoing challenge we face: achieving policy collaboration among various stakeholders interested or involved in human security activities. This is a must read for academics and practitioners alike."
Dr. Tsuyoshi Kawasaki, Assistant Professor Department of Political Science, Simon Fraser University, Vancouver, Canada

"… a significant and indeed timely contribution to a better understanding of Human Security both in terms of providing different theoretical perspectives and practical findings. A must reading for anyone who cares deeply about how to advance effective cooperation on this issue."
Pranee Thiparat, Ph.D., Department of International Relations, Faculty of Political Science, Chulalongkorn University, Bangkok, Thailand

"… Human security has become a popular theme for students, scholars and – at least rhetorically – in some policy circles, but it has not yet found full acceptance within academic security studies. This collection of chapters – written by prominent academics in the field – takes the debate forward in new directions, applying the concept to new areas and new theoretical enquiries. It attempts – with some success – to resolve some of the remaining analytical conundrums found in the human security movement, and is well-written. It will be of interest to all those who seek to follow this fast moving debate."
Dr. Edward Newman, Senior Lecturer, Department of Political Science and International Studies, University of Birmingham

Human Security in East Asia

Since the end of the Cold War, the number of interstate wars has remained relatively low, although while states may be more secure than ever, this does not mean individual human beings are too. This has led to a growing recognition of the importance of human security, in contrast to the traditional realist focus on state security. This book explores human security in East Asia, focusing in particular on the challenges to collaboration among actors involved in the process of human security promotion. It examines the theoretical complexities of conceptual arguments about human security, drawing on the ideas of scholars from Asia and the West, to provide a global perspective on what causes human insecurity and how security can best be achieved. It considers in detail case studies of military interventions in East Asia, in particular East Timor (later called Timor-Leste), and assesses how successful collaborative efforts have been in providing human security. It also explores case studies of non-military intervention, including international criminal justice in Cambodia and Timor-Leste. It discusses the relationship of regional great powers such as China and Japan to human security promotion, arguing that it will be better served if these powers engage less in the traditional game of geopolitics, and if human security objectives do not work against actors' interests. It shows how interventions to uphold human security have not always succeeded to the extent that was hoped, despite the best of intentions, and considers how improved collaboration can be achieved, so that future interventions enjoy more consistent success.

Sorpong Peou is Professor of International Security and on the Graduate Programme in Global Studies, Sophia University, Tokyo, Japan. Security and democracy studies are his main areas of expertise. His most recent book is *International Democracy Assistance for Peacebuilding: Cambodia and Beyond* (2007).

Routledge Security in Asia Pacific Series
Series Editors
Leszek Buszynski, *International University of Japan,* and
William Tow, *Australian National University*

Security issues have become more prominent in the Asia Pacific region because of the presence of global players, rising great powers, and confident middle powers, which intersect in complicated ways. This series puts forward important new work on key security issues in the region. It embraces the roles of the major actors, their defense policies and postures and their security interaction over the key issues of the region. It includes coverage of the United States, China, Japan, Russia, the Koreas, as well as the middle powers of ASEAN and South Asia. It also covers issues relating to environmental and economic security as well as transnational actors and regional groupings.

Human Security in East Asia

Challenges for collaborative action

Edited by Sorpong Peou

Routledge
Taylor & Francis Group

LONDON AND NEW YORK

First published 2009
by Routledge
2 Park Square, Milton Park, Abingdon, Oxfordshire OX14 4RN

Simultaneously published in the USA and Canada
by Routledge
711 Third Avenue, New York, NY 10017

First issued in paperback 2014

Routledge is an imprint of the Taylor and Francis Group, an informa business

Typeset in Times New Roman by
Exeter Premedia Services Private Ltd.

British Library Cataloguing in Publication Data
A catalogue record for this book is available from the British Library

Library of Congress Cataloging in Publication Data
   Human security in East Asia : challenges for collaborative action/edited
by Sorpong Peou.
      p. cm. – (Routledge security in Asia Pacific series; 8)
   Includes bibliographical references and index.
1. National security–East Asia. 2. Peace-building–East Asia.
3. Regionalism–East Asia. 4. International cooperation. 5. Security,
International–Social aspects. 6. Quality of life–East Asia. I. Peou,
Sorpong.
UA832.5.H86 2008
355'.03305–dc22
2008018787

ISBN 978-0-415-46796-4 (hbk)
ISBN 978-0-415-54283-8 (pbk)
ISBN 978-0-203-88863-6 (ebk)

To my wife Chola

Contents

Acknowledgements

This volume would not have been possible without the partial financial support of the Japanese Ministry of Education 'Center of Excellence' grant to Sophia University's 'Area-Based Global Studies' (AGLOS) and the Institute of Comparative Culture (ICC) at Sophia University and the various types of contribution made by individuals. Professors Koichi Nakano of the Faculty of Liberal Arts and Okada Yoshitaka, Director of the ICC, offered us moral support. A number of participants in our workshops made helpful comments, including Professors David Wessels of Sophia University and Lam Peng Er of the National University of Singapore. We also would like to thank my students Masayasu Tsuzuki and Magdalena Ionescu for their research assistance and William Woods for helping me edit the final manuscript. We are also grateful to the Routledge series editors in Asian Security Studies and the reviewers' suggestions for improvement. Each one of us in this volume, however, takes full responsibility for any errors of fact or judgment that may still be evident in our work presented here.

Sorpong Peou
Graduate Program in Global Studies &
Faculty of Liberal Arts
Sophia University, Tokyo

List of contributors

Mely Caballero-Anthony is Associate Professor of International Relations at the S. Rajaratnam School of International Studies (RSIS), Nanyang Technological University, Singapore. She is also Coordinator of the School's Programme on Non-Traditional Security in Asia, and Secretary General of the newly established Consortium of Non-Traditional Security Studies in Asia at RSIS.

Paul Evans is the Co-CEO and Chairman of the Executive Committee of the Asia Pacific Foundation of Canada, on secondment from the University of British Columbia where he is cross-appointed as Professor at the Institute of Asian Research and the Liu Institute for Global Issues. A specialist on regional security issues on the Asia–Pacific region, he was the initial director in 2001 of the Canadian Consortium on Human Security.

Akiko Fukushima is Senior Fellow, The Japan Foundation. She is also adjunct Professor, Law School, Keio University. She also serves as a member of numerous committees, including the Defense Agency's Council on Defense Facilities.

Maiko Ichihara is a Doctoral Candidate, Department of Political Science, George Washington University (USA).

Sorpong Peou is Professor of International Security and on the Graduate Programme in Global Studies, Sophia University, Tokyo, Japan. Security and democracy studies are his main areas of expertise. His most recent book is *International Democracy Assistance for Peacebuilding: Cambodia and Beyond* (Palgrave Macmillan, 2007).

Oliver Richmond is Professor of International Relations, University of St Andrews, Scotland and Director, Centre for Peace and Conflict Studies, and is Series Editor of *Rethinking Peace and Conflict Studies* (Palgrave Macmillan). He is the author of several major publications on peace and security studies.

Simon Springer is a Doctoral Candidate in Geography at the University of British Columbia and a holder of the Canada Graduate Scholarship from the Social Sciences and Humanities Research Council of Canada.

Introduction

Collaborative action problems in human security

Sorpong Peou

This study investigates challenges to collaboration among actors in the field of human security. We focus on the reality that global efforts to promote this type of security have not always succeeded to the extent that we might have hoped. This introduction briefly considers a normative commitment to human security with some policy implications, justifies East Asia as a major region in the world in need of further investigation, defends the need for theoretical eclecticism, and sketches the volume's structure.

As a normative concept, human security remains highly contested, as is evidenced throughout this volume, but it seems to have staying power. First, the concept has an enduring legacy, which can be traced back to the classical era of ancient Greece,[1] whereas the concept of national security was formally adopted only after World War II. Ramesh Thakur points out that 'We tend to assume that the phrase "national security" has been around forever. In fact, it was only in 1945 that Secretary of Defense James Forrestal invoked the concept as a guiding principle of US foreign policy'.[2] Self-protection against endemic violence has always been part of human history.

Second, although it was eclipsed by the concept of collective defense as the international system began to evolve from the medieval to Westphalian eras, the ancient idea of human survival regained strength over time. The individual fear of death gave rise to the Hobbesian and Lockean concepts of a social contract requiring state (illiberal or liberal) protection of individuals by way of keeping anarchy at bay. MacFarlane and Khong note: 'What we now consider to be human security concerns grew significantly stronger in the nineteenth and early twentieth centuries, despite the primacy of the sovereignty state.' European norms, associated with human security, became universalized then. In their words, 'By the end of the nineteenth and early twentieth centuries, we see an unmistakable move toward the universalization of such norms [as those on the conduct of war, the treatment of minorities, and individual rights]'.[3]

Third, the concept of collective defense/national security has been increasingly challenged, especially since the end of the Cold War. Although some leading realists see continuity in international politics,[4] others believe that national security is no longer the most pressing problem in the affairs of states. Stephen van Evera, for instance, observes that 'the number of interstate wars has remained relatively low',[5] and further contends that 'States are seldom as insecure as they think they are ... . The rarity of real insecurity is suggested by the low death rate of modern great powers. In ancient times great powers often disappeared, but in modern times (since 1789) no great powers have permanently lost sovereignty'.[6] Personal insecurity remains, though; states – big and small – have become more secure than ever, but human beings have not. Other political realists have now taken note of security problems *within* states. Some advocate peace through partition,[7] others reject the strategy of peacekeeping neutrality,[8] and still others support rearmament of ethnic groups,[9] or even argue that 'nation building' in failed states 'is not such a bad idea after all'.[10] Earlier, classical realists regarded the need to ensure personal security as a key condition for, or component of, international security. One may revisit Hans Morgenthau, who spoke of 'individual frustrations' and 'anxieties' and saw the great dangers of 'personal insecurity' within unstable societies. He hypothesized that 'The greater the stability of society and the sense of security of its members, the smaller are the chances for collective emotions to seek an outlet in aggressive nationalism'. When induced by social instability and disintegration, personal and mass insecurity can lead to 'emotional outbursts' and to aggressive foreign policies or wars.[11]

Humans will not soon become as secure as states. The number of civil wars rose after World War II and then declined after the end of the Cold War,[12] but human beings remain insecure. According to *The Human Security Report*, 'The risk of new wars breaking out – or old ones resuming – is very real in the absence of a sustained and strengthened commitment to conflict prevention and post-conflict peacebuilding'. The *Report* warns that 'The post-Cold War decline in conflict numbers was not inevitable – and it is certain not irreversible'.[13] Michael Barnett and his associates underline this reality: 'Nearly 50 percent of all countries receiving assistance slide back into conflict within five years, and 72 percent of peacebuilding operations leave in place authoritarian regimes'.[14] If more states do not become more stable or liberal and democratic, some realists and Kantian internationalists can say with certainty that human insecurity will remain. To Hans Morgenthau, totalitarian regimes are capable of projecting individual frustrations and fears, not identified with nations, onto the international scene.[15]

Last, but not least, even the concept of collective security has also been challenged. The UN system has become less of a 'collective security' and more of a 'human security' system. According to Joseph Nye, collective security 'was a miserable failure in the 1930s, was put on ice during the Cold War, and then, like Lazarus, rose from the dead in the Persian Gulf in 1990. But it was only a minor miracle'.[16] If there is a greater miracle that can now be observed, it is that the ancient idea of human survival has made a comeback and seeks to overshadow modern ideas. What the UN has done since the end of the Cold War falls more comfortably within the realm of human security.

Overall, there has been general consensus among both scholars and policymakers that human security as a normative concept takes the individual as the referent object of security. Because it differs from collective defense and collective security, human security also rests on the assumption that states are not the only actors in global politics. International and non-state actors are just as important, if not more so: they include intergovernmental organizations,[17] epistemic communities, civil society groups (including non-governmental organizations),[18] and market forces. The concept of human security also differs from that of neoliberal institutionalism, which tends to define international cooperation as collaboration for mutual advantage. Actors in human security are supposed to act in the interest of human beings everywhere, including 'strangers' in every corner of the world.[19] This shared sense of neo-idealism relies on a degree of altruism based on a set of common values embedded in the logic of 'other-help'.

Still, there are at least three challenges to the study of human security. Critics find the concept itself problematic in analytical and policy terms. First is the question of where we should place human security in security studies. A powerful critic of human security, Roland Paris (who developed a two-by-two 'matrix of security studies') argues that human security should be one of four subfields in security studies. In his view, human security should be placed in cell 4 (the bottom right-hand corner) because of its exclusive focus on non-military threats to groups and individuals.[20] Second, even proponents of human security have quarreled among themselves over what constitutes human security. There are two competing approaches to this type of security, as noted throughout this volume: the so-called broad and narrow approaches.

In my view, the third challenge to human security lies in whether actors involved in human security activities can ever hope to achieve collaborative action. Much of the literature widely acknowledges the difficulties associated with the limits of collaboration among numerous actors actively involved in efforts to promote human security. Global efforts to promote this type of security by various actors have not yet succeeded as they should. To my knowledge, even advocates of human security very often fail to collaborate with each other. This poses an empirical challenge to the concept.

These challenges remain serious, but can be somewhat minimized. On the first and perhaps easiest challenge, regarding where human security should be placed in contemporary security studies, I prefer to regard it as inclusive of national security (see Chapter 1). Paris's taxonomical effort overlooks the fact that threats to human security can also be of a military nature. His exclusion of human security from cells 1, 2 and 3 overlooks the historical reality that military threats to the national security of sovereign states (cell 1, top left-hand corner) also pose a military threat to humans identified with their nations. States can still provide security for their peoples at the national level: they defend their national sovereignty and territorial integrity because they regard these principles as the best available national means to protect the institutions, lives and values of their citizens. Proponents of human security do not ignore the need for defending national security, but seek to broaden it. In many countries, military forces also do not always defend their states as they should, but instead engage in violence against their own peoples.

On the second challenge for human security studies, this volume seeks to find a concept that is neither too broad nor too narrow. If human security is to stay analytically useful as a concept that can be operationalized and relevant in policy terms, we need to prioritize policy commitment, motivate policy action, and assess policy outcomes. We must thus capture some eclectic middle ground between the broad and narrow approaches: the broad approach has become too elastic; the narrow one remains too restrictive.

Regarding the third challenge to human security, the existing literature pays scant attention to the problem of collaborative action among various actors, yet this is an old problem afflicting globalism that seems to grow bigger rather than diminish. Realists do not deny that international collaboration is possible, but regard such behavior in the context of fear shared by a group of state actors working together in the form of collective defense. Such collaboration among states ends as soon as their common fears disappear. Rational-choice institutionalists have sought to solve collective action problems by making an appeal for cooperation among self-interested egoistic actors on the premise that cooperation helps maximize their gains. Such cooperation ends when their institutional creatures no longer serve their self-interest. Human security defies the logics of self-help and mutual help, but rests on the logic of other-help.

The question raised in this volume is whether actors in the West and East can collaborate to ensure better human security. East Asia has witnessed severe human security problems. Cambodia, East Timor and North Korea provide good examples. East Timor illustrates the point that the Indonesian invasion of this state in 1975 posed a direct military threat not only to its territorial integrity, but also to its population. The atrocities committed under the Khmer Rouge regime, and under the Suharto regime in East Timor and Indonesia, also constituted a form of direct violent action against humans: they involved the actual use of force by armed forces (including militia) to destroy individuals. Cambodia and East Timor demonstrate political violence: the Pol Pot leadership and the Indonesian occupiers, respectively, caused Cambodians and Timorese to fear the threat of violence. These peoples lived in great fear when they lost the right to determine their political futures, and still experience extreme poverty and criminal violence.

We focus our attention on East Asia also because it is a complex region that has emerged as a major center in world politics. Russia was part of a former superpower. Some regarded Japan in the 1970s to be the world's economic superpower. Most observers agree that China is on the rise as a world power, although we still do not know if it will ever become a regional hegemon pushing the USA out of East Asia, eventually emerging as a global hegemon. Nevertheless, Russia, Japan and China are still major powers in East Asia. If we want to promote human security in this region and around the world, it is important that major regional powers such as China, Japan and Russia be counted as part of this collective endeavor. Without their collaboration, human security is likely to have its limits. During the Cold War, East and West remained divided ideologically (capitalism versus communism), but the immediate end of the Cold War has witnessed the rise of a cultural division (universalism versus relativism). The post-Cold War 'East-Asian challenge' to 'Western human rights' comes readily to mind.[21] The concept of human security – increasingly advocated in East Asia – reveals the region's continued resistance to the Western approach. According to Amitav Acharya, 'Some

Asian governments and analysts see human security as yet another attempt by the West to impose its liberal values and political institutions on non-Western societies.'[22] East Asia 'remains a tightly sovereignty-oriented region'.[23] East Asian nations tend to promote freedom from want, rather than the freedom from fear associated with the ideas of human rights and humanitarian intervention, as the narrow approach emphasizes.

Japan, China and Russia have challenged the Western liberal concept of human security in different ways. Japan, the champion of human security in East Asia, has not collaborated with Canada, the champion of human security in the West. Tokyo insists on the need for sustainable human development. Its human security agenda – driven by 'developmentalism' – reveals its 'discomfort with the seemingly interventionist thrust of the evolving discourse on human security' and its 'unhappiness ... exacerbated by the emerging consensus of the International Commission and State Sovereignty on "the responsibility to protect"'' as promoted by Canada and others in the West.[24] China is reported to have hindered the peace process in Sudan. When the military government in Myanmar conducted a series of violent crackdowns on protesters in September 2007, many governments (especially those in the West) urged the UN Security Council to take stern action against the junta's leadership, but both China and Russia objected.

Is there any hope for effective collaboration in the field of human security among actors in the West and East, especially those in East Asia? Liberal scholars put their faith in democratization. Collaboration improves when states in East Asia become democratic. Constructivists tell us that norms are not fixed. States in East Asia have defended national security and non-intervention, but these norms have their European roots in the 1648 Westphalian Peace Treaty. The Westphalian principle of state sovereignty and the norms of equality and non-intervention were first accepted by European states after a series of wars among them, but were not immediately and voluntarily adopted in East Asia. Modern European norms have never been part of China's cultural framework; hierarchy and domination have been part of a Confucian system that had 'no role for international cooperation or law'.[25] These cultural norms (manifest in its claim to higher culture and universal kingship) were undermined by the Qing dynasty's internal weakness, the rise of Japan as a great power, and the Western powers' rejection of Chinese cultural superiority.[26] Japan traditionally shared the same principles and norms, but it was '[c]olonial rule and the struggle against it' that 'contributed to the rise of the norms of nation, nation-state, and sovereignty in Asia'. It was also the experiences of Western colonial domination and exploitation and the Asian struggle for independence that helped 'strengthen their [the Asian people's] attachment to the principles of sovereignty, territorial integrity, and non-interference in domestic affairs'.[27] For some, historical shocks are a major source of normative change: new norms will not become acceptable to states in a particular region unless they experience immense destruction or until more states disintegrate into anarchy, chaos and violence, as some in Africa have experienced.[28] Cultures of antimilitarism can take root in events and ideas or through collective memories.[29] Still others emphasize the need for socialization.

Some contend that actors in the West no longer seriously object to the East Asian understanding of human security, while those in East Asia appear to be softening in their objection to the Western approach. This volume reveals that a growing number of states in this region are at least learning to tolerate ideas of human security when this does not seriously affect their regime or personal security. For instance, three methods for the promotion of human security – humanitarian intervention, intrastate peacekeeping and international criminal justice – are no longer regarded as strict taboos in East Asia.

Overall, whether proponents of human security in the East and West will reach normative consensus on human security and act upon it collaboratively and effectively, or whether actors in East Asia will take more effective collaborative action for human security, remains uncertain. The literature offers a long list of complex challenges to collaborative action in the region, including political isolation from formal international institutions (Taiwan),[30] national sovereignty, past humiliations, fear of potential intervention into states' domestic affairs, non-democratic ideologies,[31] and so on.

I have thus mounted an effort to draw insights from theoretical eclecticism, by inviting some scholars to reflect on the possibility of effective collaboration among actors working on human security. By no mean do I suggest that the concept of national security found in the age-old wisdom of realism has now been relegated to the dustbin of history, but I feel the need to suggest that we 'soften' it by learning to listen to critical voices, without accepting anything at face value or questioning anything that puzzles us.[32]

We must listen to each other more often and more closely and learn from the strengths and weaknesses of each other's thinking, if we hope to enhance collaborative action for human security. How scholars can reconcile national and human security remains a challenge. William Tow and Russel Trood suggest that 'the best that may be accomplished is to sharpen and refine both agendas in ways that they complement each other more effectively'.[33] They make the case that 'both the traditionalists and human security proponents must be prepared to concede that they need each other's support and expertise if their common objective of a better and more stable world is to be realized'[34] and if their 'mutual intellectual disdain'[35] is to be effectively overcome.

In my view, scholars from different theoretical traditions may be unable to 'concede that they need each other's support and expertise', but they need to at least moderate their expectations regarding the conceptual boundaries of human security. National security can still be enhanced without arming states to the teeth so that more resources can be allocated for non-military purposes. At the same time, human security should not simply be about undermining the concept of national security, promoting egalitarian development, and eliminating all existing structural inequalities.

I define human security within what I call the MPCE framework (military, political, criminal and economic): human freedom from the fear of direct and indirect physical harm resulting from military, political, criminal and economic violence (not only the realist fear of foreign aggression against states, military defeat, political submission or subjugation to foreign forces, and the loss of political and economic independence in the form of either colonialism or imperialism). My hope is that the concept, which remains highly contested, can be better accepted and applied if we succeed in building a concept that is neither too elastic nor too restrictive, combining theoretical insights into one that is neither too parochial nor too eclectic.

This volume contains several theoretical perspectives on human security drawn from different intellectual traditions, mainly realism, liberalism, constructivism and critical theory (including neo-Marxism and postmodernism). The work is more of a dialogue among scholars than the imposition of one theoretical perspective on the rest. Theoretical eclecticism, therefore, does not mean that we engage in an intellectual imperialism, nor does it mean that we embrace mindless empiricism or naive methodological pluralism.

Scholars are free to follow in the footsteps of their theoretical traditions, but must be open-minded enough to examine the results that competing perspectives have produced. From an ontological and epistemological viewpoint, we may not be able to fuse the different positions we take as we like, but we can draw insights from each other in a mutually beneficial way. Realism proves unable to offer us a helpful prescription for the promotion of human security at the global level, but it can offer us some insight into power, diplomacy and the perils of anarchy. Liberalism has much to say about political violence against groups and individuals under dictatorial regimes. Constructivism offers useful insights on the crucial role of cultural norms and social identity in democratic statebuilding. Critical theory that includes postmodernism and neo-Marxism may be too critical of realism and liberalism, and not prone to giving policymakers a clear direction, but it can be usefully critical and creative in terms of telling us more about the nature of socioeconomic violence, and can help shed further light on the need to reduce it. Realists and liberals may not agree with their critical theorist colleagues, who see evil in the Leviathan or capitalist state, but they can learn from the latter how socioeconomic injustices and inequalities give rise to violence that threatens state and human security. In a nutshell, theoretical eclecticism requires that we become more interactive or communicative than isolative, more pragmatic than ideological, and thus generally more eclectic than parochial.[36]

A word of caution is necessary, though; just as we must not make the concept of human security too elastic and amorphous, so also we must not carelessly combine competing insights from different theoretical perspectives, rendering our arguments unintelligible. There are limits to eclecticism or pluralism.[37] If possible, clear theoretical statements should be made to allow us to test our theoretical insights against empirical evidence or to keep critically evaluating our normative commitment to human security.

This volume adds expansiveness to a growing body of scholarly work on human security in East Asia that tends to focus on a few actors and non-military security issues, and does not give serious consideration to democratic and human rights issues (as pointed out in this volume, especially Chapter 5, and by other scholars).[38] One of the staunchest defenders of non-liberal Asian values, Kishore Mahbubani, considers democracy 'evil'.[39] Perhaps the best known book on human security is *Asia's Emerging Regional Order: Reconciling Traditional and Human Security*, published in 2000.[40] It is excellent in terms of its comprehensive inclusion of non-traditional security issues and its focus on one regional institution (the ASEAN Regional Forum) and one country case (Indonesia).

I felt the need to produce an additional volume that would remain theoretically eclectic, but more inclusive in terms of both the methods used for human security promotion and the various actors involved. This volume includes Asian and Western perspectives on human security, highlighting the theoretical debates and fleshing out the nuances that are embedded in the so-called East–West divide. It also focuses on Cambodia and Timor-Leste, where human insecurity remains intense, and on actors such as states and regional institutional actors (such as ASEAN, ASEAN+3 and Asia–Pacific Economic Cooperation) and civil society. Moreover, this volume covers specific methods for promotion of human security: military peace operations, international criminal justice, democracy-building and economic development. This volume thus distinguishes itself from much of the existing literature by placing more emphasis on the need to investigate the collaborative action problems in human security, examining the role of more and different actors in East Asia, and paying more attention to the countries that have experienced serious human security problems in Southeast Asia.

The volume is divided into two major parts. Part I covers four chapters. Chapter 1 elaborates on the MPCE conceptual framework, outlining the four types of human insecurity, and contends that globalism (as the theoretical challenger to political realism) and liberal internationalism face some obstacles in terms of different actors' willingness and abilities to take collaborative action for human security. Chapter 2 shows that the liberal norms of human security rooted in Western tradition have never been fixed, but have changed over time. The Western roots of human security continue to evolve, from liberalism to something inspired by postmodernism. Influenced by critical theory advocating the politics of emancipation, the chapter shows the limits of liberalism and seeks to advance an argument that goes beyond the need for protection of the individual to include the urgent task of empowering the individual. Chapter 3 discusses the competing approaches to human security, especially between states in Northeast Asia and those in Europe. The gap between the two camps remains wide, but it has narrowed. The time for debate over the concept is over; what matters more is how to operationalize human security. Chapter 4 shares the constructivist optimism that Southeast Asian actors have moved in the policy direction of intervention, but contends that they tend to accept a type of international intervention defined in more comprehensive terms.

Part II contains an additional four chapters dealing with human security issues in East Asia. Chapter 5 takes note of the region's resistance to the Western idea of human security, especially in the context of 'responsibility to protect'. The author finds reason for optimism that the level of regional resistance has weakened. In fact, thinking on human security, especially in the context of military intervention, is more complex than has been realized. Even China, still leading in the defense of state sovereignty, has in recent years proved less resistant to the need for intervention in war-torn societies. Chapter 6 examines the case of East Timor, revealing the limits of collaborative action on the humanitarian crisis on this territory. States and other actors in the region have shown a greater degree of willingness to collaborate on military intervention. However, various regional and domestic factors still inhibit regional states and actors from taking the lead in human security efforts. Chapter 7 assesses the normative and empirical merits and policy utility of international criminal justice as it applies to East Asia, and whether actors in the region have increasingly conformed to this UN-driven and Western-based method for the promotion of human security. Chapter 8 attempts to reconcile the structural approach of Marxism with postmodernism's concern for agency. The author questions the need for collaborative action in the context of neoliberalization, as the dominating interests of capital have been promoted at the expense of human security.

The conclusion demonstrates some of the progress in and the limits of collaborative action for human security, and offers concrete directions for policy action to promote more effective collaboration. Some perspectives are prescriptively more explicit than others. When it comes to humanitarian intervention and peacekeeping, UN leadership, led by big powers in the Security Council, remains essential to ending military violence. Regional states can do their part by strengthening their regional institutions. But the collective exercise of coercive military power alone, even when possible, may prove counterproductive and costly. International peacekeeping looks far more promising. The best way to promote human security through criminal justice is to build and sustain institutions in a forward-looking fashion by reforming judiciaries and other legal bodies capable of deterring political and criminal activities that threaten human security. Moreover, if human security is to be fully enhanced and sustained, economic development must become more equitable or more favorable to non-elite individuals. Capitalism may hinder this prospect, but some East Asian capitalist policies, such as those adopted by Japan, have helped promote more equitable development.[41]

Part I

Human security

Theoretical and conceptual contentions

1 Critical challenges for globalism in human security studies

Sorpong Peou

The study of human security is driven by the process of globalization. Globalism, as a theoretical perspective, has its intellectual roots in Western liberalism (see Chapter 2). According to two leading American liberal scholars, Robert Keohane and Joseph Nye, globalism is 'a state of the world involving networks of interdependence at multi-continental distances, linked through flows and influences of capital and goods, information and ideas, people and force, as well as environmentally and biologically relevant substances'.[1]

Globalism is also associated with the multiplicity of threats to security – a growing set of actors and methods. It presents itself in different forms of threat: military, political, legal, socioeconomic and cultural. The number of actors in this new global politics has increased: states are no longer the key actors, but only one of many; the role of international organizations has become more significant; non-governmental actors (including non-governmental organizations, NGOs) have become more vocal and influential. Market forces have now become more recognizable. Methods for dealing with these threats to security have also multiplied. According to globalists, old-fashioned military globalism in the forms of imperialism, colonialism and interstate rivalry has been on the decline, while a new form of military globalism, the different forms of intervention for peace, arose. Legal globalism is spreading across the world in such forms as international or global criminal justice. Political globalism spreads ideas about power and democracy. Economic globalism sprang from Western capitalism and continues to spring into life in remote corners of the world through the process of marketization.

Globalism in the context of human security as a 'public good' faces tough challenges, though. Because the number of threats has grown, the number of actors involved in this type of security has increased, and the number of methods for dealing with human insecurity has multiplied, the question is whether collaborative action among the multiplicity of actors has grown – or can ever become – more effective.

The globalist referent object for, and sources of threat to, human security

Collaborative action for human security differs from collective defense and collective security in terms of the referent object for security. In collective defense, the concept of security is defined in military terms, with the state as the referent object for security. States are what need to be protected from external threats.[2] States, treated as 'black boxes' or 'billiard balls', must think strategically about their national survival under international anarchy. They are assumed to behave in a 'self-help' manner in their pursuit of self-interest and in defense of independence and work to protect their territorial integrity by way of maximizing their material power and enhancing their relative position within the international system, where only sovereign states reign supreme.

In collective security, states also remain the main referent object for security, but the concept is broadly defined in an internationalist context. Immanuel Kant and his disciples, in particular, have envisioned the possibility of a 'perpetual peace' among republican states, and their political vision has influenced contemporary idealism or liberal internationalism in the context of collective security,[3] whose referent object for security remains the state. On collective security, Inis Claude explains that it 'purports to provide security *for* all states, *by* the action of all states, *against* all states which might challenge the existing order by the arbitrary unleashing of their power'.[4]

Globalists, however, have made the case that states are no longer the only referent object for security, due to the decline in old-fashioned militarism. They would draw comfort from the fact that the overall rate of state 'death' has slowed. Since 1415, states (recognized as sovereign by European states) have experienced less insecurity defined in terms of loss of sovereignty. They would agree with the 'soft' realist argument that state aggression in the modern world has become rare.[5] Both Keohane and Nye also observe that 'interstate use and threat of military force have virtually disappeared in relations in certain areas of the world, notably among the advanced, information-area democracies bordering the Atlantic and the Pacific and among a number of their less wealthy neighbors'.[6] In this brave new world, even small states stay alive and well.

Insofar as acknowledging that the pursuit of national security may still be legitimate,[7] globalists give greater attention to the individual. According to a UN Development Programme (UNDP) report, the 1990s saw only about 220,000 people killed in conflicts between states, whereas about 3.6 million people died in wars within states.[8] It no longer makes sense to talk about the state as the only referent for security. People (defined as individuals and groups or communities) should become the analytical focus in security studies.[9]

Globalist proponents of human security have now agreed on one conceptual aspect: people, not sovereign states, are the main referent object for security. The UNDP has been most responsible for formally advancing the concept of security concerning the daily lives of 'ordinary people' or how they live and – safely and freely – exercise their choices.[10] In the mid-1990s, the Commission on Global Governance also redefined security by making the following point: 'global security extends beyond the protection of borders, ruling elites, and exclusive state interests to include the protection of people'.[11] Canada, one of the early champions in human security, also defended this people-centered approach to security. When still Minister of Foreign Affairs, Lloyd Axworthy contended that '[e]ssentially, this is the idea that security goals should be primarily formulated and achieved in terms of human, rather than state, needs'.[12]

However, it should be pointed out that everyone does not receive equal attention in human security studies. Victims of war, refugees, women, children in war situations, and poor individuals stand among the most vulnerable groups and thus receive the most attention. Women face various forms of violence rooted in gender-based injustices, such as sexual discrimination and abuses. Children are caught in armed conflicts and exploited when forced to serve as child soldiers. Some further argue in defense of the need to protect vulnerable civilians, including young men and the elderly.[13]

As to the question of what threatens human security, globalists again differ from proponents of collective defense/national security and collective security. For political realists, interstate war is the main source of threat. As Walt puts it, 'The main focus of security studies is ... the phenomenon of [inter-state] war. The study of traditional security assumes that conflict between states is a constant possibility and that the use of military force has far-reaching effects on states and societies'. He also makes the case that 'security studies may be defined as the study of the threat, use, and control of military force'.[14] (This does not suggest that realism pays no attention to non-state sources of threat. Some have noted the threats of terrorism[15] and ethnic violence.)[16] Collective security also rests on the rationale that external aggression against states remains the main source of military threat to international peace and security. Certain member states within the international community are expected to violate the norms of world peace.

While looking at a broader picture, proponents of human security disagree among themselves as to what constitutes the main sources of threat. The narrow 'protection-based' approach (championed by Canada and others in the West,[17] including the International Commission on Intervention and State Sovereignty, ICISS) clashes with the broader 'development-based' approach (championed by UNDP and the Commission on Human Security supported by Japan).[18] The broad approach became an extension of an old paradigm known as 'basic human needs', developed in the 1970s,[19] but is thought to be analytically less vague than the concept of human development, which 'provided no clear guarantee for individuals. Many could be still sacrificed in the course of bringing the broad range of good things to the majority, by governments who warmly adopted the language of human development'.[20] In 1991, Ken Booth argued that humans' security means 'emancipation', defined in terms of 'the freeing of people (as individuals and groups) from the physical and human constraints, which stop them carrying out what they would freely choose to do'. In his critical perspective: 'War and the threat of war is one of those constraints, together with poverty, poor education, political oppression, and so on'.[21] More recently, initially led by the UNDP, the broad approach has gone beyond war or armed conflict to include other non-military threats to 'human dignity', such as unemployment, hunger, disease and natural disasters, said to kill more people than bombs and bullets. The list of threats to human security is indeed long, and the sources of threat are numerous, ranging from those that are human-made to those that 'stem from the forces of nature'.[22]

Most scholars and state leaders in East Asia have adopted this approach. Woosang Kim and In-Taek Hyun, for instance, define human security as 'a condition of relative safety that is free from humanitarian emergencies caused by natural or man-made disasters'.[23] The Commission on Human Security lent more legitimacy to this approach when it issued a major report contending that 'the protection of the vital core of all human lives in ways that enhance human freedoms and human fulfillment ... It means creating political, social, environmental, economic, military and cultural systems that together give people the building blocks of survival, livelihood and dignity'.[24]

The narrow approach, however, emphasizes freedom from actual violence and the fear of war and violent crime (such as genocide, politicide, democide and terrorism). *The Human Security Report*,[25] for instance, defines human security as 'freedom from actual violence' and 'the fear of violence' in political, criminal and economic terms. Political violence includes armed conflict, genocide and international terrorism. Criminal violence, which kills far more people than both war and terrorism combined, includes homicide and rape. Although not explicitly stated, the *Report* seems to define violence in economic terms. For instance, human trafficking is 'a cause of human insecurity' because '[t]raffickers seek to exploit their victims for long-term profit'.[26]

We may need to find some middle ground between the two competing but complementary approaches. The broad approach is too elastic if it includes such terms as 'human dignity', which is a matter of personal and cultural interpretation that can never be evaluated or shared by everyone. For some, it means 'emancipation from oppressive power structures – be they global, national, or local in origin and scope'.[27] For others, it means something rather vague. An Asian scholar, for instance, refers to dignity as rulers' acceptance of their people's role within society. Rulers must accept advice from their people.[28] If we go down this road, we will end up going 'beyond measurable limits',[29] and perhaps nowhere. The narrow approach is too restrictive to allow the concept to be defined more broadly than the structural causes and consequences of war or armed conflict, nor does it explicitly include others forms of economic violence.

We need to stick with the UNDP's key (if unelaborated) statement: 'Without peace, there may be no development. But without development, peace may be threatened'.[30] Although still a highly contested concept, peace defined as the absence of military, political, criminal and economic violence (not human dignity or safety or livelihood *per se*) serves as the conceptual boundary of human security. Natural disasters (such as the tsunami that devastated the coastal regions of Southeast and South Asia and claimed hundreds of thousands of human lives) should not be construed as a human security problem. Car accidents and health problems such as cancer – which kill millions of people each year, but do not result from the conscious policy decisions and actions of individuals or collective bodies – do not constitute challenges to human security, either.

We need to define human-made violence in a more restrictive fashion by placing emphasis on its organizational character. According to Kofi Annan, the fear of violence includes different forms of organized violence: genocide, war crimes,

crimes against humanity or the 'wholesale slaughter' of civilians,[31] civil, especially ethnic, conflict, and terrorism. Both MacFarlane and Khong focus on organized violence as the threat to human security, with an emphasis on the agency
of 'individual perpetrators' (or a collection of them) who violently intrude on the
'bodies' of individuals.[32]

In my view, the military, political, criminal and economic (MPCE) framework
for human security is reasonably restrictive. The cases of Cambodia and East
Timor enable us to conceptualize human security in a way that is analytically possible, policy-relevant and practical. In *military* terms, humans are insecure when
directly subject to the actual use of armed force in such forms as military attack
(external and domestic) and other brutal acts, such as genocide or 'ethnic cleansing'. Military violence remains the traditional form of human fear – a military
threat to states as well as to individual human beings, their citizens. This type
of fear is still in line with political realism, the key concept of which is national
security. The arch-classical political realist Hans Morgenthau regarded the inten-
sification of individuals' personal anxieties, fears and insecurities to be rooted in
domestic instability, which leads people to identify themselves with the power
and foreign policies of their nations.[33]

The Human Security Report (2005) further contends that 'Protecting citizens
from foreign attack may be a necessary condition for the security of individuals, but it is certainly not a sufficient one. Indeed, during the last 100 years far
more people have been killed by their own governments than by foreign armies'.[34]
Indeed, the dictatorial regimes in the socialist world were responsible for at least
100 million deaths during the Cold War. East Timor illustrates the point that the
Indonesian military invasion of this Portuguese colony was based on the actual
use of force against its territorial integrity as well as its population. The atrocities
committed under the murderous Khmer Rouge regime in Cambodia and under the
brutal Suharto regime in Indonesia also involved the actual use of force by armed
forces (including militia) to destroy target individuals.

The use of threat to terrorize or threaten individuals or groups is distinguished
from armed violence, primarily because it does not involve the actual use of force
to kill or wound the human body. *Political* violence is based on the threat of
physical violence rather than its actual use, whether directed at individuals or
groups. Political power used to suppress human rights is a psychological attack.
Viewed in this light, political violence takes place when individuals or groups use
whatever means available (personal or institutional) to exert strict control over
the thoughts and actions of people. Terrorism is a form of political violence aimed
primarily at instilling fear in civilians for political purposes. Cambodia and East
Timor also demonstrate political violence, in that the Pol Pot leadership and the
Indonesian occupiers caused people to fear the threat of violence. Cambodians
and Timorese also came under threat when they lost the right to determine their
own political futures. Colonial powers, terrorists and dictators thus 'rule by fear',
based on the perceived threat of punishment.

In *criminal* terms, humans remain insecure as long as they are subject to physical violence for non-political purposes. Criminals create fear without seeking

political gain. Individuals commit homicide or rape for personal reasons. Those who deliberately, unlawfully, directly or indirectly, commit murder or sexual violence are criminals, as they do not challenge the state, nor do they have any military purpose. However, soldiers may violently enslave or rape women during wartime (such as the use of women as sexual slaves before and until the end of World War II, and the gang-rapes by Russian soldiers during their attacks on Germany in the final phase of that war).

Economic violence is another form of threat to human security, but it should go beyond the human trafficking that proponents of the narrow approach contend should be the limit. Both MacFarlane and Khong take issue with the economic dimension of human security, but their fear of conceptual overstretching is overstated. Even political realists have long regarded the economic dimension of national security to be important.[35] When individuals or groups engage in economic exploitation or violent oppression, such as land-grabbing or depriving people of the means of survival, they commit economic violence.

In economic terms, human security is under threat when individuals or groups are deprived of the means of survival, such as land-grabbing and forced eviction from property. Each year, extreme poverty also kills more than 8 million people around the world. These victims die needlessly, not simply because diseases such as malaria, tuberculosis and AIDS kill them, but because these killer diseases 'prey on bodies weakened by chronic hunger'.[36] Extreme poverty is a form of violence against human security, because the victims possess no means to earn enough to live, and because extreme structural inequalities are deeply rooted in unjust policies controlled by ruling elites.

In short, human security improves when the actual use of armed force ends, when the threat of terror or political tyranny disappears, when criminal activities decrease, and when extreme poverty rooted in highly structural inequalities is eradicated. Of these four types of violence against humans, the use of armed force should rank highest because it tends to produce ripple effects that create or exacerbate the other three. Military violence tends to result in fears of political terror or punishment, extreme poverty, and criminal activities (such as homicide and rape). This can be seen, for example, in the atrocities that took place in Cambodia after a civil war, and in East Timor after the Indonesian invasion. These wars also caused severe destruction and impoverished the people in these two countries, which are endowed with rich natural resources.

Globalist means and agency

In terms of means, globalists reject traditional balance-of-power and balance-of-aggression mechanisms. Collective defense seeks to secure states through power balancing, and collective security is about power management among states to ensure international security. On collective security, as Inis L. Claude puts it: 'the problem of power is here to stay; it is, realistically, not a problem to be eliminated but a problem to be managed'.[37] The realities of power in the international system remain, but balancing against aggression is more effective than balancing under anarchy. There is 'a legally binding and codified commitment on the part of all members to respond to aggression whenever and wherever it might occur'.[38] The rationale is that 'when it works, it confronts aggressors with preponderant as opposed to merely actual force'.[39]

Globalists' means for achieving human security are not always incompatible with realist and internationalist prescriptions for national and international security. According to *The Human Security Report* (2005), 'protecting citizens from foreign attack may be a necessary condition for the security of individuals, but it is certainly not a sufficient one'.[40] Globalists often treat military means to achieve national security as working against human security. The ICISS puts it this way: the realist concept of security 'diverts enormous amounts of national wealth and human resources into armaments and armed forces'. Meanwhile, 'countries fail to protect their citizens from chronic insecurities of hunger, disease, inadequate shelter, crime, unemployment, social conflict and environmental hazard'.[41]

The two best known military methods for human security are humanitarian intervention and peacekeeping.[42] Humanitarian intervention differs from the realist method of military intervention justified by the need to maintain the balance of power for stability, and departs from moral statism, which defends the principle of non-intervention in the sovereign territory of states. In human security, international humanitarian law prohibits violence against non-combatants.[43] Humanitarian intervention places emphasis on the need to end widespread starvation (for example, Somalia in 1992), to restore democracy (Haiti in 1994), to end civil war (Bosnia in 1995), and to stop 'ethnic cleansing' (Kosovo in 1999).[44] The ICISS redefines the concept by introducing the term 'the responsibility to protect'. The international community has the responsibility to intervene in situations where there is either 'large-scale loss of life' or 'ethnic cleansing'.

Intrastate peacekeeping serves as another military method for promoting human security. When peacekeepers are dispatched to maintain peace within states, they play a crucial role in helping to control and resolve conflicts between hostile domestic parties. Their role formally comes under the command and control of the UN Secretary-General, whose authority rests on the consent of the adversaries and the principle of absolute impartiality. The UN does not have an army of its own, but relies on the contribution of national troops from member states. Peacekeepers are lightly armed and allowed to use force only in self-defense. Their role includes monitoring ceasefires, the cantonment and demobilization of hostile troops, the destruction of weapons, the formation and training of new armed forces, and even the reform of the military and security apparatus.[45]

Peacebuilding in general remains a non-military approach to human security. Peacebuilding relies on specific non-violent means designed to prevent conflict from recurring. According to *The Human Security Report*, 'the risk of civil war is reduced by equitable economic growth, increased state capacity and inclusive democracy. Development is a necessary condition for security – and *vice versa*'.[46]

There are at least three non-military approaches in peacebuilding. The first is of a political nature, primarily because of its emphasis on democracy promotion based on free and fair elections.[47] The second emphasizes criminal justice issues; for instance, recent efforts by various actors have been made to build the International Criminal Court (ICC) and *ad hoc* criminal tribunals, viewed as an effective way to build international and domestic peace through the promotion of justice for individual victims.[48] The third relies on the means to promote socioeconomic reconstruction and development; top advocates remain those working at the World Bank and the International Monetary Fund (IMF), who strongly believe in the power of market-based solutions to political problems, such as violent conflict.[49] Together, they form the liberal doctrine of a secular trinity: democratization, criminalization of political violence, and marketization. Together, they serve the liberal mission to promote human security.

Regarding providers of security, conventional theoretical perspectives include mostly states and international organizations. For realists, in particular, states are the principal providers of national security. According to Barry Buzan, states may not always protect their citizens; some may even use violence against them – however, the real problem is not states as such, but rather types of state. In his view, 'strong states', defined in terms of internal stability and cohesion, are capable of providing their citizens with the security they need.[50] In collective security, member states and their international organizations become the collective providers of security.[51] According to US President Woodrow Wilson, collective security is 'not a balance of power, but a community of power; not organized rivalries, but an organized common peace'.[52] Members of this international community are sovereign states presumed to behave as a 'great mass' whose behavior is driven by a 'positive commitment to the value of world peace'.[53]

Proponents of human security, however, invoke the universal notion of global solidarity (solidarity among people, no matter where they live) on the basis that 'no-one is secure as long as someone is insecure anywhere'.[54] In advancing the 'responsibility to protect' as the key concept for human security, the ICISS argues that national or 'state authorities are responsible for the functions of protecting the safety and lives of citizens and promotion of their welfare'.[55] It does not argue that states have been relegated to the dustbin of history, but adds that when states fail to protect their citizens, outside actors must step in. And states may need to work in partnership with other actors.[56]

Proponents of human security recognize the contribution of international organizations such as the UN, its specialized agencies and regional organizations, and other non-state actors. The role of the Security Council in the maintenance of international peace and security remains prominent, but the General Assembly has become necessary, especially if the Council fails to act. The role of the UN Secretary-General in the field of international peace and security, according to Article 99 of the UN Charter, has been expanded in practice to include his activities in providing Good Offices imperative to the peaceful settlement of disputes, in sending fact-finding missions to troubled areas, and in supporting peacekeeping and peacebuilding operations.[57]

Regional and subregional organizations also have a role to play.[58] Although the relationship between regional organizations and the UN 'has received remarkably little attention', it has been argued that security organizations operating at the regional level 'may be the best – although not perfect – answer the international community can provide'.[59] A handful of regional organizations – namely the Organization of American States (OAS), the Organization for Security and Co-operation in Europe (OSCE) and the North Atlantic Treaty Organization (NATO) – have, since the end of the Cold War, engaged in various human security activities such as humanitarian intervention, peaceful settlement of disputes, and the promotion of democracy and human rights.

NGOs have also claimed to represent people, rather than states, thus making them actors for human security, and their number has expanded in recent decades. To be fair, most proponents of human security do not argue unrealistically that NGOs have now replaced states' role in promoting human security. In 1914, only 1083 NGOs existed; by the end of the twentieth century they had increased to more than 37,000, with nearly one-fifth of them formed in the 1990s alone.[60] Transnational NGOs include the International Crisis Group, Amnesty International, Human Rights Watch, and the Fédération internationale des ligues des droits de l'homme. Some NGOs are now recognized as human security actors that enjoy the support of states in the process of civil society-building around the world.[61] They provided useful input into drafting the Universal Declaration of Human Rights.[62] They also play their part in helping the UN carry out its post-conflict peacebuilding work, and serve as channels for development assistance. They help build civil society groups capable of maintaining a democratic balance between state and society. According to Washburn, 'The UN could not carry out many of its programs without NGOs as partners – this applies especially to economic and technical assistance, humanitarian relief, human rights, and election monitoring'.[63]

Market forces are also said to play a helpful part in both conflict and postconflict zones, especially during the process of peacebuilding, involving democratic institution-building. There is a growing understanding among business actors, policymakers and academics that certain types of business and private sector behavior may, either intentionally or unintentionally, 'adversely affect the incidence, intensity and duration of violent conflict'.[64] Rather than promoting conflict for personal profit through exploitation or illicit economic transactions that can fuel or prolong violent conflict, private sector actors can serve as a force for promoting democratic governance. Firms have the potential to take corporate responsibility by doing any of the following: ending their financial and commodity business with state and non-state combatants, abiding by transparency regulations against corruption that perpetuates conflict, creating jobs, and sharing revenue with national and local governments as well as local communities.

Collaborative action on human security

The need to 'open intellectual doors to peer in on international collaboration, cooperation, welfare'[65] was once voiced by Kalevi Holsti, and has now been adopted to advance the concept of human security.[66] Political realists do not say that collaboration is impossible, but that it is always temporary and based on the logic of self-help. In collective security, states collaborate to provide mutual assistance.[67] 'Mutual help' is central, and cooperation is defined as 'collaboration for *mutual* advantage'.[68] Collaboration in the context of human security, however, is based on the logic of other-help or altruism: actors collaborate to provide security for all individuals under threat. Human security is generally treated as a global public good, where individuals who cannot provide security for themselves can still benefit from its provision for free.[69]

But the provision of this public good is not the act of one actor, as there are a myriad of actors involved in this endeavor. The concept of collaborative action in human security further suggests that a large set of actors must begin their mission with some normative convergence on the need to help others. The question is the extent to which states, non-state actors and international organizations can agree on the methods that include peace operations, economic sanctions, international criminal justice and economic development. Collaboration further means coordination of policy activities by actors in a particular method, and 'requires the actions of separate individuals or organizations – which are not in pre-existent harmony – to be brought into conformity with one another through a process of coordination'.[70] Neoliberal institutionalism seeks to overcome collective action problems by adopting a rationalist method of analysis, looking into how actors can coordinate activities for reduction of transaction costs.[71] Coordination may be important to the process of global collaboration, especially when actors seek to reduce transaction costs, but collaborative action on human security has more to do with altruism and selfless purposes, shaped or driven by the collective need to promote the personal security of individual human beings, including 'strangers' in faraway lands. Normative convergence and coordination are strange bedfellows, but one without the other will not lead to success in human security promotion. In 1995, the then-UN Secretary-General Boutros-Ghali wrote that 'If UN efforts are to succeed, the roles of the various players need to be carefully coordinated in an integrated approach to human security'.[72] Shahrbanou Tadjbakhsh and Anuradha Chenoy contend that 'There have been too many examples of fragmented and uncoordinated interventions that have actually led to more problems down the lines.' They then emphasize that 'The best that international organizations can do for the cause of human security is actually not to increase insecurities by failing to coordinate properly between partners and between sectors'.[73] NGOs also seem to have reached a general consensus that their activities would be far more effective if they could 'operate in a multidimensional and "multi-track" framework in which local actors, external NGOs, governments and international organizations undertake complementary actions'.[74] This goal can be reached if they can achieve 'concerted and consistent coordination and a commonality of objectives'.[75] Material contribution is always the empirical test of collaborative action. Actors may agree on collective norms and the need to provide public goods such as military intervention, democracy promotion, international criminal justice and economic development, but their normative commitment proves unhelpful if they provide little in material terms. Normative convergence is thus a good start and effective coordination is the next helpful step, but material support is perhaps the most crucial element.

Recent trends reveal that a variety of actors involved in the field of human security – state, non-state and international – have made a normative, policy and material commitment. In normative terms, a growing number of states have made a commitment to the promotion of human security. Previously, they had agreed only on the individual right to be free from starvation.[76] In recent years, more positive signs have become increasingly evident: a growing number of states have shown greater interest in the promotion of human security. In policy terms, they have also sought to coordinate their activities. The 'Human Security Network' (originally a bilateral arrangement between Canada and Norway) has expanded to include a dozen other countries, especially in the West. The G8 has now placed on its agenda human security issues such as conflict prevention, arms control and disarmament, terrorism, crime and the environment, all of which are said to have an adverse impact on human life.[77] Even leading American political realists, such as Stephen Walt, have recently urged the USA to help rebuild failed states, and advised Washington to 'rely more heavily on multilateral institutions, even if this policy reduces its freedom of action in the short term'.[78]

Within the UN system, there also appears to be more normative convergence on human security. During the Cold War, there was little evidence of international intervention on behalf of individuals and groups, despite massive human suffering. After the Cold War, promoting human rights and building democracy has become a norm. A number of key reforms were proposed to identify and achieve 'the larger goal of the United Nations as human security'.[79] Christopher Joyner notes: 'the UN Secretariat has assumed the impressive role of international agent for democratization'.[80] According to Nigel White, 'democracy and support for democracy are grounded in the UN Charter' and 'the norms governing support for democracy have come from the HRC [Human Rights Committee] operating under the ICCPR [International Covenant on Civil and Political Rights]'.[81] The UN Security Council also increasingly advanced into the uncharted territory of human security. After the Cold War, the Council became more interventionist in humanitarian terms. More specifically, normative convergence on military intervention became evident in the early 1990s. After the massacres in Rwanda in 1994 and Srebrenica in 1995, calls have been made for the protection of individuals. The report on peace operations presented by a distinguished panel headed by Lakhdar Brahimi attempted to move the UN away from its commitment to defending its own peacekeepers, to one that would defend individuals under their charge.[82] At least in normative terms, the Council has no longer tolerated the murder of individuals by political regimes. As recently as April 2006, the Council 'issued a ringing condemnation of all violence committed against civilians during armed conflict, directing its strongest language at attacks on women and children, and pledged to ensure that all peace support operations employ all feasible measures to prevent the scourge'. The Council members then unanimously adopted a resolution condemning 'all attacks deliberately targeting UN personnel and others involved humanitarian missions, urging states to bring those responsible to justice'.[83] The UN Peacebuilding Commission (established to propose integrated strategies for postconflict recovery, focusing on economic reconstruction, institution building and sustainable development) has also become one of the UN Security Council's subsidiary international bodies (which also include the International Criminal Tribunal for the former Yugoslavia and the International Criminal Tribunal for Rwanda).

Overall, there has been a growing desire within the UN Administrative Committee on Coordination (ACC; now the Chief Executives Board for Coordination, CEB) to develop a 'United Nations voice' that would bring the UN organs and agencies under a shared vision on human security. In October 1999, for instance, an ACC meeting considered 'that the broad concept of sustainable human security and development captured well the broad objectives of the UN system to promote peace, development, democracy, social justice, the rule of law and human rights'. It stated that 'Sustainable human security and development can serve as the overarching objectives of a common agenda for the UN system'.[84]

A growing number of regional organizations, including the OAS, are believed to have played a role in complementing those of other actors such as the UN, and in enhancing human security in much of Central America. Other regional organizations have now taken humanitarian issues into their agendas as well. The OSCE, for instance, has shifted its security agenda to one based on humanitarian questions. As a regional organization, NATO evidently began to assist in cases against political criminals in the former Yugoslavia, especially when it carried out the first round of arrests in 1997.[85]

NGOs have also been regarded as having an expanded role in the UN system, especially in peace operations, having encroached upon not only the Economic and Social Council (ECOSOC), but also the General Assembly and the Security Council. The number of NGOs within the UN system (on the ECOSOC roster) has also grown, from only 41 in 1948, to 377 in 1968, and to 1350 in 1998.[86] More recently over 1600 NGOs had consultative status at the UN. Within the UN system, since the 1990s the status of NGOs has changed from 'consultative arrangements' (a role secondary to that of states) to social 'partnership' (equality).[87]

A growing number of NGOs have become increasingly involved 'in humanitarian activities closely related to UN peacekeeping operations'.[88] The establishment of the ICC resulted from 'a rising tide of consensus over humanitarian law, driven by global and "indigenous" NGOs, international organizations, international lawyers, consumer groups, and, not least, state governments'.[89] The ICC agreement no doubt resulted from collaborative efforts by a coalition of 200 NGOs and some 60 governments in favor of an independent court. Eventually, 120 governments voted for the Treaty of Rome to establish the ICC. The UN and NGOs or civil society organizations, such as Amnesty International, Human Rights Watch and the International Committee of the Red Cross have established a symbiotic relationship and played complementary roles in the promotion of human security. In Thakur's words, they 'acting in concert have helped to establish the principle that states are responsible for the protection of human rights of their citizens and internationally accountable for any failures to do so'.[90] NGOs seem to have reached a general consensus that their activities would be far more effective if they could 'operate in a multidimensional and "multi-track" framework in which local actors,

external NGOs, governments and international organizations undertake complementary actions'.[91] This goal can be reached if they can achieve 'concerted and
consistent coordination and a commonality of objectives'.[92]

Last, but not least, markets have received recognition within the UN system in
the process of economic development, and are assumed to play a collaborative
role in peacebuilding. They should be able to coordinate multilateral initiatives
and activities. Close to 700 companies pledged their support for the UN's 'global
compact'. On the economic front, international organizations such as the IMF and
the World Trade Organization 'are beginning to accept the necessity to establish
links with NGOs'.[93]

UN attempts at enhancing global collaboration among other international and
transnational actors sharing a vision for human security are viewed as 'growing'.[94]
Although they still need to enter into 'expanded partnerships' among themselves,[95]
states, the UN, regional organizations, civil society actors, the private sector and
academics have sought to enhance their collaboration on human security.

The challenge for collaborative action

If there is real 'madness' in the globalist approach to human security, it has much
to do with the multitude of human security issues and ongoing collaborative
action problems. In reality, the norms of human security have not yet effectively
transformed those of national security. Moral statists still argue in favor of state
sovereignty as the protective shell against intervention by powerful states. Con-
sequentialists further make the case that humanitarian intervention does more
harm than good: it leads to chaos and breeds violence.[96] The USA, the world's
most powerful democracy, 'is second to none in the jealous defense of national
sovereignty against international encroachments'.[97]

Global norms of intervention remain fragile. UN members have not reached
consensus on the question of when humanitarian intervention is warranted, nor
have they agreed on who gets to decide. Convergence on this method for the
promotion of human security was weakened after the NATO bombardment of
the former Yugoslavia in March–June 1999 (which took place without authorization from the UN Security Council), and the military intervention in Iraq. While
some see humanitarian intervention as a 'right to secure the delivery of humanitarian assistance by force',[98] others view this type of intervention as far from
valid. The cases of intervention in Somalia, Rwanda and Iraq, some argue, offer
'no more than the most tentative support for the descriptive claim that the concept of humanitarian intervention is now seen by the international community
as legitimate'.[99] Whenever they agree on the need for humanitarian intervention,
'they often disagree on the size, tactics, and mission of an intervening force and
whether intervention does more good than harm'.[100] Consequently, the decade of
humanitarian intervention in the 1990s has been transformed into a decade (the
2000s) that has 'not seen effective humanitarian intervention by anyone'.[101] Intervention by major states, most notably the USA, Britain, and France, has become
less and less frequent. After the failure in Somalia during its military intervention

in October 1993, the USA has done virtually nothing to help end civil wars in Africa; it even 'actively prevented the UN from obtaining military forces from other countries', 'did almost nothing in the case of Liberia', 'has done nothing in the Congo', and 'has done nothing' for the people in Darfur besides issuing official statements describing 'human rights as genocide'.[102]

Post-Cold War coordination efforts to promote human security have no doubt become more evident but far less than is desirable; even governments within the international community have complained 'about the lack of effective coordination for the past half-century, [but] they have done little about it'.[103] Country-level donor coordination within the UN system has improved, but remains poor. This is a common complaint: 'While some minor pooling of bilateral aid efforts has occurred, assistance from the community of donor countries remains largely uncoordinated'.[104] Even though '[t]he United Nations remains our one and best hope for unity in diversity in a world in which global problems require multilateral solutions' and 'the locus of collective action',[105] it has now become clear that its member states still refuse to collaborate effectively. Even one of the staunchest supporters of the UN, Ramesh Thakur, still acknowledges that it has 'demonstrated a failure to tackle urgent collective action problems due to institutionalized inability, incapacity or unwillingness'.[106] There have been a few exceptional proposals regarding the need to establish an Economic Security Council and a Human Security Council, but no progress has been made.[107] Other recent work raises more questions about the need for better coordination between NGOs and other actors, such as states, militaries and international organizations. There still exist 'demands for more effective relationships between NGOs and other actors involved in conflict zones, including the militaries and international organizations'.[108] Critics of global corporatism point to the problem of policy coordination between the UN and other actors, particularly NGOs and the private sector. Some have called for less partnership and urged NGOs to stay outside the UN system and apply more pressure on the UN.[109] Others even see corporate responsibility as the problem of 'wolf in sheep's clothing', and even accuse promoters of corporate responsibility of ignoring 'corporate criminals' and companies of polishing their images and reputations by flying the UN flag.[110]

There are also limits to what states, international/regional and non-governmental organizations can provide in terms of making concrete, material contributions to human security activities. The European Union and NATO, for instance, during the summer and autumn of 2005, limited their action to that aimed at providing 'airlift and training support to several thousand AU [African Union] soldiers charged with monitoring the situation (no peacekeeping or peace-enforcement) in Darfur'.[111] The 53-member African Union still has little financial and logistical capacity, and has no standing collective force up to modern military standards. Other regional organizations provided little assistance. Peacebuilding funds still represent small percentages of national budgets: 'peacebuilding looks highly supported on paper, [but] in fact it receives little meaningful financial and political support relative to the costs of renewed conflict'.[112] NGOs can play a vital role in ending and transforming conflict in developing countries, but their 'participation in conflict zones is *ad hoc* and privately initiated and managed through funds coming from international sources'.[113] As pointed out by Hampson and others, they lack resources and capabilities, and remain largely dependent on their governmental allies.[114]

One thing is clear: collaborative action based on normative consensus, policy coordination and material contribution cannot be forged and enhanced unless it also serves actors' own interests. Scholars continue to note problems with collective action. Roland Paris observes that 'different members of the human security coalition have customized the definition [of human security] to suit their own particular interests'.[115] Peacebuilding remains an ambiguous concept that can 'camouflage divisions over how to handle the postconflict challenge' and 'can facilitate collective action' among different actors, who 'can support the symbol without necessarily achieving consensus on the substance'.[116] In *Building Sustainable Peace*, both Tom Keating and Andy Knight further concede that 'one cannot swim against the current of national interests',[117] and how we can harness them to human security objectives remains a daunting task.

Norms seem to matter significantly only when they also promote actors' interests. Japan is known as a civilian power increasingly involved in peacebuilding, but in August 2003 the Diet (legislature) revised the law governing its overseas development assistance (ODA) with the aim of ensuring 'Japan's own security and prosperity'. According to a leading Japan scholar, 'It was not the first time that Japan's strategic interests were factored into its ODA calculus, of course, but it was the first time that ODA was openly identified with national security'.[118] When it met in early 2005 to discuss whether to join the peacekeeping force in Darfur, Japan's Cabinet Office reached this decision: 'Sudan was too far away and Japan had no national interest at stake there.'[119] Powerful donors remain conscious of their relative position in the world. US foreign policy often proves this point: 'Americans are far more interested in maintaining US global hegemony ... solely by further opening foreign markets to [their] goods and culture ... than they are in the promotion of democracy *per se*'.[120] Martha Finnemore, a leading constructivist, further contends that 'norms, rules and routines ... will serve the interests of powerful actors; they will not survive long if they do not'.[121]

In short, then, norms do not seem to operate independently from material power, and can be best promoted if and when they do not work to undermine the interests of actors, especially those of states, which still play a crucial role in the security arena.

Conclusion

The chapter shows that human security goes beyond both realism and liberal internationalism, and theoretically can be located in globalism, when examined in the light of the referent object for security, sources of threat, providers of security, and the means involved. By no means do I suggest that the new 'human security paradigm' has prevailed over that of national or international security. Thakur seems quite premature when exhorting realists to 'get real'[122] and noting that 'the turning points in human history have come from the efforts of those unreasonable people – Gautama Buddha, Jesus Christ and Mahatma Gandhi – who set out to change the world instead'.[123]

After several thousand years (since the day of Buddha to our modern day), global norms remain as fragile as ever, and self-interest still trumps altruism. Although it is chipping away at the theoretical foundation of realism, globalism has potential but remains theoretically weak. Challenges for collaborative action on human security remain formidable: altruism has become a force in the new global politics, but it has not yet superceded self-interest. To measure progress in the direction of altruism, one must ask if actors reach normative convergence, take policy action to coordinate their activities for human security outside their national borders, and make more material contributions.

Perhaps the greatest challenge for the study of collaborative action for human security is of a methodological nature. We might try to hypothesize that collaborative efforts have had some positive impact on the global stage, and seek to measure it. Since the late 1980s, for instance, some have argued that there has been a 'globalization of liberal market democracy'.[124] We have been encouraged to look at other worldwide or global trends, such as shrinking global gaps in gender inequality and global levels of socioeconomic development. This globalist approach, however, risks establishing a spurious relationship between global progress and human security activities.

The regional approach can still shed more light on progress in human security, or the lack of it. East Asia is one region in need of further investigation into the question of how this type of security can be promoted through collaborative action among actors. We thus make some effort to put to the test the optimistic proposition that global collaboration for human security can be enhanced: namely that liberal norms can be learned and internalized; global coordination improved; and more material contributions provided.

2   The western roots of human security

Oliver P. Richmond

'Security', like 'justice', is an essentially contested concept, not just in terms of its meaning, but also in application. The concept has now broadened considerably to incorporate military, political, economic, societal and even environmental dimensions, and the interlinkages between them. The debate on security has tackled a number of conceptual questions regarding the unit of analysis, or object, of security: the tools for achieving security; the relationship between development and security; and the place of ideas such as dignity and equity in security, as noted in Chapter 1.

When Mahbub ul Haq, a Pakistani, first articulated the concept of human security in a 1994 UN Development Programme (UNDP) report as an alternative to territorial and military security through a focus on individual security and sustainable development, he was drawing on a range of antecedents that had long been critical of realist thinking.[1] Indeed, realist responses to his work can be seen in the reluctance of some states to accept it for fear that it might undermine their sovereignty.[2] Its later reincarnation as a crucial element of a liberal international system can be seen in the 'Responsibility to Protect' usage of the concept, and in the subsequent High-level Panel Report.[3] Today, human security is taken to be a central concept across much of the UN system and by many member states and donors, although when it comes to the concept of humanitarian intervention, the consensus appears weaker.[4] Many have written about the roots of human security from the perspective of the post-Cold War environment, or its links with the UN system,[5] but little has been written that examines the deeper roots of the concept emanating from a genealogy of mainly western political thought.[6]

In its broadest incarnation, human security is broadly defined as freedom from want and freedom from fear: positive and negative freedoms and rights. This has broadened the level of analysis in international relations, and brought social and economic insecurities to the fore. Discussion of human security has occurred in the context of the wide acceptance of the liberal peace as being the objective of most forms of intervention in conflict zones, ranging from democratization to human rights, the rule of law, development, and free-market reform. This has entailed normative changes that have transformed the nature of political community. These developments, and the issues related to human security, have raised the need to consider collaborative action. This also raises the problem of agency *vis-á-vis* human security in the context of the securitization of the individual, and in the context of the many actors involved in its provision.

There have been criticisms of the concept of human security, as noted by other contributors in this volume. Some have wondered if human security issues are more appropriately considered as 'domestic' issues of welfare and governance. Why are human security issues international security issues? Human security challenges can and do spill over territorial borders, and cause a range of wider security threats and sources of regional and local instability. These include refugee flows, illegal trafficking in narcotics and humans, environmental degradation, the disruption of international markets, and perhaps even terrorism (if we consider that deprivation provides a breeding ground for extremism). Human security threats are therefore interdependent and very much a global concern that requires international and local cooperation among a range of actors. Yet the concept is regarded by positivist and reductionist analysts as hopelessly broad and all-inclusive, and therefore without analytical usefulness.

This chapter argues that there are two clear dimensions of human security theory emerging from these debates and that lead on from developments in international relations theory more generally. The first is derived from the intersection between realist and liberal thinking in international relations and in policy more recently, and in particular is associated with a peacebuilding consensus on the 'liberal peace'.[7] This institutionalist approach certainly aspires to human security in its broader forms, but in fact focuses narrowly, and in positivist terms, on basic security plus the construction of effective institutions of governance through which human security can be developed in postconflict development settings. This top-down perspective takes human security to be dependent on security, on strong states, and on international intervention driven by hegemonic states, which establishes the necessary institutions to provide for very basic forms of human security – mainly physical security. The second approach derives from the critical impulse in international relations, and offers a focus on emancipation as the aim of human security. This bottom-up, emancipatory approach means that individuals are empowered to negotiate and develop a form of human security fitted to their political, economic and social needs, and provided with the necessary tools to do so. This, by necessity, focuses on a broad notion of human security, on external providers of human security, but aims at local agency as its ultimate expression. Human security is thus focused on emancipation from oppression, domination and hegemony, as well as want. It is thought of as a universal project, but one capable of being shaped by and reflecting local interests and particularities.

The following section maps out some of the antecedents of the contemporary debates on human security with a view to explaining these in relation to key strands of western thought. It does not purport to go beyond western thought, nor should this be taken to imply that these are the only contributors to human security:

> ... the concept's origins are partly, if not equally, rooted in Islam, Eastern thought and a range of indigenous traditions previously un-penetrated by Western thought and customs. From the teachings of the Prophet Mohammed,

the Buddha and Confucius to the centuries-long struggles of indigenous groups, such as those culminating in the efforts led by Rigoberta Menchu and José Ramos-Horta, strong notions of social justice, communal responsibility, inter-generational equity and harmony with nature emerged to challenge – and sometimes change – Western-held beliefs. They further shaped international dialogues that preceded and informed the introduction of the modern concept of human security in the 1990s.[8]

Furthermore, much contemporary work on human security, if broadly defined, is being carried out in a Southeast Asian context (see Chapter 4).[9] However, the institutions that have been used to develop human security in practice, including non-governmental organizations (NGOs), have been predominantly liberal since the 1990s, even if the idea itself draws on broader themes. While what follows is not exhaustive, it underlines the fact that the evolution of human security and of human security actors has an extremely long and sophisticated intellectual provenance, which has often found itself in opposition to dominant simplifications of western or liberal international relations. What is more, its most powerful evocation today lies in its emancipatory characteristics that produce a great deal of tension with the liberal institutionalist approach, which many assume should reproduce human security.

Antecedents of the debate on human security

It would be quite wrong to suggest that human security is new, given its obvious roots in the tradition of political liberalism and the enhancement of the freedom and security of individuals. Human security is normative: it argues that there is an ethical responsibility to reorient security around the individual, but it is also cognizant of the fact that security issues at the individual level have implications for the stability and legitimacy of the international system. Human security is also based on empirical observations of the relationship between a society and state, regional and international stability. It also provides a methodological position through which security for the individual can be constructed by private as well as public action, through empowerment, assistance and aid. These strands can be observed in much of the canon of texts dealing with international relations throughout history; in the works of Aristotle, Plato, Augustine, Confucius and Ibn Kaldun, a concern can be seen with the exercise of power and its impact on society.[10] What is more, it is clear that from the Bible to the Koran, from Roman law to later European writings, there is always an awareness, expressed openly or not, of the sanctity and rights of the person (although with some exceptions, such as slaves), and the need to respect this to have a stable polity. For Aquinas, this was expressed through a natural law in which states had a limited role focused on justice, peace and protection for individuals.[11] The approach of Aquinas to tyranny was an implicit acceptance of the limitations of rule and the need to incorporate the interests of the governed.[12] This was famously incorporated in the *Magna Carta* of 1215. The emergence of the 'just war' doctrine in theological and political thought and philosophy, in the context of war within and between European states, was also a step towards thinking about the broader implications of war, not just in terms of whether war was just, but also how it should be conducted, with a view to mitigating its effects on individuals.

The Treaty of Westphalia, often credited with establishing the modern states-system – by which is meant the realist states-system – created a discursive framework in which security was thought of solely in terms of national survival, and this became the driving force behind much orthodox theorizing about security henceforth. In Thomas Hobbes' view, this led to the reliance of individuals on the state to provide them basic security, which could never be achieved alone.[13] The state came to dominate discourse about security in a doctrine of 'absolutism'.

In response, more liberal modes of intellectual thinking began to develop an alternative position on the concept of security. John Locke, for example, noted that the state was a voluntary association of individuals who required mutual security.[14] This is associated with the notion of a contract between rational individuals who create a commonwealth to maximize their liberty and security.[15] This represented a balance between the natural law that included constraints on sovereigns and human rights. Both Gentili and Grotius also were concerned with the treatment of civilians, both in and out of war.[16] Rousseau also argued famously that sovereignty lay with the people, implying that consent was necessary between people and sovereign, which would not be forthcoming if their rights were abused.[17]

Consequently, key thinkers in European political thought provide an early basis for contemporary debates on human security.[18] Most notably, Immanuel Kant provided an important insight into the early evolution of a more humanistic mode of political thought, in which individual rights and representation were also to be considered. This found its contemporary character initially in the 'Peace Project' associated with the Enlightenment.[19] The *Project for Perpetual Peace* of the Abbé de St-Pierre (1713) spurred Kant to expand these ideas further. Kant developed an account of the social and moral world that would incorporate an understanding of the types of relations required between polities if a moral life were to be possible.[20] This is exactly what Kant tried to achieve in *Perpetual Peace: A Philosophical Sketch*, and it continues to be a project that preoccupies most, if not all, actors engaged in the 'international'.

Kant based his understanding of peace on his belief that a 'categorical imperative' exists as an innate moral law. This universal law allows for universalization and dictates that human beings must be treated as ends rather than means.[21] What he offered, and what has become popularized in contemporary international relations, the media and international organizations and instruments, is that people are ends in themselves and that they have rights and needs in any location. Furthermore, actors not directly associated with non-citizens are subject to a normative requirement to consider attending to these rights and needs. What this implies is that individual rights are being developed in a security and civil context; and what is more, that individuals being viewed as ends rather than means indicates that both have agency and are referents of security. Kant's contribution to the human security debate is clear – individual security must be considered in the construction of a liberal version of peace.

As to the question of who provides for human security, we must also remember that Kant feared that a world government representing a universal peace would be as unpleasant as a Hobbesian world, as it might culminate in worse despotism.[22] Thus *Perpetual Peace* sets out the conditions by which peace can be attained between states, some of which are clearly reflected in the UN Charter. Of course, in a Kantian context, his perpetual peace was to be provided by a 'pacific union' of democratic states, security by free trade, and regulated arms exchanges, rather than by specific organizations, public or private, tasked with human security-oriented roles. There is no mention of the task of providing human security for those who do not yet have it in other states, although this must be implicit in perpetual peace theory and, to a lesser extent, in democratization theory. Kant specified that states should be republican (democratic), that international order should rest on a federation of free states that would be able to abolish war among themselves, and that non-citizens should be afforded 'universal hospitality'. This argument also gave rise to the 'democratic peace' thesis.[23]

A Grotian discourse on natural law has also made an important contribution to this intellectual debate in that it introduces the foundation of natural law: the rights of self-preservation and to own property. These rights were extended to states that protect themselves, but in the context of norms and rules as opposed to the Hobbesian version of a state of nature.[24] Where states cannot do so, the implication is that such rights are still a requirement of the individual and must be provided for by their own endeavours or by outside actors. Clear parallels with the human security debate are obvious here, in that human security is constructed as a condition that can be guaranteed and transferred by external actors, where local actors lack any such capacity. Furthermore, this is seen as a requirement for those external actors operating in the human security realm.

From such approaches, there emerged the roots of the institutional version of human security, whereby rights and needs for individuals are catered for by liberal institutions, probably multilateral in nature, which govern or intervene where necessary.

Another key strand can be seen in the emergence of nationalism, which is based on John Stuart Mill's understanding of the right of people to determine their own government.[25] His thinking was part of a developing human rights tradition, often argued to be the key to human security thinking. However, self-determination, once associated with the protection of specific territory, soon became a prescription for war between groups laying claim to the same territory, rather than for peace. Still, the debate about self-determination, in which individuals residing in groups define their own security and political rights, is important for our understanding of human security, because it enables people to determine their political rights and confers a responsibility on the international community to facilitate this. Political rights in this sense were envisaged in relation to decisionmaking about security, and because these rights were devolved to the individual, it is implicit in this framework that self-determination was partly a human security-oriented framework in which individuals were empowered to make decisions about their own security and needs. The territorial and highly politicized nature of self-determination meant that its operationalization often undermined human security in multi-ethnic states, where identity-based conflicts emerged.

As the Enlightenment project progressed, the earlier view that war was part of the natural fabric of life was replaced by the new view that peace should be so, rather than an ideal to be aspired to – and that this peace should be thought about in the context of nations.[26] Of course, the counter-Enlightenment unleashed the opposing view that peace should be derived, as Burke or Herder might say, from the uniqueness of the nation and tribe rather than universalism, meaning nationalism.[27] Construing this sentiment in the context of nationalism might also be a cause for war. But what is important here is the notion that war needed to be curtailed, and that peace could be constructed by states and between states for the benefit of their citizens. From here, it was a short step to the beginnings of the institutionalization of activity related to the construction of peace by states, international organization, and non-state actors, which even by the nineteenth century were beginning to emerge in the shape of the Congress System, the International Committee of the Red Cross (ICRC), the ending of the slave trade, and disarmament discourses. Again, the antecedents of contemporary human security thinking can be clearly seen.

The creation of social movements began to occur on a large scale during the nineteenth and twentieth centuries. The peace movements, disarmament movements, human rights movements, trade unions, and groups advocating the end of slavery or the broadening of the franchise, with which we are now so familiar, were largely a product of the western secular experience. Two distinct pathways can be observed here. Early and contemporary peace movements often have a religious orientation. The second, and also perhaps most recent, pathway is the secular emergence of liberal-internationalism, associated with cosmopolitan movements, disarmament and democratization, coordinated by international organizations such as the League of Nations and the United Nations. Other campaigns of significance can also be pointed to as a product of the western secular experience. These include campaigns against conscription, ideological and feminist movements against war, the campaign for nuclear disarmament, and the environmental movements.[28] It is also important to note the significance of the philosophy behind the French Revolution, which sought to devolve power to the population away from the lineage of royalty and liberate an entire nation. The American War of Independence also contributed a philosophical strand on personal freedom and the role of government, embodied in the resulting constitutional framework to the debate on how peace and security can be attained. At the same time, the construction of an international community, which was intended to prevent the use of violence and the use of war as an extension of politics, also gathered pace. It is important to note that the era of European imperialism was crucial for both the use of force by states in pursuit of prestige and economic interest, and at the same time the *mission civilisatrice* that went with it, involving missionaries, campaigns against slavery or such as those conducted in the Congo against King Leopold's ruthless exploitation of the territory, often largely run from within civil society rather than by states.[29] From 1816 to the 1860s, Britain deployed a naval squadron against slave trading on the west coast of Africa. This reversal in the British approach to slavery meant a reinterpretation of international law to allow vessels to be boarded and searched. This attack on state sovereignty meant that, for the first time perhaps, a humanitarian principle took precedence.[30]

This did not mean a rejection of imperialism as a significant contributor to a peaceful world order at this time, but it seemed to represent an uneasy collusion between humanitarianism and domination.[31] Increasingly, an emancipatory version of human security can be seen to be emerging, in which individuals are deemed to have certain inalienable rights and the capacity to act on them if empowered.

These different traditions, including political and civil rights and antiwar movements, were and are indicative of the move towards an understanding of security issues in the context not just of states, but also individuals. The development of human security actors and their associated normative and legal regimes provides the next strand in this debate. Henri Dunant's work, which led to the Geneva Convention of 1864, delineated what was lawful in war in order to bind states to certain standards of behavior during conflict and led to the creation of the ICRC. Out of this emerged what came to be known as international humanitarian law, of which the ICRC is the guardian. Despite debates over the efficacy of its neutrality, it is clear that the non-state actors who were required to operate in the realms of human security were now beginning to crystallize. From this, the two key thrusts of human security thinking can be gleaned: the move to develop institutions to provide human security (incidentally a key aspect of the contemporary liberal peace); and the recognition of individuals' capacity to lobby, advocate and bring about change reflecting their own emancipatory version of human security.

The importance of Woodrow Wilson's Fourteen Points at Versailles in 1919 must be noted as a contributing factor to contemporary notions of human security, although self-determination and its association with nationalism have turned out to be somewhat counterproductive in their attempts to end conflict. Tribal nationalism and the 'old world' conservative order had been repulsed, and the USA had emerged as a global force. Wilson was opposed to European imperialism and its contradiction of the values inherent in the American constitution, as well as the legacy of imperial relationships with North America (although such impulses overlooked the treatment of the indigenous communities). He pointed out that France and Britain had different views of 'peace' when compared with the American view, and proposed to 'force them to our way of thinking'.[32] The peace he had in mind, an 'ultimate peace of the world', was reminiscent of Kant's republican states that went hand-in-hand with democracy.[33] This was to rest on a 'community of power' and represent an 'organized common peace'.[34] This was underlined when Wilson spoke to the US Congress early in April 1917, when he famously stated that the 'world must be made safe for democracy'.[35] This was a task that, in his eyes, was philanthropic rather than self-interested on the part of the USA, and it was ultimately to be based on the self-determination of peoples.

Unfortunately, the conduct of the representatives at Versailles in 1919 seemed to betray this ethos.[36] However, Wilson's Fourteen Points outlined what he saw as a mechanism for a sustainable peace. Outlined to the US Congress on 8 January 1918, they included the foundation of the League of Nations to guarantee the sovereignty and territorial integrity of all states.[37] Added to these points, and among others, was the principle he outlined before Congress on 11 February 1918, that territorial adjustments should be of benefit to the populations concerned – namely, self-determination. The League also brought with it mechanisms for dealing with refugees and for promoting the wellbeing of colonized peoples. With the foundation of the International Labour Organization in 1919, the link between welfare and security was also acknowledged.[38] Security was now being formally thought of as also existing at the level of the individual and group, rather than solely at state level. Providing individuals with agency also implied an engagement with their security concerns.

Peace and human security in the UN system

As with the Versailles Treaty, the new peace after World War II was developed by a mixture of public and private thinking on the matter of security.[39] This time, non-official input was much more developed, most notably in the context of the Dulles 'Commission to Study the Basis of a Just and Durable Peace', the Council for Foreign Affairs and in the work of Chatham House.[40] The new peace after 1945 was to be securely based on both security guarantees and a degree of economic redistribution derived from Marshall Aid and the Truman Doctrine, but in the context of a global body that could establish the degree of consensus among states for a particular course of action. This provided yet another reaffirmation of the broadening of the security debate away from a state-centric notion that peace was also derived from economic and social security, and that the new multilateralism would be ascribed with associated duties within this broad framework. Although not widely recognized as such at this time, human security became an integral part of the notion of peace in the postwar environment. The 'idealist' peace engendered in Wilsonianism was now to become firmly institutionalized in organizations that would work constantly to provide military security, legal guarantees, political consensus, humanitarian resources, and development and financial investment. These activities were to be coordinated by and around a set of institutions emanating from the UN. The UN clearly elucidated its conception of peace in the preamble to its Charter, driven by the permanent five members of the Security Council. In the context of the UN system, peace came to engender the rejection of interstate war, the provision of humanitarian resources, development, financial regulation and adjustment, and human rights. Thus far, security was still conceptualized for states, with states as its agents, but it is also clear that there was both official and private pressure for a non-state discourse on security. This brought about the still unsettled tension between non-intervention and territorial integrity for states and the protection and empowerment of the human subject, both in the UN system and at the international and domestic levels. This debate highlights the emerging tension between an institutionalist approach to human security as it developed via the Charter, the Declaration of Human Rights, and various covenants and conventions, and an emancipatory approach to the empowerment of individual human security.

The UN system, and its genesis in the discussions between British Prime Minister Winston Churchill and US President Franklin Roosevelt during World War II, was essential to postwar developments and, more specifically, to the emergence of peacebuilding and humanitarian intervention in the post-Cold War environment. This was not a wholly new phenomenon. A humanitarian explanation had been given for European intervention during the Greek War of Independence in the 1820s, and others. David Rieff, for instance, argued that during the nineteenth century, '… the morality play of humanitarian intervention in which a victimised population must be rescued from warlordism and tyranny was already well elaborated'.[41]

The defense and construction of the liberal peace as a sum of Security Council, General Assembly, Secretariat, international agency and financial institutional development became a legitimate and legitimating objective in this context. The evolution of international humanitarian law has also been crucial. Once the multiple layers of the creation of a liberal peace in conflict zones became too much for the UN alone to achieve, as was evident in the 1990s and beyond, key components of that system took over. This reflected the need for a 'good peace' between and after both world wars.[42] This was to be not a peace rooted in the threat of force, bitter negotiations or complex government, but a 'natural peace'.

This has been strengthened by the development of a human rights discourse, derived especially from the work of western thinkers such as John Locke and John Stuart Mill. This dictates that states have a duty to meet the rights of citizens and, by extension, if they do not do so, others may then become bound to do so. As Christine Bell points out, the evolution of what have become known as human rights instruments is predicated on a relationship between peace and justice.[43] This line of thought can be seen as a natural evolution of the universalism apparent in Enlightenment thought.[44] As Chris Brown has also pointed out, there are two key antecedents to this rights discourse: one based on a universal natural law tradition, and the other based on a particularistic, contractual, legal account.[45] He, concurring with Michael Ignatieff's position on liberalism and its linkages with humanitarian intervention, argues that the fiction of universal rights is not harmfully misleading, although he acknowledges that if particularistic rights discourses are presented as universal, then this problem is far more significant.[46] As Brown points out, the *Universal Declaration of Human Rights* was constructed in such as way as to represent a universal consensus, although it ultimately reflected the rights enshrined in western constitutions.[47] Henry Shue conceptualizes the development of these rights in terms of 'basic rights', which include security rights and subsistence rights.[48] Basic rights denote 'everyone's minimum reasonable demand upon the rest of humanity'. This is reflected in the *Covenant on Economic, Social and Cultural Rights*.[49]

A key question is whether such rights are indeed intrinsic to the individual, or require delegation to, or the guardianship, of states or international institutions as duties. Similarly, rights of individuals can also be seen as duties.[50] Again, one can clearly see the emergence of a human security discourse and of a requirement for human security actors to become engaged, in terms of both emancipation and the creation of the necessary institutions for the provision of human security. Both of the above-mentioned documents place the discussion of peace and rights in a developmental, welfare and cultural context, again indicating the *long durée* of the concept of human security.

This aspect of the debate raises the question as to whether individuals should expect other actors to take the lead in providing them with the resources (as the recent report of the High-level Panel and *The Responsibility to Protect* outline), or whether they should exercise their agency in this regard. International consensus seems to rest mainly with the former, although most think that empowerment should be provided so that individuals can become responsible for their own security. Again, a tension between liberal approaches and emancipatory approaches emerges.

In parallel to these conceptual developments, non-state actors began to gain more of a role in responding to conflict, specifically in the context of human rights and humanitarian assistance. One of the notable early organizations that illustrated the problems such activities faced was the International Rescue Committee, which began its life rescuing Jews from Europe during World War II, and was later involved with retrieving Hungarian refugees after the failure of the 1956 rebellion, and Cuban refugees after Fidel Castro came to power in Cuba in 1959.[51] Other such organizations followed, including the Catholic Relief Service, World Vision and the Oxford Committee for Famine Relief (OXFAM). OXFAM's first major campaign focused on relieving the city of Athens from a British Navy blockade in 1941–42, which led to an estimated minimum of 100,000 deaths from starvation.[52] Although human security actors were clearly derived from the view that humanitarianism had to be included in any construction of peace, many of these organizations soon added the mantras of development to their repertoire,[53] further broadening the conception of security.

As is well known, the norm of non-intervention effectively allowed human rights abuses, humanitarian disasters, ethnic cleansing and genocide, phenomena that undermined the assertion of a liberal international order. Such difficulties emerged in multiple contexts: in the Middle East after the declaration of the state of Israel in 1948; in India and Pakistan during Partition in 1948; in the attempted secession of Katanga in the Congo in the early 1960s; during the war between East and West Pakistan in 1971 and the subsequent intervention; in the attempted secession of Biafra during the Nigerian Civil War 1967–70; and in numerous other cases. It was the case of Biafra that brought to international attention the issue of intervention on humanitarian grounds. The very controversial role of humanitarian organizations such as ICRC and OXFAM was to aim at preventing genocide if Biafra was defeated. When, in 1968, the Nigerian federal government forbade assistance to the rebels, the ICRC withdrew, but OXFAM and others continued.

This led to the continuation of the war; however, on the defeat of Biafra, genocide did not actually take place. Humanitarianism was given an early political lesson. Henceforth, non-intervention became a much-disputed norm in unofficial human-itarian intervention, with some NGOs deciding to work only within the context of state consent. Famously, a splinter organization from ICRC, led by Bernard Kouchner, broke with these norms and rejected the ICRC's historical status and guardianship of humanitarianism. He articulated his 'right of humanitarian inter-vention'. Whether this is seen as a legal right or norm is ambiguous, but the intent was clear: humanitarianism and peace were too important to be left solely within the domain of state activity.

Despite these developments, Wheeler shows, humanitarian intervention as a right was not exercised in the cases of the West Bengal crisis of 1971, the Viet-namese overthrow of Pol Pot in Cambodia in 1979, or Tanzania's overthrow of Idi Amin in 1979.[54] As Brown points out, the 1990s brought the return of an occasional practice of international humanitarian intervention,[55] heralded by UN Security Council Resolution 688 and humanitarian action on behalf of the Kurds in northern Iraq. The 1990s were further marked by several major attempts to start the institutionalization of human security, in the context most notably of the UNDP, but also of the foreign policy engagements of donor states such as Canada and Japan, among others.

Contemporary contributions to the debate

Human security has now become a well used concept in policy documentation and speeches referring to the commitment of major states to conflict zones and the developing world. What has been most important about this policy develop-ment is the contribution human security has made to the development of gover-nance regimes, with peacebuilding processes increasingly being used to transfer and install. Human security has thus become a policy target for international and regional organizations, states, agencies and NGOs across the world. It is in the interplay of the different policy agendas of these actors that problems with the concept of human security begin to emerge, both as a theoretical approach and as practice.

The institutionalization of human security through the reconstruction of social, economic and political governance has been the result of a peacebuilding 'con-sensus' among these actors. Their attempt to construct a more inclusive terrain for the notoriously narrow and simplistic debates that have disfigured the discussion of security has appeared, in some ways, to have fallen into the same trap that classical debates on security did. Indeed, the narrowness of classical debates was configured to *prevent* collaborative action, and hence the undermining of state sovereignty. Classical debates, as illustrated by multiple versions of realism and liberalism, often culminate in the protection of the concept and framework of the Westphalian state, rather than the populations they house. In contrast, human security – particularly in its emancipatory version – broadens the agents and struc-tures identified as being causes of insecurity and responsible for its eradication so far that it becomes very difficult to prioritize crucial areas that may be most effective in ameliorating insecurity. Thus the concept has been likened to 'carrying a band aid' to deal with humanitarian crises caused by war. Ultimately, the debates about human security constitute a dual attempt: to move away from the purely rational approach embedded in the concept of state security, and to incorporate the diverse elements that are involved in a theoretical understanding of security. The problem here might be that, as Khong argues, this may lead to a paralysis of our ability to provide security, comparing it to 'speaking loudly about human security but carrying a Band-Aid'.[56] This is clearly an important criticism in the context of the role of NGOs and their increasing use as subcontractors. It is clear that, as Terry has argued, there is a contradiction between the discourse and practices of human security. Humanitarian assistance is not apolitical, of course, but it does provide states with a tool with which to avoid foreign policy engagement[57] through the work of the many agencies and NGOs involved in conflict zones. Yet the implication of the human security discourse is that intervention has become part of the means by which this can be achieved. Perhaps this is why it is more accurate to argue that the work of these actors has become part of foreign policy in the general sense of constructing a liberal peace.

Supporters of human security would argue that 'prioritization' is simply an excuse for the substitution of interests for human life. Yet the human security debate is derived from a set of previous and concurrent debates, which leads inexorably to the position that human life cannot be considered secondary to narrow sets of interests. Such a realist response to the emergence of the human security debate should not be unexpected, as it stems from the desire to limit and prioritize security concerns in which individuals are secondary to states and their institutions. Also problematic here, however, are the different levels of influence and resources and differing capacities of the multiple actors engaged in the provision of human security. This raises the question of which types of actor drive human security provision, and therefore which agenda dominates collaborative action?

The human security debate[58] has been notable mainly because of its acceptance in some key policy circles (such as within the UN organization) and in global civil society. Its call for the subjects of security to be redefined from the state to the individual – in other words, from managing interstate relations to building peace by introducing social, political and economic reforms – represents not a radical shift, but a culmination of a lengthy evolution. Its initial acceptance was mainly because liberal state and international organization objectives shifted from *status quo* management to the multidimensional approaches of peacebuilding, in which strategies are applied that aim to transform conflict '... into peaceful non-violent process of social and political change...'.[59] One of the side-effects of this, particularly in the context of UN organs and the humanitarian community, is that the provision of basic human needs in conflict zones has been privatized. This process has been characterized by their complex and multilevel, multidimensional nature and, as Mark Duffield points out, represents a securitization of development, economy and human rights, as well as politics.[60] More importantly, the process represents the securitization of the individual. This development, guided by the notion of human security, has had a major impact on the practice and efficacy of intervention. In this, the UN, and its relationship with NGOs, has become crucial because of its recognition of the multiple political, social, economic and humanitarian dynamics of 'peace' via the concept of human security.

Boutros Boutros Ghali's *Agenda for Peace* was an important early post-Cold War attempt to engage with this shift. *Agenda* presented early warning systems, preventative diplomacy, peacemaking, peacekeeping, peacebuilding and peace-enforcement operations as enabling the UN to become engaged in addressing the '… deepest causes of social injustice and political oppression…'. Thus what was required was a coordinated strategy that spanned these approaches. This involved a long-term commitment to postsettlement environments, including disarmament, the repatriation of refugees, the restoration of order, election monitoring, the protection of human rights, reforming and strengthening governmental institutions, and '… promoting formal and informal processes of political participation'.[61] Humanitarian assistance and monitoring, developmental, educational and conflict-resolution NGOs emerged as crucial actors in the controversial development of peacemaking, peacebuilding and, indeed, humanitarian intervention in the post-Cold War order, both within and alongside the UN system. One of the key questions, at the most basic level, is whether NGO involvement in the provision of human security should function on a rights basis, or on a needs basis.[62]

This outlines the differing positions taken by humanitarian pragmatists and humanitarian idealists, in which regulation of such activity to preserve an over-arching normative framework is contrasted with the liberalization of NGOs to provide assistance to those who need it, regardless of their position as victim or aggressor, or their location within the overall normative framework of the international system. Furthermore, what is often overlooked in both views is that making humanitarian decisions is itself a hegemonic act made by third parties about 'others'. This opposition can be observed in the position of the ICRC and Médecins Sans Frontièrs.[63]

Clearly, it has been disillusionment with the role of states in constructing peace in conflict zones that has led to an increased role for non-state actors, organizations and agencies. In this sense, human security is a critique of traditional Westphalian forms of sovereignty. This evolution has been based on the need for expertise in the field working on the different aspects of human-oriented security. This type of assistance has been enabled by the development of transnationalism and the recognition of non-state actors as key agents in this area.[64] Gradually, they have become important not just in providing technological expertise, but also in a normative sense, in fulfilling a role in the construction of what Galtung would term a 'positive peace'. In this sense, such actors are 'moral entrepreneurs'.[65] As Anderson points out, understanding how NGOs operate in the realm of aid and assistance is crucial.[66] Indeed, understanding the role of NGOs opens up the possibility of a private, civil society account of peacebuilding and of its tense relationship to work by agencies, international organizations, institutions and states. Such an understanding also sheds light on what disputants and societies in conflict want from both their wars and the coming peace, to which they are assumed often to be committed. Advocacy movements, epistemic communities, non-state actors, NGOs and humanitarian actors seem to be what Wallace and Josselin have described as 'norm entrepreneurs', that privilege democracy, human rights, and forms of development in their microlevel interventions, as well as in their discourse in the realm of international relations.[67]

Part of this evolution has been the growth of institutions, organizations, regimes, norms and law pertaining to the rights of groups and individuals as ends in them-selves. This is illustrated by the developing role that NGOs have played, made possible by a series of UN General Assembly resolutions that called for access for humanitarian assistance where it was required:[68] humanitarian assistance to victims of emergencies and natural disasters, access for accredited agencies, the establishment of relief corridors, and the establishment of the UN Department of Humanitarian Affairs to coordinate humanitarian intervention (although bound to the rules of sovereignty).[69] Gradually, a space has opened for broader forms of peacemaking, peacebuilding and humanitarian intervention, and the fact that NGOs have become part of this illustrates that there is increasingly a normative level to both local and international politics relating to the wider existence of political communities in terms of human security. Although problematic in terms of the rule of law and political interests, humanitarian intervention of both an unofficial and official nature is clearly increasing – especially on an unofficial level – often substituting for state interests and capacities in ways that have not yet fully been revealed. NGOs derive their legitimacy at both local and global level, and they tend to engage in projects relating to human security rather than state security in situations where the state is often perceived, from inside or out-side, to have failed its population. This human security ethos on which the work of NGOs is based has had significant implications for global politics, and highlights a growing gap between humanitarian issues and state practice. NGOs may now have become a third category of subject in international law, along with states and international organizations.[70]

The implication here is that human security has similarly become normatively established. Yet this assertion is the target of pragmatic arguments that NGOs can have a role in state-rebuilding as long as they are monitored and controlled by intergovernmental institutions and their member states, and normative arguments that a global civil society has now transcended state control and represents a cos-mopolitan desire for human security. The notion of human security in particular has been attacked on the grounds that as a nodal point for directing state, interna-tional governmental organization (IGO) and NGO activity, it obfuscates the kind of prioritization that is required to preserve state security and stability.[71]

Thus the dynamics of a familiar dispute between independent, transnational actors (disillusioned with the ability of states to provide security to the margin-alized) and the state-centric belief (that margins must be sacrificed in order to preserve order and security) becomes clear. But human security has emerged as a compelling alternative to the traditional notion of state security, opening up fur-ther possibilities. Both versions of security imply different conceptions of interna-tional relations, of the responsibilities of state and non-state actors, of the nature of the international system, and of what kind of ethical order is viable. While such debates preoccupy policy and academic communities, NGOs continue to raise funding and work in the field to ameliorate the impact of political, social or economic 'abnormalities' and other disasters, using human security as their key referent.

Human security has also been included in debates on globalization. Scholte argues that globalization has highlighted broader understandings of security and, in particular, of human security. In his view, 'in some respects globalization has promoted increased human security, for example, with disincentives to war, improved means of humanitarian relief, new job opportunities, and greater pluralism'. He adds that, 'in other ways globalization has perpetuated or even deepened warfare, environmental degradation, poverty, unemployment, exploitation of workers, and social disintegration'.[72] This is illustrated by the polarized debates about the links between globalization and security, and by the possibility that globalization raises normative questions about security well beyond the traditional limits of the state (although it also tends to highlight global social hierarchies). This raises questions about whether globalization enhances or undermines popular participation and consent procedures.

If globalization has made security indivisible and human suffering an irrevocable universal concern, this indicates a normative and practical role to governments, world markets, communicational facilities, civil society, IGOs and NGOs in facilitating better conditions for those caught up in violence or disasters. But we can point to the Washington Consensus as an aspect of this development,[73] which, as with debates about globalization, has been linked to both neoliberalism and 'market fundamentalism'.[74] This is important in the context of the globalization of responses to conflict because of the conditionality associated with the work of the World Bank and International Monetary Fund in conflict zones. This conditionality is mirrored by the broader activities of states, organizations, institutions and NGOs when they construct interventions, gather funding for those interventions, and develop relationships with actors involved in conflict through the various political, economic, developmental and social reform projects that peacebuilding entails.

Again, the tension between the top-down, hegemonically constructed version of human security and the emancipatory version, in which individuals are empowered or develop their own agency, is apparent. This tension is also apparent in international relations theory's approach to human security. The broad, emancipatory approach to human security, as defined by ul Haq, rests on its important normative implications, which many realist–liberal-inclined scholars do not want to engage with.[75] As Ponzio argues:

> By positing that 'human beings count', human security helps scholars and practitioners balance the traditional preoccupation with the state as the main 'unit of analysis' with the urgent needs of people. In doing so, the concept introduces a missing ethical dimension in the study of international relations and related subjects.[76]

Conclusion

The human security debate has so far come about partly because of the emergence, during the twentieth century in particular, of discourses concerning non-state actors, human rights, international human rights law, international humanitarian law, feminism and development. All these different strands of thought and policymaking have effected the redefinition of security to include the individual and the establishment of norms, regimes and institutions to protect individuals, meet their material needs, and realize their dignity.[77] International organizations and specialized agencies have played a major role in constructing this whole intellectual process.

Where this becomes problematic is in the little-examined question of how much human security discourses, regimes, norms and associated institutions enhance, or substitute for, the agency of individuals in providing for their security. In many cases, it seems that the provision of these soft security frameworks has been delegated, subcontracted, and in some cases privatized in the context of a global civil society. This effectively has meant the empowerment of such actors in defining and providing the human security requirements of target populations. This is where an understanding of both versions of human security I have outlined is crucial. Although the liberal version, which focuses on institutional provision, is significant, the emancipatory version is necessary if these institutions are to be effective in empowering civil society actors rather than merely becoming ends in themselves. The goals of human security in an emancipatory form cannot be achieved by states alone (if at all); its provision is also privatized, localized and indigenized. This means that a broad definition of human security is thus required; otherwise, if we revert to a narrow version, as proposed by some scholars and practitioners in order to make it more practical for policymakers, human security loses its emancipatory potential.[78]

As this paper has sought to illustrate, however, the human security debate has a long provenance both in theoretical terms and also in the more surprising area of the creation of a capacity to address human security issues. The emergence of non-state actors, their networks of a human rights discourse, a development discourse, and the establishment of international organizations, institutions, and agencies all long pre-date the start of the formal human security debate. Yet they further imbue human security with a practical application and capacity. Furthermore, the conservative responses of those who have sought to undermine human security as a research and policy agenda are nothing new. It is all the more surprising that the capacity that currently exists to address human security issues has emerged to such a large extent. In contrast to, and in opposition to, state security, human security provides a body of actors with an agenda for capacity-building, cooperation, entrepreneurship and intervention. Reductionist thinkers, who want to appease state power and the status of officialdom, will always find difficulties with this concept, despite that fact that such a parsimonious mapping of security does not represent the complexity of peacebuilding, nor does it provide the necessary tools. Indeed, such 'pragmatic' approaches really represent appeasement and the ontological acceptance that violence is inevitable and cannot be redressed. Yet contemporary human security approaches also effectively contribute to the eventual rebuilding of state capacity, because in their relations with IGOs, regional organizations, states, and donors in general, they, too, become part of the liberal conditionality associated with the construction of the liberal peace. This is partly because human security-oriented actors are caught up in a web of collaboration with other actors perhaps more focused on regional or state interests, or on neoliberal development, democratization and human rights agendas.

The question of collaboration indicates that conditionality and dependency are a problem not just between peacebuilders and recipients, but also between donors and the various actors operating to enhance human security. The implication of this is that while donor–peacebuilder relations are necessary, they are also open to manipulation. While collaboration between multiple actors for the provision of human security is therefore necessary, as elaborated in much of this volume, it also remains problematic. This is because, although human security has the potential to be emancipatory and recognize difference within diverse postconflict societies, liberal institutions and actors have operationalized it as a liberal form of biopower in which social engineering focuses on a broader peace, rather than on the peace experienced by the individual. This means that liberal human security cannot respond adequately to a range of problems, such as culture, agency, dependency, conditionality, welfare and inadequate coordination, without making the next step to a much more sophisticated engagement with the identity and needs of individuals in postconflict settings on their own terms, rather than those driven by the peacebuilding consensus and epistemic community of human security-providers derived solely from neoliberal internationalism or institutionalism.

3 East versus West?

Debate and convergence on human security[1]

Akiko Fukushima

As noted elsewhere throughout this volume, the term or concept 'human security' was introduced to the international community when the seminal *Human Development Report*, authored by the United Nations Development Programme (UNDP), was published in 1994. As the concept was finally adopted by a small number of governments in the East and West and then spread into academic circles, skeptical political realists (such as Professor Seizaburo Sato in Japan) began to question whether human security would soon be in a credible position to replace national security. In Sato's view, the concept was simply flawed.[2] These critics have a point in terms of their intellectual bias toward the concept of national security. No one can make the case that states no longer exist and no longer care about their national security, but I contend that human security has become increasingly relevant to the world in which we now live, largely because of the growth of interdependence among states and their peoples.

This chapter further argues that there has been a degree of normative convergence in academic and policy debate over conceptual complementarity between national and human security, as each is now recognized as indispensable to, or not regarded as exclusive of, the other. By convergence, I do not mean to suggest that the conceptual divide no longer exists. In my view, however, the competing conceptions of human security within the narrow and broad approaches have increasingly come to some sort of a truce based on mutual recognition, or reached a higher degree of consensus based on the need to focus not on their definitional differences, but on operationalization of the concept. More specifically, this chapter contends that states and other actors in Europe and East Asia have now made some progress when assessed in terms of the extent to which their views on human security have now converged. My arguments are advanced as follows. The first section reviews the historical development of human security and the debate on its analytical merits. After that, the chapter focuses on the different positions states in Europe and East Asia have adopted, and assesses the extent to which their positions and expectations have converged. The last section reviews the possibilities of regional institutional efforts to operationalize human security policy objectives.

The concept of human security: emergence and academic debate

Why did the people-centered dimension of security – human security – emerge in the early 1990s? There are at least four major factors that have given rise to this concept. The first was the end of the Cold War. After the unexpected collapse of the Soviet Union, the likelihood of interstate war declined dramatically. Intrastate wars, which had been kept in check by the irrepressible 'glacier' of the Cold War, erupted in Africa and south-eastern Europe, whose atrocities Europe and Canada have been exposed to first-hand. With some of these conflicts resulting in geno-cide and 'ethnic cleansing', most of the victims were ordinary citizens or unarmed civilians/non-combatants. In many of these intrastate conflicts, failed or failing states denied their citizens access to the means of dealing with the various forms of insecurity they faced on a daily basis. Moreover, these states often provided breeding grounds for extremism or terrorism, leading to senseless atrocities, not least of which was the string of attacks on the USA on 11 September 2001.

The second factor was the impact of the new global war on terrorism waged in both Afghanistan and Iraq since the early 2000s. After the terrorist attacks on the USA and after Washington announced its 'war on terror', state leaders and their people offered their support for the war against Afghanistan. But when the war was expanded to Iraq, many raised critical voices, questioning the legitimacy and appropriateness of this war. In addition, internal stability has not taken hold in the two countries. The Taliban insurgents in Afghanistan were resurging; armed factions in Iraq were regrouping; fatalities among foreign military and civilian personnel and local populaces rose.

The third factor was related to the fact that the sources of threat to security became more diverse. In addition to military security threats, a new category of threats emerged, ranging from climate change and natural disasters to infectious diseases, to name a few. Not surprisingly, these threats, which affect individuals and communities in ways that are different from the more traditional security threats, have intensified the debate on whether they should even be regarded as security threats in the first place.[3] But these non-military threats hit industrialized and developing countries alike, and it became increasingly clear that they could even undermine national security.[4]

Last, but not least, is the globalization factor. The development of information and communication technologies has resulted in the swift cross-border transfer of capital, goods and information. Thomas Friedman referred to this phenomenon, which is most prevalent in economic activities, as a 'flattening of the world'.[5] This flattening has extended to other, less welcome developments, such as proliferation of terrorism, weapons, narcotics, pollutants and disease-carrying bacteria. In a globalized world, threats are no longer confined to the regions in which they flare up, but rather emanate out like a tsunami to neighboring regions and other parts of the globe. Thus peoples around the world now share a common global vulner-ability, anxiety, and thus insecurity. This so-called flattening has been uneven, resulting in 'an unflat world'. Friedman observes that 'children in the developing world are ten times more likely to die of vaccine-preventable diseases than are children in the developed flat world'.[6]

These four factors together have given rise to a new global awareness that 'hard' security associated with state survival is no longer capable of providing security at individual and community levels, and thus came the new framework on security.

However, there has probably never been a security-related concept that has caused such incandescent debate over its definition as human security. In Japan, there were debates over how to translate the concept into Japanese, over the various merits of different translations, and over how to communicate the most appropriate nuance. Japan seems to have settled on *ningen no anzenhosho* as the accepted translation of 'human security', but the discussion reflected the broader debate on the interpretation of the concept itself. A fierce debate over whether to rely on the broader or narrower approach also unfolded. The debate, discussed elsewhere in this volume, initially had been framed as one focusing on freedom from fear and the other on freedom from want. The serious divide between the two approaches was whether the use of force in the name of human security, known as humanitarian intervention, is permissible.

The broader approach was found first in the UNDP's 1994 *Human Develop-ment Report* and later in the report of the Commission on Human Security (CHS). The CHS was established by Japan and chaired jointly by Sadako Ogata (former UN High Commissioner for Refugees and current President of the Japan Inter-national Cooperation Agency, JICA) and Amartya Sen (former Master of Trinity College Cambridge and current Lamont Professor at Harvard University). The commission's report, entitled *Human Security Now*, defined human security as protecting 'the vital core of all human lives in ways that enhance human freedoms and human fulfillment', with the following characterization:

> Human security means protecting fundamental freedoms – freedoms that are the essence of life. It means protecting people from critical (severe) and pervasive (widespread) threats and situations. It means using processes that build on people's strengths and aspirations. It means creating political, social, environmental, economic, military and cultural systems that together give people the building blocks of survival, livelihood and dignity.[7]

With this definition, the concept of human security includes three freedoms: 'freedom from fear', 'freedom from want' and 'freedom to live in dignity'.[8] The commission opted not to itemize which elements are included in human security, arguing that what people consider 'the vital core of all human lives' varies by individual and society.

Meanwhile, the narrower definition limits human security to freedom from violence, namely freedom from fear. One of its advocates, Andrew Mack, who has been compiling an annual report on human security, initially at the Univer-sity of British Columbia (Canada) and now at Simon Fraser University (also in Canada), has noted the difference between the broad and narrow definitions in the following words:

All proponents of human security agree that its primary goal is the protection of individuals. However, consensus breaks down over precisely what threats individuals should be protected from. Proponents of the 'narrow' concept of human security focus on violent threats to individuals.[9]

Mack and others have criticized the broader definition as being all-encompassing, making the notion too ambiguous and unwieldy to be of any use for policymaking.

The war of words in the decade-long debate over the broader versus narrower approaches is still quite unsettled. Nevertheless, some normative convergence is now more evident than ever. Advocates of the broader definition have now embraced freedom from fear, while those in the narrow camp have come to recognize the merits of freedom from want. This convergence is reflected in a paragraph on human security with the broader interpretation covering both freedoms that was inserted into the UN Outcome Document of the World Summit in September 2005.

> We stress the right of people to live in freedom and dignity, free from poverty and despair. We recognize that all individuals, in particular vulnerable people, are entitled to freedom from fear and freedom from want, with an equal opportunity to enjoy all their rights and fully develop their human potential. To this end, we commit ourselves to discussing and defining the notion of human security in the General Assembly.[10]

Furthermore, with regard to the contentious issue of humanitarian intervention, including the use of force – one of the issues that polarized the debate between the broad and narrow definitions – some degree of convergence in the debate has been witnessed by the introduction of the concept 'Responsibility to Protect'.

'Responsibility to Protect' – originally recommended by the Independent Commission on Intervention and State Sovereignty, which regarded the responsibility to protect as an alternative to the 'right to intervene' – was inserted into the World Summit Outcome Document in 2005. The Document clearly states that each individual state has the responsibility to protect its population from genocide, war crimes, ethnic cleansing and crimes against humanity, and that in accordance with chapters VI and VII of the UN Charter, the international community, through the UN, also has the responsibility to use appropriate diplomatic, humanitarian and other peaceful means to help protect populations from such crimes.

The same document also states that if national authorities fail to protect their populations from such crimes, the international community has a responsibility to take necessary coercive measures, based on a Security Council resolution and in accordance with chapter VII of the UN Charter. Under this description, military intervention is restricted to that requiring a resolution by the UN Security Council. The notion of responsibility to protect lessens concerns harbored by some countries about the need for intervention in domestic jurisdiction in the name of human security.

These developments have elevated the politics of defining human security to a new realm. Consensus has emerged on the point that, regardless of how discussions develop concerning the definition, the question is how to operationalize human security. In addition to defining human security, there are other debates on the terminology, including whether human security is really a concept, or whether it simply provides a policy framework or a label thereof. The latter does not perceive human security as a single ideological standpoint, but rather as a label for a policy for dealing with issues of peace and security in a holistic manner. In other words, this view posits that if, by incorporating a human security standpoint, it enables effective responses or approaches to the resolution of real issues, then there is real and important value in applying a policy label of human security.[11] This is the view that is becoming mainstreamed.

Debate has also taken place on whether human security is really about security, or whether it is a concept relating to development aid; in other words, where do the differences between human security and human development lie? Some have even questioned whether human security as a concept is advanced simply to get more budget appropriations to development aid. But if human security contains the three freedoms (freedom from fear, freedom from want, and freedom to live in dignity), the concept definitely includes elements other than development aid.

One should further note that the concept of human security has altered the *modus operandi* of development aid. For example, the Trust Fund for Human Security, which the Japanese government established in the UN in March 1999, initially disbursed the funds in accordance with Japanese Official Development Assistance (ODA) modalities, which contained only a slight flavor of human security in its early years. However, during the years since its creation, and particularly since the publication of the CHS report in 2003, the Fund has gradually placed greater emphasis on human security. Especially with the revision of the guidelines for the fund in November 2005, UN agencies seeking funds are required to meet specific criteria: projects must be multi-agency, target multiple sectors, and adopt an integrated approach rather than simply coordinating their activities. In designing projects, those seeking funding from the trust fund must look at the local needs in their entirety, instead of simply picking one aspect of the local area that fits the mandate of an agency, thereby reflecting the interconnectedness of various causes of vulnerability. For example, instead of demining unexploded ordnance alone, such a project would need to be linked to the use of cleared areas for farming. Accordingly, these revised guidelines attempt to ensure that local needs are assessed thoroughly and require multiple UN agencies to engage in projects from the dual aspects of protection and empowerment. To use the above example of demining, the project would need to train local people to remove bombs and mines for their personal protection as well as to build local capacity for conducting mine-clearing. Moreover, projects that combine income-generating activities such as farming with other activities tend to help empower local populaces. This is in line with the 'One UN' approach as well as with two aspects of human security recommended by the CHS.

Another example can be found in the way Japan has now used its ODA, the charter for which was revised in August 2003. One of its basic policies is described as follows: 'In order to address direct threats to individuals such as conflicts, disasters, infectious diseases, it is important not only to consider the global, regional and national perspectives, but also to consider the perspective of human security, which focuses on individuals.'[12] The ODA medium-term policy formulated in February 2005 posited human security as an item on which development aid as a whole should be based. This ODA policy has subsequently led to the reform of JICA, which is responsible for providing technical assistance and granting aid, and which had previously concentrated on specific individual fields and tended to break down aid into segments. JICA now focuses on human security on the ground, with approaches such as empowering local people through economic activities that are developed based on their assessed needs and capacities as well as developing soft infrastructure, such as legal systems.

Some have questioned whether threats included in the broader definition of human security are actually threats to humans, and others have criticized it as a move toward excessive securitization. But the impact of climate change and infectious disease has emerged in both industrialized and developing countries, and there is growing recognition that diverse threats are threats that could undermine national security.[13]

Policy divergence and convergence

This section further explores how Asia and Europe have approached human security, pointing out differences and similarities and some evidence of convergence. It may be helpful to point out that Europe was slower than Asia when it came to the official adoption of human security in the policy agenda. In Europe, with the exception of the Nordic countries, the Netherlands and Switzerland, policy attention to human security emerged only in recent times. The European Union recently adopted human security. Antonio Missiroli observes in his foreword to the European Policy Centre's publication in 2006 that, 'Finally, [human security] has made inroads into the EU policy arena, first by influencing some of the analytical parts of the European Security Strategy (ESS) of December 2003, then through the dedicated report on *A Human Security Doctrine for Europe* drawn up for High Representative for the Common Foreign and Security Policy, Javier Solana, in September 2004 by a study group chaired by London School of Economics Professor Mary Kaldor'.[14] Benita Ferrero-Waldner, EU commissioner for external relations, also alluded to human security in a speech in 2005, saying that 'there can be no long-term peace and global security without human security'.[15]

States in Asia had paid attention to human security earlier than Europe – soon after the UNDP introduced the concept. Human security was introduced to the policy debate as early as 1998. Then-Foreign Minister of Thailand Surin Pitsuwan, finding the idea relevant to Asia, served as a member of the CHS. In Japan, the late Prime Minister Keizo Obuchi introduced the term 'human security' in two policy speeches in December 1998. Prior to these speeches, in May 1998, a study group entitled '21st Century Foreign Policy Challenges' was convened by the Japan Center for International Exchange (JCIE), at which the issue of clearly positioning human security as a new guideline for foreign policy was recommended. The group concluded that in a world in which anxiety and instability were expected to increase, there was a strong possibility that 'human security' would come to be a key term. Based on their recommendations,[16] Obuchi framed it as Japanese foreign policy toward Asia, especially in the context of Japanese assistance to countries and vulnerable populations hit by the Asian financial crisis in the previous year. At the 'Intellectual Dialogue on Building Asia's Tomorrow', organized by JCIE in Tokyo on 2 December, he noted the following in his speech:

> While the phrase 'human security' is a relatively new one, I understand that it is the key which comprehensively covers all the menaces that threaten the survival, daily life, and dignity of human beings and strengthens the efforts to confront those threats ... To support Asian countries in this economic crisis, we have pledged and steadily implemented contribution on the largest scale in the world. With human security in mind, we have given, as one of the most important pillars of our support, assistance to the poor, the aged, the disabled, women and children, and other socially vulnerable segments of population on whom economic difficulties have the heaviest impacts.[17]

Two weeks later, on 16 December, Obuchi delivered a policy speech entitled 'Toward the Creation of a Bright Future for Asia' to the Institute for International Relations in Hanoi on the occasion of his official visit to Vietnam to attend the ASEAN+3 Summit Meeting. In his speech, the Prime Minister announced Japan's assistance to protect the lives, livelihoods and dignity of people, particularly in the wake of the Asian financial crisis, describing this assistance in terms of Japan's approach to human security.[18]

Furthermore, Prime Minister Obuchi announced that his government would contribute 500 million yen for the establishment of the Trust Fund for Human Security at the UN. The fund was created in the following year and, as of June 2007, approximately US$297 million had been contributed by Japan and Slovenia, funding more than 170 projects for a variety of purposes, such as postconflict support for victims, removal of landmines and unexploded ordnance, community rehabilitation, education, poverty reduction, reintegration of former combatants, and food security.

There has been a clash between East Asia and Europe over the policy of human security. Most Asian countries discuss human security along the lines of the Japanese broader definition, although the reaction to the terminology has varied in Asia. This difference in defining human security might have emerged from exposure to the post-Cold War conflicts. Europe and Canada have been exposed to the atrocities in Rwanda and Darfur as well as in the Balkans directly, which led them keenly to feel their responsibility to protect people in conflict areas. Asians, in contrast, have not been exposed to the atrocities of the similar magnitude. Japan and Thailand have been enthusiastic promoters of the terminology.

For Japan it had the tradition of comprehensive security, which looks at security from a broader perspective, from energy to food security, although at state level, and the term 'human security' provided a new standpoint for a proactive foreign policy that Japan was searching for without violating its constitutional constraints regarding contributions to international security.

Other Asian countries were initially circumspect about human security, with some being indifferent and others being downright hostile to the terminology. Considering the fact that the concept of human security was first espoused by Mahbub Ul Haq of Pakistan, why should the countries of Asia have reacted so adversely to the concept? One reason, already mentioned, is that the concept itself was ambiguous and hazy, and there were criticisms that an accurate understanding of the terminology was difficult to attain. Second, in Asia the word 'security' has a normative meaning, and this has aroused feelings of suspicion that there is a possibility of losing national sovereignty in the name of human security. This is a considerable hurdle in Asia, where many countries achieved sovereign status only following the end of World War II, and therefore the perception of not wishing to lose sovereignty is very strong and deep-rooted, in contrast to the case of Europe. Third, there are many countries that persistently cling to the notion of national security, along with national sovereignty. Given the various territorial disputes that have still to be resolved, and also the fact that there are countries that have the potential to plunge into civil war, it is unsurprising that arms build-up continues in Asia. ASEAN's iron-clad rule of 'non-intervention in internal affairs', although still undergoing metamorphosis, provides further evidence of this.

Lastly, there is the concern in some countries, including China, that the term 'human security' is simply a smokescreen to allow other countries or, more broadly, the international community, to intervene in their internal affairs. The result has been that those concerned in China termed post-Cold War expanded security threats as 'non-traditional security', and have recommended and promoted this in a collaborative approach as a 'new security concept'. In Chapter 5 in this volume, Paul Evans points out that Japan and Thailand have been more receptive to human security than many of their neighbors, and that interest in this type of security has been strongest in some of the new democracies in East Asia, especially Thailand, South Korea and the Philippines. It is not surprising that most negative reactions have come from undemocratic North Korea and Myanmar.

However, the posture of Asian countries toward human security is gradually shifting to a more positive one. Mely Callabero-Anthony has observed that one of the reasons for Asia coming to accept human security in a more positive light is that '… the idea of human security, which provides an alternative approach to re-think security by highlighting the threats and insecurities of individuals and communities, has gained more resonance and credence in the light of emerging threats and uncertainties'.[19]

This shift from negative to positive is due to a series of recent incidents and factors: the Asian financial crisis of 1997; bombings in Indonesia and southern Thailand, including the Bali bombing of 2002; repeated terrorist incidents in

Mindanao in the Philippines; the prevalence of infectious diseases such as the SARS outbreak of 2002 and the recent threat of avian influenza; and the Sumatra and Indian Ocean tsunami of 2004. These common experiences for Asian countries have served to promote regional cooperation, transcending traditional concepts of security and moving toward a perspective similar to the broad definition of human security. With the exception of the tsunami disaster, each of these incidents began in a domestic environment and emanated outwards. These events have therefore made it painfully clear to countries in the region that, although they may harbor predilections for state sovereignty, unless these threats are faced through visible and effective regional cooperation, countries will find that alone they are unable to bring the situations under control. In addition, the UN World Summit Outcome Document included reference to human security and to the responsibility to protect, and this has served to lessen concerns about interference in domestic affairs.

Non-democratic China, which was initially hostile to the notion, has also come to accept the idea of human security. Wang Yizhou, director of the Institute of World Economics and Politics, Chinese Academy of Social Sciences, mentioned that 'It should be clarified that human security and social security are the foundations for national security.... . To seek national security at the expense of human security and social stability is to treat the symptom rather than the root of the problem'.[20] However, not all Chinese agree with this statement, certainly not in policy circles, where there is still a preference for non-traditional security. In response to threats that are generally covered under the broad definition of human security, the terminology 'non-traditional security' has come to be used rather than human security – and not only in China. According to Amitav Acharya, the terminology 'non-traditional security' is less loaded and is less easily connected with human rights. He points out that countries in Asia prefer nation-states to be clearly both the main actor in, and the main subject of, security considerations. He noted, 'If we refer to human security, we focus upon military and non-military threats to the safety of societies, groups and individuals, thereby securitizing human welfare in general'.[21] An Asian study group was established within the Institute of Defense and Strategic Studies (now called the S. Rajaratnam School of International Studies) at Nanyang Technological University in Singapore to conduct further research on non-traditional security issues; information has now been exchanged.

In Europe, it seems the terminology was accepted more on the basis of the narrower definition, as originally advocated by the liberal government of Canada. John Kotsopoulos observes that the broader definition 'is useful for re-framing and expanding the scope of the debate ... However it reduces human security to a "laundry list" of actions that should be taken to enhance security, with little policy utility or immediate impact'. He further argues that the broad definition 'creates three separate problems: double standards, an unworkably-ambitious agenda and the need for legal constraints'.[22] This is often echoed by other Europeans. It is also argued that Europe has practiced elements included in the broader definition of the terminology under specific programs, such as development aid, environmental protection, human rights and disease. Thus Europeans often ask what value added can be offered by using the label 'human security'.

Nordic countries and Switzerland, in particular, have been known for their proactive promotion of human security. Norway has been instrumental in promoting the narrow definition of 'human security', along with Canada. Canadian Foreign Minister Lloyd Axworthy, when appointed in 1996, highlighted human security as one of the new pillars of Canadian foreign policy in the post-Cold War era, based on its narrower definition. The Canadian government has worked fervently to advance the cause of human security, although with less vigor in recent years. Canada has undergone a transformation in its narrow approach to human security. In the first generation of human security, it prioritized the creation of norms and institutions for the protection of individuals embroiled in armed conflicts, based on international humanitarian and human rights law. Such norms and structures are exactly what were witnessed in the conclusion of the Convention on the Prohibition of the Use, Stockpiling, Production and Transfer of Anti-Personnel Mines and on their Destruction (Mine Ban Treaty), the establishment of the International Criminal Court, and regulations on small arms and the protection of child soldiers, among other norms. In the second generation, Canada focused on monitoring and implementation of the norms and institutions established in the first generation. Currently, in the third generation of human security, Canada targets urban violence. Officials illustrate the issue by explaining that more people died in the 1990s through acts of violence in the city of Rio de Janeiro than died in the civil war in Columbia in the 1980s. Thus Canada clearly bases its understanding of human security on the narrower definition.[23] Under the Conservative government today, the phrase is never used, although on practical issues such as Darfur and in trying to generate attention for the concept of responsibility to protect in the UN context, the Harper government is closer in actions, if not in rhetoric, to earlier Liberal policy.

Norway's Foreign Minister Vollebaek also worked with his Canadian counterpart Lloyd Axworthy on the Mine Ban Treaty. Capitalizing on their successful efforts on landmines, they launched the Human Security Network (HSN), which has since worked to promote human security, focusing on issues relating to conflict, such as landmines and the protection of children in conflict. The HSN holds a ministerial meeting every year at which human security themes are deliberated. There are 13 countries participating in the HSN: Canada, Australia, Chile, Greece, Ireland, Jordan, Mali, the Netherlands, Norway, Slovenia, Switzerland, Thailand, and South Africa (as an observer).

The Swiss government has also been known for its emphasis on human rights, humanitarian affairs and migration concerns, which naturally led it to take up human security. Its Department of Foreign Affairs has an explicit human security agenda and even has a Human Security Division. Its foreign policy documents explain that it takes both definitions of human security, and has programs 'to combat poverty, improve health care and strengthen good governance' as well as to ban antipersonnel mines, control small arms and light weaponry, and pursue other agendas such as child soldiers. Switzerland is also a founding member of the HSN. Although the Swiss government accepts the broader interpretation of human security, it seems closer to the Canadian approach with its focus on human rights and its rights-based approaches. It is also keen to prohibit landmines and to control small arms and light weaponry. Thus these European countries found the Canadian narrower definition more workable.

Turning to Asia, the Thai government has created a Ministry of Social Development and Human Security, which focuses on issues of domestic social safety nets. Thailand has also been an active member of the HSN. Japan has promoted human security based on its broader interpretation through three paths: dissemination of the concept, operationalizing it through aid, and implementing it through cultural relations. Nevertheless, one should note that Prime Minister Obuchi also agreed with the Canadian-led efforts toward realization of the Mine Ban Treaty, and while quelling domestic opposition, he signed it and saw that it was also ratified swiftly. Japan has made various efforts to disseminate human security through intellectual dialogue, and the very first of such efforts took place in December 1998 with the previously mentioned 'Intellectual Dialogue on Building Asia's Tomorrow', where Obuchi gave his seminal speech. Since then, Japan has organized numerous track I and II symposiums and dialogues on human security. The ultimate expression of such dialogue came in 2001 with the establishment of the CHS. The CHS itself was proposed and supported by the Japanese government, and on 1 May 2003, co-chairs Madame Sadako Ogata and Professor Amartya Sen presented their final report to Secretary General Kofi Annan, entitled *Human Security Now.*[24] As for the path through aid, Japan has taken two avenues, namely through the Trust Fund for Human Security at the UN and through its own ODA, as described above. The third path is through its cultural activities and cultural relations. The CHS included in its report a description of culture as a means of realigning human security. Moreover, the Japanese Council for the Promotion of Cultural Diplomacy announced in its report entitled *Establishing Japan as a 'Peaceful Nation of Cultural Exchange'* in 2004 that Japan advocates 'cultivating mutual understanding and trust between different cultures and civilizations to prevent conflict'.[25]

The Japan Foundation, whose mission is to promote cultural exchange and cultural relations, promotes human security through its cultural activities. In other words, the Foundation uses a part of its programs as a catalyst or a facilitator for cross-cultural tolerance and dialogues in various stages of conflict prevention, conflict resolution, emergency assistance, and postconflict peacebuilding and reconstruction. As an illustration, parties to conflicts may find it difficult to meet and discuss difficult issues in their own territory, but it is easier for them to meet in a more neutral location. In some ethnic conflict cases, their respective cultures may have historical baggage, but a third culture can offer joint experiences among disputing parties and communities, which may lead to reconciliation or confidence-building. In this way, postconflict psychological scars of people in conflict areas can begin to heal through cultural activities. Thus it is a very broad interpretation of human security that Japan engages.

Because of Japan's broader interpretation of human security, Japan and Canada have been portrayed as competing champions of the concept, and their divide on the interpretation has been so large that they could no longer collaborate on any practical applications. In fact, Japan has not participated in the HSN that Canada led, giving the following reasons: 'To varying degrees, the countries in this Network focus on human security in conflict situations, and in cases in which human security cannot be ensured by the state, they tend to emphasize that in some such cases humanitarian intervention, including the use of force, is permissible. Japan's understanding is that human security is a comprehensive terminology, including also development aspects.'[26]

However, on the occasion of the HSN ministerial meeting in Austria in May 2003, the then-co-chair of the CHS Sadako Ogata was invited to attend as a guest speaker, and she introduced the CHS report. Since then, Japanese ambassadors responsible for human security have attended the annual ministerial meetings as guests. Moreover, in 2006 the Japanese government proposed the creation of the Friends of Human Security forum, which held its first meeting in October of the same year and the second in April 2007, both in New York. The second meeting was attended by a total of 40 countries, including all the permanent members of the Security Council except China. The Friends forum provides an open and unofficial forum for concerned countries to come together regardless of their support for or opposition to human security, including the members of the HSN, and engage in discussion on human security. Even Canada did not voice any strong objections to the creation of the Friends forum, which is an indication that the gap between the broad and narrow definitions is now narrowing and that they are focusing more on operationalizing, rather than debating, the concept.

Acting on human security at the regional level

The question of operationalization has now become important. Because of its transnational nature, human security offers a platform for regional cooperation. In Europe, many argue that regional institutions such as the EU have long adopted human security, even though they have not always used the label. More conspicuous reflection on human security can be found in the aforementioned study group, chaired by Mary Kaldor in the report *A Human Security Doctrine for Europe*, announced in September 2004, which is the doctrine for the ESS and which recommended the creation of a human security response force to be composed of 15,000 individuals.

Although it seems the recommendations in the report itself have so far not been implemented, it has been widely discussed in Europe. The study group has reconvened, with funding from the Finnish government, to conduct further research on human security. Meanwhile, other regional institutions, such as the Organization for Security and Co-operation in Europe (OSCE), are interested in the concept of human security; the OSCE convened a side event dedicated to human security in the autumn of 2007.

Chapter 4 in this volume discusses at greater length the role of regional institutional actors in East Asia, but it is worth pointing out here that some of them began to accept the concept of human security earlier than those in Europe, although the concept has not so far been quite mainstreamed. ASEAN in particular alluded to human security in its Eminent Persons Group's report in 2000,[27] in the context of HIV/AIDS in 2001,[28] and in its *Socio-Cultural Community Plan of Action* in 2004.[29] ASEAN+3 (China, Japan and South Korea) Summits have not mentioned human security in their Chair's Statements, but a regional group known as the East Asia Vision Group set out a vision for ASEAN+3 in its report in 2001 entitled *Towards an East Asia Community*, and advocated human security as one objective in constructing an East Asia community.[30]

The East Asia Study Group, which was an intergovernmental organization established to review the vision, also mentioned human security as a theme for regional cooperation in 2002, although its tone was somewhat weaker than that of the Vision Group.[31] China also participated, and accordingly agreed to the inclusion of the concept of human security in these documents. On the other hand, in the case of the ASEAN Regional Forum, which is tasked with addressing Asian security, there has never been any reference at all to human security in the Chair's Summaries following its ministerial-level meetings, although it was mentioned in a report on side events in the context of illegal trafficking of drugs[32] and security cooperation.[33]

In contrast, the Asia Pacific Economic Cooperation (APEC) conference, after a great deal of discussion on the human security issue, included in the 2003 APEC Leaders' Declaration in Bangkok a section on 'Enhancing Human Security', with the following text: 'We agreed to dedicate APEC not only to advancing the prosperity of our economies, but also to the complementary mission of ensuring the security of our people.'[34] Since then, human security has appeared in all subsequent Leaders' Declarations, in 2004, 2005 and 2006. Human security, however, has been used in the context of specific threats such as terrorism, protection of air travelers, energy, HIV/AIDS, and other infectious diseases such as SARS and avian influenza. One could say that the APEC perception of human security is a hybrid between a concept distilled down to the US focus on terrorism and the broader interpretation of the terminology by Asian countries. What is more, human rights are listed in parallel with human security, indicating that a number of APEC members are opposed to incorporating human rights into the concept of human security.

Furthermore, in the track II process led by an association of ASEAN think tanks, the ASEAN Institute of Strategic and International Studies has convened what it has called the ASEAN People's Assembly (APA). Scholars, think tanks and policymakers from the ASEAN countries and dialogue partner countries have been invited to participate in the Assembly. The third APA was held in Manila, the Philippines, in September 2003, and the declaration adopted at that meeting included reference to promoting human security toward the realization of the ASEAN Vision 2020, which advocates the formation of an ASEAN community.[35] Since then, all chair's statements and reports have included human security in the context of priority challenges that must be considered, including disadvantaged sectors, those negatively affected by globalization, indigenous peoples, cultural minorities, and the poor in general.

In addition, there are NGOs active in Southeast Asia that are working from the perspective of the broader definition of human security. For example, Focus on the Global South (with headquarters in Bangkok) and the Third World Network (with headquarters in Malaysia) have raised the issue of freedom from want caused by the advance of globalization, and are promoting a movement that focuses on labor exploitation by multinational companies, and also on environmental destruction.

In this way, although human security is gradually coming to be addressed in its broad interpretation in regional cooperation in Asia, with the exception of APEC, it still does not feature prominently or frequently in major documents, such as chair's statements of regional organizations. Its adoption is still limited to reports from various related advisory commissions. This is to be expected, because to date the regional organizations have channeled their energies into economic cooperation, and there has been little substantive debate on political and security cooperation, which is to come in the future. Asia is also engulfed by the wave of globalization, and therefore functional cooperation to respond to threats that are included in human security is already under way, including antipiracy measures, measures to combat infectious diseases, and measures against climate change. The East Asian human security approach is not a rights-based one, as it is in Europe, and does not focus on human rights, because Asians remain more sensitive than Europeans about being potentially accused of human rights violations.

For advocates of human security in the East and West, the concept has attracted policy and academic attention sufficient to stir policy interest and debate. But they have now agreed that it is infertile to look for full convergence on its definition, and that it is time to act rather than to keep debating what human security should mean.

Conclusion

Since its introduction more than 10 years ago, the concept of human security has moved toward a stage where increasing weight is being placed on operationalization. In contrast to other theories of international relations advanced by academics, the concept basically resulted from government initiatives (although the term was initially coined by a handful of intellectuals). Since then, human security has been promoted by politicians, governments, international organizations and NGO activists. During its early days, there were critics quite eager to write human security's obituary, but the concept has now survived the course of a dogged foreign policy debate and, having been incorporated in the Outcome Document of the 2005 UN World Summit, it is still commanding policy attention at the UN, and in both Europe and Asia.

The academic and policy debate over the concept of human security continues unabated. As a result of this interest, books and journal articles have been published; and seminars and university courses on human security have been established at great speed, especially in Japan. Research is now being conducted with greater analytical vigor.

Is this global surge of interest in human security transient or sustainable? Now is the time to transcend that debate and operationalize the terminology. Unless the terminology can link hard and soft security, as well as foreign and domestic polity, in order to respond effectively to the changing face of vulnerability, and unless we can move the terminology to a new realm, human security will occupy only a brief and fleeting moment in international relations discussions, and will be lost among the other ephemera of the twenty-first century. The response lies in whether or not the terminology can respond to the needs of our time. More specifically, it depends on whether human security can offer a better label for strategies and tactics to better respond to the growing vulnerabilities and anxiety espoused by people around the globe. In Europe, a 'Human Security Doctrine' has been recommended. Japan has already taken steps to operationalize human security anew, even when not using the label explicitly.

Will human security be officially operationalized by the EU in the future? In Asia, will APEC use human security as a label for its involvement in security? Will other regional institutions, such as the OSCE in Europe and ASEAN+ institutions in Asia, use human security as a label for their strategies? While human security has to date been positioned in terms of states' foreign policy, it is still incumbent on industrialized countries to attend to their domestic policies in terms of meeting human security needs. After a long decade of academic and policy debate over what human security should mean, the time has now come for all interested actors to put it into practice.

4 Southeast Asia's points of convergence on international intervention

Mely Caballero-Anthony

The extent to which actors in East Asia are prepared to translate into policy action whatever norms of human security they embrace is a matter of debate. This chapter focuses specifically on humanitarian intervention issues, and explores possibilities of policy collaboration between states and non-state actors in Southeast Asia. Let me make it clear from the outset that the concept remains highly contested, both in theory and in practice. If one were to plot certain points in post-Cold war history when the issue of humanitarian intervention has been re-examined, the period soon after the 1999 NATO-led attacks in Kosovo comes to mind. This was when the legality and legitimacy of military intervention were hotly debated in many parts of the world. The discourses that emerged were significant in that these led to the shifts in the terms of the debate regarding defining the boundaries between humanitarian intervention (coercive military interference in the internal affairs of states) and differentiating it from the act of war (military conflict between states). The NATO action typified this conundrum. While NATO's attacks on Kosovo had been considered to be 'intervention' into internal affairs to prevent massive human rights violations by Serbs against the Albanian minority, the direct attack on another state from outside looked very much like war.[1] Similar controversy was replayed a few years later with the American-led 'war' on Iraq in March 2003. Among the reasons cited for the military invasion was to protect the human rights of Iraqi citizens under the Saddam Hussein regime. Both acts raised the issue of whether the norm of sovereignty was being reformed, or whether a new norm of intervention was being established.[2]

During this tumultuous period, then-United Nations Secretary General Kofi Annan made several speeches on the evolving nature of humanitarian intervention that, in turn, added new elements to the debate. For example, at his 1999 speech at the UN General Assembly, Annan urged the international community to revisit the issue of humanitarian intervention in the light of the kinds of humanitarian crises that happened in Rwanda, Bosnia and Srebenica. A year later, in a significant speech delivered at a seminar organized by the International Peace Academy, he offered alternative ways to operationalize the contentious issue of humanitarian intervention by confining it to non-forcible actions. Notably, he declared that 'The humanitarian among us are those whose work involves saving lives that are in imminent danger, and relieving suffering that is already acute', but went on to make the case for broadening the notion of intervention: 'They are people who bring food to those threatened with starvation, or medical help to the injured, or shelter to those who have lost their homes, or comfort to those who have lost their loved ones.'[3] The speech not only heightened the prevailing debate, but also brought in the salient aspect of broadening the concept of humanitarian intervention to include actions along a 'wide continuum (of responses) from the most pacific to the most coercive'.[4] According to Michael Byers and Simon Chesterman, Annan's attempts to broaden the definition of the concept of intervention were a way of shifting the debate away from a focus on NATO-type interventions carried out without the endorsement of the UN Security Council to highlight instead the true problems at the heart of the brewing controversy at that time – the lack of political will to act.

This chapter further examines points of convergence between state and non-state actors in Southeast Asia for collaborative action within the context of broadly defined notions of humanitarian intervention. Despite the prevailing reservations in East Asia about humanitarian intervention, prospects for intervening for humanitarian purposes may not necessarily be implausible, if one accepts the earlier suggestion of Annan for a more nuanced approach to humanitarian intervention. The argument is also based on current developments in the region that lend themselves to more active engagement by states in responding to humanitarian crises, such as natural disasters (tsunami, floods), and more subtle engagements in addressing potential challenges to human security and regional stability. These developments, as will be discussed, present a challenge to the western idea that confines humanitarian intervention to the use of force without the consent of states or actors concerned. Hence, in discussing the experience of Southeast Asia in engaging with this contentious issue, the ultimate objective is to examine possible spaces where possible convergence could exist.

Humanitarian intervention: discourses and dilemmas in the context of Southeast Asia

Much of the literature on humanitarian intervention came from the perspective of international law. Through the prism of the 'legalist paradigm', the discourse on intervention is dominated and informed by the norms that proscribe intervention in the domestic affairs of sovereign states. This legalistic view has also been referred to as the 'traditional' and/or 'restrictive' view of intervention. R. J. Vincent's definition of intervention best captures this perspective, which describes it as 'activity undertaken by a state, a group within a state or an international organization which interferes coercively in the domestic affairs of another state'.[5] This view takes off from the classical definition of external intervention, 'dictatorial interference by a sovereign state, a group of such states, or an international organization, involving the use or threat of force or some other means of coercion, in the domestic jurisdiction of an independent state, against the will or wishes of the government of the targeted country'.[6] But this type of intervention is considered a crime by international law. According to Michael Walzer, the legalist paradigm regards the use of force or the threat of force against other states as a crime of aggression, justifying a war of self-defense, and considers that only aggression justifies war. Hence, 'unless something like aggression takes place, there is no legal justification for international intervention'.[7] The more restrictive legalist perspective therefore upholds the traditional norms of the non-use of force, respect for state sovereignty, and non-intervention.

At least until the end of the Cold War, the legalist perspective was the dominant paradigm. But this was soon challenged with the emergence of a normative, 'solidarist' perspective that came along with the changes that occurred in the post-Cold War era. The normative view sought to transform the notion of intervention as a means to promote the political interests of states into a mechanism for the promotion of universal norms, such as defense of human rights. Rosalyn Higgins noted that, starting from the mid-1980s, issues like human rights no longer became a matter solely within the domestic purview of states, but had become a matter of legitimate international concern.[8] Thus human rights issues have become the normative basis for intervention, which for a long time had largely been ignored by the realist perspective that looked at intervention on the basis of state's interests. From this normative perspective emerged the concept of 'humanitarian intervention'.

Conventionally, humanitarian intervention has been defined in terms of 'intervention motivated by humanitarian considerations'. An expanded, more explicit formulation is offered by J. J. Holzgrefe, who defines humanitarian intervention as, 'the threat or use of force across state borders by a state (or a group of states) aimed at preventing or ending widespread and grave violations of the fundamental human rights of individuals other than its own citizens, *without the permission* of the state within whose territory force is applied'.[9] But, while humanitarian intervention can be viewed as being normatively progressive, at least prior to the end of the Cold War, this was regarded mostly as an exception to the non-intervention principle.

So far, the lack of consensus on the principles of humanitarian intervention has hampered any significant progress in this idea being accepted by the international community. As noted by Nicholas Wheeler and Alex Bellamy, the subject is a particularly difficult one for theorists of international society because of the concern about double standards. According to them, humanitarian intervention 'is the archetypal case where it might be expected that the society of states would agree to privilege individual justice over the norms of sovereignty and non-intervention'.[10]

This concern about the selectivity of response has therefore become the main bone of contention in humanitarian intervention, leading Hedley Bull to argue that without a consensus, the international order would better be served by the principle of non-intervention than by allowing humanitarian intervention. Similarly, Chris Brown had neatly summed up the contentions on the motivations for humanitarian intervention and the questions pertaining to who should intervene. He thus observes that: 'The general problem here is that humanitarian intervention is always going to be based on the cultural predilections of those with the power to carry it out'.[11]

From the above, it follows that the concern for selectivity underscores the elusiveness of an international consensus on the principles of humanitarian intervention. As pointed out by J. L. Holzgrefe, there is the salient question of whether humanitarian intervention benefits or harms the national interest of the intervening party or parties. Holzgrefe argues that it is more often the case that the interests of the intervening state 'count for everything in assessing an intervention's legitimacy; [while] the interests of the target state count for nothing'. Citing Samuel Huntington's argument that 'it is morally unjustifiable and politically indefensible that members of the [US] Armed forces should be killed to prevent Somalis from killing one another', Holzgrefe further argues that the realities of *realpolitik* – rather than concerns of *moralpolitik* – define the motivation of the states that intervene.[12]

But if state interests largely dictated motivations for intervention and would therefore be a disincentive for states to intervene, the developments of the post-Cold War period somehow belied these concerns. Thomas Weiss, for instance, noted that from 1990 to 1994, there were twice as many resolutions passed on humanitarian intervention in the UN Security Council than during the first 45 years of its history.[13] Paradoxically, it was during the post-Cold War period that the most contentious discourses were heard on humanitarian intervention. To be sure, these developments raised a number of questions: whether these developments signaled a growing acceptance of the idea of humanitarian intervention in state practice; whether there were other motivations beyond state material interest that provided the impetus for states to agree to humanitarian intervention; and whether the rising trend was reflective of the state of affairs in the international arena in the post-Cold war era, which was defined characteristically by an increase in intrastate conflicts?

These issues became the foci of enquiry evaluating the current trends in humanitarian intervention. The recent studies that emerged reassessed the conventional wisdom that state interests, power and material factors often dictate motivations behind humanitarian intervention, rather than, or more than, the ideational factors. Among these is the work of Martha Finnemore, who examined the role of norms in international relations. In her book, *The Purpose of Intervention: Changing Beliefs About the Use of Force*, she argues that realist and even liberal conceptions of humanitarian intervention do not offer good explanations, as neither approach provides an answer to the question: 'What interests are intervening states pursuing?'[14] According to her, in most cases, particularly post-1989, the intervention of great powers, such as that of the USA in Somalia in 1992–93, was arguably without any obvious national interest – political, economic or otherwise. She further contends that the strong opposition of some American administration officials to the Somalia intervention did in fact 'underscore the realists' problem', since as the events unfolded there was no obvious US interest that was served.[15] To Finnemore, there were clearly other considerations that influenced the decision to intervene, including the impact of television images of hungry and abused Somalis seen in American living rooms. These stirring images, she argues, were powerful in swaying public opinion and in fuelling public pressures and policy impetus for states to decide to intervene. But, more importantly, she argues that state practices (in intervention) change over time, and that state motivations and interests are not given, thus there is a need to be more aware of the transforma-tive role of persuasion and debate. According to this constructivist perspective, the impact of these factors had often been ignored in the ongoing discourses on humanitarian intervention.

As these recent academic and policy debates continue to evolve, and despite the lack of international consensus on the norms of humanitarian intervention, suffice it to say that, interestingly, it has now become the most discussed yet controversial topic within the UN circle. In fact, as Thomas Weiss observed, this controversy led to the growth of an academic cottage industry on humanitarian intervention.[16] The vigorous debates on humanitarian intervention also found their way to East Asia.[17] The contestations became more pronounced, especially when the idea of human security started to gain more resonance in the region. The con-nection between this type of intervention and human security is best seen within the context of the evolving processes of reconceptualizing the very notion of security in the region.

The history of these processes is reflected in the evolution of security-related concepts, namely comprehensive security, cooperative security and human secu-rity. The emergence of these different concepts was aimed at broadening the notion of security beyond the conventional state-centric and military-oriented security of a state. These concepts had been crafted by a number of actors, both state and non-state, who have at various points been engaged in the various processes of broadening the security concepts that were reflective of the security concerns in the region, as well as in the rethinking of security approaches to advance these ideas. Although the work of the plethora of actors may have produced these con-cepts, their ideas may not necessarily be mutually reinforcing, and could at times be at odds, particularly when examined against the evolving concept of human security.[18]

Despite the attractive appeal to the region of the concept of human security,[19] multilateral efforts at pursuing collaborative human security projects/agendas have been hampered by hot contentions, primarily on the approaches to human security. This controversy is best captured in the 'freedom from fear' versus 'free-dom from want' divide that emerged among states. Countries that promote human security in their foreign policy agenda, such as Canada for example, have main-tained a distinctive focus on 'freedom from pervasive threats to people's rights, safety or lives', or freedom from fear. By emphasizing this particular aspect of human security, the Canadian approach had not ruled out the collective use of force and/or sanctions, if and when necessary, to guarantee human security.[20] In contrast, as discussed elsewhere in this volume, Japan and other Asian coun-tries preferred to adopt a comprehensive view of human security closely aligned with that of the developmental approach espoused by the UN Development Pro-gramme.[21] The differences between these approaches created an atmosphere of suspicion among states that regarded the policy instruments of human security to be a Trojan horse for intervention in the internal affairs of states. Some states in

Southeast Asia became wary of the emphasis placed on certain elements belonging to the freedom from fear category – for example, political security (freedom to exercise one's basic political rights) – that were viewed as allowing certain states to interfere in their internal affairs and adopt a more confrontational attitude in promoting regional security. Such practices were seen to go against the regional norm of non-interference. Hence, against these developments, it appeared that the idea of humanitarian intervention as a possible area of collaborative action to advance the cause of human security had been prematurely snuffed.

I argue, however, that this picture is incomplete. When viewed against the larger picture of the new global initiative on promoting humanitarian intervention through the UN-sponsored idea of 'Responsibility to Protect' (R2P) and, more significantly, when juxtaposed against the current trends in the region on conflict prevention, one can discern emerging developments that point toward some possible avenues to promote human security. As regards the latter, one notes with great interest the official discourses currently taking place in the region regarding the idea of establishing an ASEAN Security Community in 2020 and the related initiative, among others, of establishing a regional peacekeeping force. At the very least, at both state and non-state levels, one sees a growing trend and/or greater willingness to discuss issues that were once considered 'taboo', including the contentious issue of humanitarian intervention. Against these trends, which will be discussed at length, I would submit that the notion of collaborative human security in the idea of humanitarian intervention – broadly defined – is possible.

ASEAN's convergence on nuanced humanitarian intervention: lessons from Cambodia and East Timor

When one reviews cases in the region's recent history in international intervention to examine how regional actors (including ASEAN and its Regional Forum, ARF) had or had not played a role in averting massive humanitarian sufferings and grave violations of human rights, the memory of Cambodia after the Vietnamese military invasion in late 1978, and the case of East Timor 20 years later, are quite instructive.

In the case of Cambodia, some nagging questions persist with regard to the timing and motivations behind the interventions that took place. For instance, it was not until the Vietnamese occupation and the installation of a pro-Vietnam regime in 1979 that the 'problem' was noticed by states in Southeast Asia.[22] During this period, member states of ASEAN began to take up this case in the international arena and internationalized the issue through sponsorship of the UN General Assembly resolution on the settlement of the Cambodian problem. For ten years (1979–89), ASEAN had persistently mobilized international support in calling for an end to the Vietnamese occupation of Cambodia and for a political settlement to the ongoing war. ASEAN obviously lacked power projection and regional authority to influence the behavior of the Khmer factions and the major power dynamics, but these shortcomings were made up for by the group's intense lobbying in the international arena and unceasing efforts at opening and maintaining channels of communications with the armed Cambodian factions until the conflict was eventually resolved. In 1989, Vietnam eventually withdrew unilaterally from Cambodia. This was followed by the peace process under the Paris Agreement of 1991, the establishment of the UN Transitional Authority in Cambodia (UNTAC), and the holding of the first national elections to be held in the country in 1993.

It is important to note that while a number of factors eventually led to the successful resolution of the Cambodia conflict, the intervention that took place and was undertaken by different actors was significantly different from the kind of humanitarian intervention being debated now in the international arena. ASEAN's 'intervention' can best be described as belonging to the lowest scale in the continuum of acts or mechanisms of humanitarian intervention. As mentioned earlier, their intervention came in the form of internationalizing the problem and acting as interlocutor between and among the warring parties in Cambodia, in search of a comprehensive political settlement. Such intervention did not involve or require any use of force, and was limited to diplomatic means. As for the UN's role, its intervention was defined within the chapter VI provision of postconflict peace operations. The nature of UNTAC's 'intervention' ranged from a combination of the elements of peacekeeping, peacemaking, economic and social maintenance, and national reconciliation. Moreover, it is noteworthy that the ASEAN and UN 'interventions' in Cambodia were carried out with the consent of Cambodian parties. Clearly, there was willingness on the part of all parties concerned (Cambodians and non-Cambodians) to work collaboratively in seeking a peaceful end to the conflict and to rebuild a once wartorn country into a normal state.[23]

The commitment of ASEAN member states to get involved in Cambodia was tested again when Cambodia was caught in a power struggle after its second national elections in 1997. Cambodia's Second Prime Minister, Hun Sen, staged a coup to oust his coalition partner, First Prime Minister Prince Norodom Ranariddh, from the position of first prime minister. As a consequence, ASEAN decided to delay Cambodia's admission into ASEAN until a political solution was reached between the conflicting parties. The ASEAN decision was aimed at driving home the point that no leadership or form of government by violent means was ever to be encouraged, as this violated the regional norm of the non-use of force. As a consequence, ASEAN insisted that Cambodia met certain conditions before it could be admitted to the grouping, which included, among others, the holding of free and fair elections and the establishment of the Cambodian Senate. ASEAN also formed the ASEAN Troika, which comprised the ASEAN Foreign Ministers of the present, past and future chairs of the ASEAN Standing Committee, to deal with efforts at restoring political stability in Cambodia.[24] In this second 'intervention', the modalities used were still confined to diplomatic means and were not controversial.

In contrast, the East Timor case proved to be the most difficult challenge to ASEAN and even the larger regional organization, the ARF. Both organizations came under severe criticism for their inability to stem the violence and gross violations of human rights that followed. As noted in many accounts, ASEAN could not initiate any form of preventive action to stop the atrocities that occurred in many parts of the country soon after the East Timorese voted for independence from Indonesia in the plebiscite held at the end of August 1999. It was not until the UN organized a peacekeeping mission under the framework of the International Force for East Timor (INTERFET) that violence was controlled and large-scale humanitarian relief operations could be carried out.[25] By then, East Timor had suffered many lost lives and massive property destruction, while thousands of terrified people were also forcibly displaced to West Timor.

As the crisis unfolded, some member states of ASEAN and the rest of the international community, either individually or collectively through the UN, urged Indonesia to enforce law and order in East Timor. As noted in Chapter 6 in this volume, it took the Australian initiative to offer a large number of its troops for a UN peacekeeping force before any international action could begin to stop the violence in East Timor. Although some ASEAN members participated in the INTERFET, its contributions were lost in the barrage of criticism of the extent to which ASEAN 'intervened' in what was considered by the organization to be an intrastate conflict. Criticisms were even more strident of the ARF, which was silent throughout the crisis. ASEAN's inability to respond to the humanitarian crisis in East Timor was seen as a litmus test of its operational capacity as a regional institution to act in times of crisis, or to prevent crises from escalating into a humanitarian crisis.

ASEAN's perceived lack of leadership in East Timor drew comparisons with the proactive role it had assumed in the search for a comprehensive political settlement of the Cambodian conflict. One would recall that throughout the crisis, ASEAN made up for its lack of political influence over the behavior of the warring factions by internationalizing the issue at the UN and facilitating dialogues between the warring Cambodian parties, which culminated in the famous Jakarta Informal Meetings (JIM I and JIM II). Although it could be pointed out that ASEAN's swift reaction was predicated on its protest against Vietnam's invasion and occupation of a UN member state, which violated the international norms of respect for a country's state sovereignty and the right of self-determination – principles that are espoused in ASEAN's Treaty of Amity and Cooperation (1976) – as against the internal dimension of the East Timor conflict, the latter nonetheless also presented a strong case of gross violation of international norms.

But the crisis in East Timor required a different type of intervention that regional organizations like ASEAN were not prepared or meant to undertake: collective use of military force through peace enforcement and peacekeeping. The response of ASEAN officials was therefore not surprising when they declared that only the UN had the legitimacy and the capabilities to undertake any peacekeeping operation and mobilize the massive resources necessary to respond to the kind of humanitarian crisis that unfolded in East Timor. An official from the ASEAN Secretariat explained that what ASEAN had done was to 'undertake consultations, arrive at consensus and let the individual members decide on what specific contributions to make to the UN effort'.[26] While these actions were consistent with ASEAN's norms of conflict management, the responses of its members stacked against expectations reflected the stark reality that the grouping's resources or lack thereof defined the nature and capacity of ASEAN to 'intervene'.

In brief, the East Timor experience revealed the limitations of ASEAN and the extent to which it could go to 'intervene' in what was considered an intrastate conflict involving a member state. If compared with other regional organizations, such as NATO and the African Union, it becomes evident that neither ASEAN nor the ARF had peacekeeping forces that could be deployed rapidly to carry out such an intervention. In this regard, the material constraints clearly defined the inadequacy of both organizations to respond to a humanitarian crisis. At the same time, one could point to the emerging normative elements at play, as reflected in the responses by some ASEAN members that willingly sent their own peacekeepers to participate in the UN missions that were sent to East Timor, and whose troops eventually took the lead in the subsequent UN missions that oversaw the birth of East Timor as an independent state. The same normative considerations had made these countries participate in providing humanitarian assistance in the aftermath of the crisis. These included providing medical relief to the victims of violence, temporary shelters for internally displaced persons, and the reconstruction of damaged infrastructures. These facts are, more often than not, ignored in the analyses of ASEAN's role in East Timor.

Against the lessons from Cambodia and East Timor, one could surmise that the nature of international intervention by states in Southeast Asia had been confined largely to diplomatic means (such as acting as interlocutors, providing good offices as in the case of the ASEAN Troika, and so on), and providing humanitarian assistance. The latter is seen clearly in the different phases of peace operations – particularly in the reconstruction and rebuilding phases. In a situation where humanitarian intervention required the deployment of military force – enforced peace operations – as the case of East Timor shows, states would, and were only able to, work within the framework of the UN peace operations, the idea being that only the UN had the legitimacy to undertake any form of intervention and/or decision to enforce peace.

In sum, the nature of international intervention undertaken by ASEAN and the UN in responding to the problems in East Timor can be described or categorized loosely as 'lower-level' humanitarian intervention. Nevertheless, this type of intervention is salient, given the region's strict adherence to the principle of non-interference, and must not be ignored in the light of the current debates on whether humanitarian intervention is an emerging norm, and on the elusiveness of a global consensus on the norms of humanitarian intervention. From the region's experience, certain spaces had been pried open that provide us with opportunities to explore possibilities for collaborative action for human security.

ASEAN: toward humanitarian intervention

While it has been argued that humanitarian intervention was never part of the regional agenda in ASEAN, this is not to say that there are no normative shifts – at least as far as ideational developments are concerned. In this section, I argue that the view about humanitarian intervention as one of an East–West divide[27] needs to be revisited, given the emerging dynamics in Southeast Asia. In a region that has been besieged by crises, including humanitarian catastrophes, attempts to rethink the notions of sovereignty – and its flip side, the principle of non-intervention – are not new.

At the official level, there have already been initiatives undertaken by certain governments in ASEAN to respond to regional crises that required some form of 'intervention' and to prevent them from happening again. For instance, in the aftermath of the 1997 political crisis in Cambodia, the idea of 'constructive intervention' was floated by former Malaysian Deputy Prime Minister Anwar Ibrahim. How was this constructive intervention to be carried out? Anwar's proposal called for a proactive policy of involvement and assistance to Southeast Asia's weaker nations in order to prevent their internal collapse. These interventions could take the form of: direct assistance to firm up electoral processes; an increased commitment to legal and administrative reforms; aid in the development of human capital; or the general strengthening of civil society and the rule of law. A year later, former Thai Foreign Minister Surin Pitsuwan proposed the idea of 'flexible engagement', which was later amended to 'enhanced interaction', to set the conduct of interstate relations in ASEAN. An important result that came out of these semantic exercises was the announcement at the 1999 ASEAN Ministerial Meeting that ASEAN leaders will have an annual retreat to enable them to discuss problems, be they domestic or regional, among themselves and on a more regular basis. This announcement was seen as a significant departure from the traditional ASEAN practice of 'sweeping issues under the carpet' for the sake of regional unity.

These initiatives and processes of finding a more acceptable modality to 'intervene' indicated a desire by ASEAN members to be more proactive in addressing regional challenges stemming from either domestic or interstate issues that would affect regional peace and stability. Arguably, these modes of intervention are different and may not be relevant to the current debate on humanitarian intervention that require the use of force. But they are, nevertheless, relevant to the current initiatives and attempts by the UN to expand the conventional notion of intervention. Of particular reference here are the statements by Annan arguing for the widening and re-operationalization of the concept in order to explore possibilities for a wider range of options for the international community to take action and enable other actors to get involved to stop widespread and systemic human rights violations 'prevent them early, and to stop or seek justice for them'.[28]

Within this broader context of humanitarian intervention, it is reasonable to argue that intervention for humanitarianism must not be confined to military options alone. As case studies have shown, more could have been done by states and non-state actors if a range of options were laid out for others to 'intervene' in ways other than military action to avert humanitarian disaster. These include the often-ignored processes of conflict prevention and postconflict rebuilding, and it is in these types of operation where state and non-state actors in Southeast Asia can find a role, given the kinds of constraints and resources available to them.

Despite these limitations, there are significant developments in pushing states to confront the idea of humanitarian intervention, and the necessary response for it.

One of these is the attempt by non-state actors, specifically members of the track II organization Council for Security Cooperation in the Asia Pacific (CSCAP), in defining the principles of humanitarian intervention.[29] This was initiated in the light of the bitter debates that ensued following the NATO intervention in Kosovo in 1999, and the UN intervention in East Timor. Against these developments, a workshop was organized by the CSCAP Working Group on Comprehensive and Cooperative Security to reflect on the challenges posed to the principle of non-intervention. The findings of that workshop, which were outlined in the Summary of Discussions, were instructive in that it was perhaps one of the pioneering attempts to reflect some of the emerging thoughts and ideas on the controversies found in the region with regard to calls to review the principles of non-interference in the domestic affairs of states. Some of the points that emerged from that Summary Report are highlighted below:[30]

1. Clarifying the concept of non-intervention: according to the CSCAP document, 'intervention' refers to intervention in the domestic affairs of the state without the government's consent. It is not the same as, and cannot be confused with, the alternative concepts of 'constructive intervention', 'constructive involvement', 'flexible engagement' or 'enhanced interaction', which have been recently proposed by some states in ASEAN.
2. Conditions for intervention: humanitarian intervention is permissible in cases of gross violations of human rights, but must meet the following criteria.

    i. There must be consent from the local people.
    ii. There must be support from the international community.
    iii. There must be a clear and limited objective.
    iv. There should be a high probability of success.

3. Outstanding issues: these refer to important questions on the issue of (military) intervention, which include the role and effectiveness of the UN and the Security Council; the mechanisms for intervention (how and in what form to intervene); timing of intervention; resources and the role and legitimacy of regional organizations.

Given that one of the difficult hurdles in humanitarian intervention is consensus on principles and procedural safeguards to ensure that it is properly carried out, the CSCAP efforts in this regard are notable. It belies the assumption that states in the region are unwilling to discuss this issue in multilateral forums.[31]

Furthermore, these discussions are not only found in the track II, unofficial circles. Interestingly, these issues have also been discussed widely at track III level (civil society organizations). For example, at the 2002 ASEAN People's Assembly (APA), there was a special session devoted to debating the ideas propounded by the R2P Report and obtaining the reaction of civil societies in the region on the various proposals related to the responsibilities to protect, react and rebuild.[32] It is interesting to note that at the discussions on humanitarian intervention at the first APA meeting, the cases cited where intervention was needed centered largely on Myanmar. Many NGOs represented at APA issued calls to governments in the region to 'intervene' in Myanmar to stop alleged cases of human rights abuses. But while the language of humanitarian intervention was often used, the types of intervention suggested did not include deployment of military force against the regime in Yangon.[33] Other related concerns discussed in this forum were pushing ahead with the establishment of regional human rights mechanisms, human security, the role of civil society, and social conflict prevention.[34] Discussions on various types of intervention within the context of R2P have continued to be a regular feature as noted in Chapter 3 in this volume. Of particular interest to advocates of humanitarian intervention were the discussions pertaining to the role that civil society groups/NGOs could undertake prior to and following intervention phases. For instance, at the APA III, one of the interesting points raised on the R2P was how women's issues NGOs could make use of the R2P proposals to promote the construction of new norms on the protection of women and children in conflict areas, and how to refocus the R2P doctrine away from an emphasis on reaction, and instead to think more about the responsibilities to prevent and to rebuild.[35] As an offshoot of the APA discussions, focused group discussions have taken place in some capitals in ASEAN to continue the exchange of views and perspectives in the region on R2P.[36] Similarly, APA has also been closely involved in other related initiatives, such as developing a regional human rights scorecard and a Southeast Asian Human Development Report.[37]

When put together, these types of regional discourse, albeit at a non-official level, are indicative of the willingness by several actors in the region to address the difficult issues related to humanitarian intervention. They also reflect the growing constituency of non-state actors in the region who are seriously examining intervention issues and how multisectoral actors can play a collaborative role.

These activities therefore dovetail well with the ongoing efforts by other actors to promote the adoption of proposals within the broader framework of the UN Reforms, specifically those that are outlined in the UN Report on *A More Secure World*, which included the R2P ideas on sovereignty-as-responsibility.[38]

While definitive statements that would reflect the official sentiments in the region with regard to the R2P since its launch, attempts to rethink the notions of sovereignty and the principle of non-intervention have already started and are no longer a novel enterprise. Governments have had to confront the issue of intervention even before the R2P report was introduced, in response to having to address new challenges in the region. As a result, new initiatives had been undertaken by certain governments in ASEAN that required some kind of 'intervention' in order to prevent certain crises from happening again (for example, ASEAN on Cambodia in 1997). While it could be contended that these 'official' initiatives may not have directly challenged the principle of non-interference and state sovereignty, it could also be pointed out that in actual practice, these initiatives and processes had already impinged on those principles.[39] More recent examples include ASEAN's official communiqué that urged the Myanmar government to resolve the political impasse and, more significantly, the slew of initiatives that were deliberated at official levels to promote the idea of an ASEAN Security Community.

A number of observations can thus be made from the official and non-official initiatives that have taken place in the region in relation to R2P and humanitarian intervention. First, contrary to the impression that discussions on non-intervention and sovereignty are frowned upon, or that the subjects are regarded as taboo, there have actually been dynamic movements toward the understanding and promotion of an evolving concept. These can be seen in the increasing tendency to debate these issues at both official and non-official levels – at both track II and even track III. These developments did not happen in a vacuum. The numerous crises that followed the Asian financial debacle had exposed the lack of capacity within the region to respond to and manage problems that could potentially lead to humanitarian crises. There was also the need to respond to the criticisms and pressures from the international community for ASEAN to be more effective. And more importantly, the pressures from citizenries pushing their own governments to respond had propelled both state and non-state actors to debate and rethink the principles of interstate conduct that were seen to hamper effective responses to humanitarian crises.

Second, there appears to be an emerging normative regional consensus on the idea of human security, broadly defined to be the security of individuals and societies. The idea that human security must be protected and ensured bridges the perceived gap between states promoting the notion of 'responsibility to protect'/ humanitarian intervention, and states that are recipients of this notion. This is very significant in a region where political developments are perceived to be at odds with the emerging normative order in other regions (EU and North America), which emphasizes the observance and promotion of human rights.

Third, there also appears to be broad agreement on the intervention issues of just cause, right intention, last resort, reasonable prospects and, most importantly, the right authority. One notes, for example, the guidelines set out by CSCAP, which broadly cover the same principles that the R2P had laid out. From both official and track II discourses, there is agreement that the 'responsibility to protect' must be a multilateral exercise, and that this responsibility should be carried out within the framework of the UN system. There is also the shared recognition that only the Security Council has the ultimate authority to sanction humanitarian intervention.

Against these examples of emerging regional trends and practices and their policy implications, what are the prospects for convergence of norms on humanitarian intervention? What are the possibilities for collaborative action to promote human security within the context of intervention through the R2P framework?

As alluded to earlier, the notion of humanitarian intervention has to be understood and appreciated in its broader context, even to the point of reconceptualizing what this type of intervention would entail if collaborative action for human security is to take place in East Asia. Hence, this calls for a more nuanced operationalization of the concept of humanitarian intervention. I had argued that for possible spaces to open for collaborative action, one should seriously consider

Annan's arguments, noted earlier, as the concept of humanitarian intervention. Humanitarian intervention should include humanitarian assistance in crisis prevention, crisis management and other humanitarian disasters – if the ultimate objective is to promote human security. Unless we move beyond the confines of 'armed military action', then states and societies in the region that have their own constraints will not be able to participate in any substantive way to avert possible humanitarian crises. Similarly, insistence on the strictures of humanitarian intervention definitions could only become a non-starter in the region. Thus, by following the lead set by Kofi Annan and/or the UN in broadening the range of activities under the rubric of 'reconstructed' humanitarian intervention, multiple actors can be enjoined to explore a range of ideas on how to collaborate and work towards human security for states and societies within and outside the region.

Whether or not intervention – as seen through the prism of 'responsibility to protect' – is an evolving norm that can reshape interstate relations, this has yet to find traction not only in Asia, but also in the rest of the global community. Hence acceptance of this norm remains uncertain and questionable even in the West, given the lack of progress in resolving issues of principles and legality of intervention.

More importantly, it must also be recognized that the development of any norm is usually preceded by ideas and state practices, and it is from these ideational elements that we are able to explore possible spaces wherein a regional fit and/or a role for regional actors can emerge. Thus, while some scholars have asserted that the prospects of R2P to be the defining framework for collaborative humanitarian intervention are hamstrung by the prevailing material and power-based structure of interstate politics, as well as the lack of reforms in the UN,[40] it could also be argued that the emergence of new ideas and norms in the region, coupled with new developments in interstate relations, could temper such reservations.

Most noteworthy was the launching of Bali Concord II, endorsed in October 2003 at the ninth ASEAN summit, wherein the introduction of the ASEAN Security Community (ASC) project has been most instructive. Together with the creation of similar economic and sociocultural communities, the Concord lays the foundations for the creation of an ASEAN Security Community by 2020. Of the three pillars identified, the ASC proposed by Indonesia has been the most interesting, insofar as it provides some insights on the new modalities ASEAN is planning to adopt in order to manage regional conflicts beyond its so-called 'ASEAN way'.[41] The concept of a security community is 'meant to provide a sense of purpose, a practical goal, and a future condition that all [ASEAN] members should strive for'.[42]

The ASC was to be realized based on five strategic thrusts: political development, norms-setting, conflict prevention, conflict resolution, and post-conflict peace building.[43] Of these five areas, the mechanisms being proposed under conflict resolution are particularly interesting within the context of our discussion on intervention. For instance, in plans to enhance regional cooperation for the maintenance of peace and stability in Southeast Asia, the notion of building capacity for regional peacekeeping operations has been mooted. This idea was originally proposed by Indonesia. In explaining the rationale for this proposal, a spokesperson for the Indonesian government remarked that 'ASEAN countries should know one another better than anyone else and therefore should have the option ... to take advantage of an ASEAN peacekeeping force to be deployed if they so wish'.[44]

While some ASEAN states had objected to the peacekeeping force proposal, on the grounds that it was 'too early' to consider setting up a force, and highly problematic because 'each country has its own policy about politics and the military',[45] this proposal has not been completely rejected – at least if one were to go by what is outlined in the 2004 Voluntary Action Plan. Instead, in lieu of a regional peacekeeping force, the possibility of establishing a regional peacekeeping centre is currently being deliberated among ASEAN officials. In fact, military officials attached to the peacekeeping units in some ASEAN states, such as Thailand, have openly endorsed a similar idea of having a regional coordinating centre for regional peacekeeping units, including other measures such as joint training exercises and joint peacekeeping operations courses.

Thus, while the ideas on building regional peacekeeping capacity (including peacebuilding) do not exactly fall strictly within what we call humanitarian intervention, they are nevertheless relevant if seen within the broader context of what humanitarian intervention entails. This includes the important yet complex tasks of peace operations – arguably a critical part of a host of activities involved in any kind of military intervention – with or without consent. What is often missed in the discussions of humanitarian intervention that get bogged down by legalities are the nuts and bolts of what happens before and after such operations take place, who goes in, and what else happens. These series of operations therefore command different sets of strategies, methods, resources and skills. As argued by one scholar, '[any] peace operations is not an activity, it is a project'.[46]

More recently, ASEAN adopted a historic Charter. Announced in 2005 and formally adopted at the thirteenth ASEAN Summit in 2007, it is aimed at enhancing ASEAN's capacity to deal with security challenges. Aside from conferring a legal personality on ASEAN, the Charter 'strengthens its institutions and organizational structure'.[47] Among the institutions outlined in the Charter, albeit modest, are the dispute-settlement mechanisms, the enhanced role of the ASEAN Chair and Secretary General to deal with conflicts through good offices, and the need for an effective and timely response to urgent issues or crisis situations affecting ASEAN.

Conclusion

This chapter argues that the notion of collaborative action for human security in Southeast Asia framed within the idea of humanitarian intervention – broadly defined – is possible, but only if one adopts a more nuanced approach to this notion of security that allows for convergence of interests among various actors. This would call for a reconceptualization of humanitarian intervention, as has been argued by Kofi Annan and defined within the kinds of measures of 'responsibilities' outlined in the R2P report. As discussed throughout this chapter, we have already seen many of these measures in regional efforts at providing constructive intervention, conflict prevention and post-conflict rebuilding, and more recently in the kinds of measures introduced in the ASEAN Security Community Plan of Action.

In the Southeast Asia region, where humanitarian intervention has never been on the agenda of regional state actors, one cannot ignore the significance of these ideas, and how they might then evolve into a norm espoused under the R2P report where more responsible states would be willing to prevent, react and rebuild the welfare and security of the greater humanity. These ideas, which have since been translated into regional endeavours such as the ASC, can be viewed as concrete examples of an 'Asian brand' of intervention, where careful efforts towards finding a more acceptable base, or middle ground, have been made to balance the concerns for state sovereignty and the compelling need to respond to humanitarian problems. These initiatives, either from the latest ASC proposal or those being initiated by civil society groups, can be considered part of the emerging yet important building blocks progressing toward the ultimate objective of promoting human security.

Nevertheless, the challenges of getting these normative ideas translated into concrete actions and modalities remain – particularly those that would have a bearing on intervention – for both military and non-military aspects. But given the impediments on pushing ahead with the conventional notion of humanitarian intervention, more focus should be given to developing the other possibilities of preventing conflict at the earlier stages – for which efforts, especially at the ideational level, are already abundant. As already argued, these broadly defined efforts at intervention to prevent conflict from escalating into humanitarian crises are more effective and no doubt more realistic, given the ongoing realities in the region.

Part II

Collaborative Action on Human Security in East Asia

5 Human Security *in extremis*

East Asian reactions to the responsibility to protect[1]

Paul M. Evans

Although human security has a growing number of academic and practitioner adherents, a cursory skim of titles and subjects in mainstream security journals in North America and Europe indicates that the phrase remains far less popular than more familiar concepts such as national security or cooperative security.[2] Human security operates on the margins of security thinking except in a handful of countries such as Canada and Norway.[3]

The impact of human security on intellectual and policy circles in East Asia is still growing, but remains limited. The conventional wisdom regards Asia as resistant to innovative concepts of security that, in normative terms, have the potential to erode traditional conceptions of sovereignty; and in policy terms demand a new allocation of resources to manage an array of non-traditional security challenges well beyond military threats to territorial integrity. States in the region jealously safeguard their sovereign prerogatives. Especially in Northeast Asia, a neighbourhood where the Cold War continues, where historical legacies remain unresolved, where divided states exist, where defence spending remains high, and where there is little experience with regional institutions or cooperative security, human security appears to many an alien and even dangerous transplant.

This chapter argues that after facing initial opposition, human security is finding a niche in regional discussion and policy behaviour. The regional preference is for the broader approach to human security that looks at multiple 'new' threats to human wellbeing. But there has been a subtle shift toward the narrower understanding of human security, which is related to protection of individuals in situations of violent conflict, as embodied in the logic of the 'responsibility to protect'. Human security is playing a catalytic role in changing the normative framework related to state obligations and the principles of sovereignty and non-interference. Collaborative action among actors in East Asia involved in human security activities is only at a nascent stage, but the future prospects are encouraging.

This chapter first outlines some of the conceptual and policy debates about human security, and identifies two main variants identified as the broad and narrow approaches. It pays attention to the idea of the responsibility to protect as it connects to the concept of human security. The special focus is the pattern of discourse and practice in China in the context of its new approaches to participation in peace operations. This country, widely identified as 'the high church of *realpolitik* in the post-Cold War world'[4] and as nurturing hegemonic ambitions, serves as a useful window on the interactions of older conceptions of state sovereignty and new forces of regional integration and global awareness.

The responsibility to protect and the challenges from states in East Asia

There have been frequent disagreements about the nature and meaning of human security – its what and how – but far fewer on its why and when. Advocates regularly point to changes in the post-Cold War security environment; the increasing significance of intrastate as compared to interstate conflict; the emergence of a new form of diplomacy that connects states, international institutions and civil society actors; and, more fundamentally, the deepening of globalization that brings with it new information networks and media capacity, that has exacerbated the problems faced by failed and failing states, and that has produced new forces for democratization. Most security specialists are now familiar with the term, even if some dismiss it as analytically problematic, morally risky, unsustainable, counterproductive, and 'so vague that it verges on the meaningless'.[5]

Part of the problem is that the concept emerged to challenge the traditional concept of national security only after the Cold War had ended. The term was used occasionally before 1994, but only after its formulation in the UN Development Programme (UNDP)'s *Human Development Report* in that year did the concept begin to penetrate academic and policy discourse.[6] Portrayed alternatively as a new theory, concept, paradigm, analytical starting point, worldview, political agenda, normative benchmark and policy framework, human security has inspired a shelf of books, hundreds of journal articles, several government reports, and scores of new seminars and teaching programs.

Human security raises a host of conceptual, philosophical and political challenges for both its adherents and detractors. Conceptually, it challenges mainstream understandings of security by changing the referent point and introducing issues and means that extend beyond conventional security strategies. Philosophically, it raises fundamental issues related to conscience, obligations beyond borders, development and domestic legitimacy. Politically, it raises questions about sovereignty, intervention, the role of regional and global institutions, and the relationship between state and citizen.[7] Insecure states almost certainly produce insecure citizens, but secure states do not necessarily produce secure citizens. Beyond this point, human security fragments into a variety of approaches on how broadly to define the threats, how to prioritize them, and whether to emphasize the complementarity or tension between the state and the individual.

As also discussed by other contributors, there are two basic approaches to human security. The most influential expression of the logic of the narrow approach to human security was outlined by the International Commission on Intervention and State Sovereignty (ICISS) in its final report, *The Responsibility to Protect* (R2P).[8] Against the background of contested humanitarian interventions (and non-interventions) in Somalia, Sierra Leone, Rwanda, Bosnia and

East Timor, the ICISS was a response to the request by Kofi Annan for the international community to forge a consensus on the principles and processes for using coercive action to protect people at risk. Created in September 2000, co-chaired by Gareth Evans and Mohamed Sahnoun, and officially supported by the Canadian government and several private foundations in the West, the ICISS carried out extensive research and consultations before issuing its report in October 2001.

R2P explicitly eschewed the vocabulary of 'humanitarian intervention' and 'the right to intervene', and instead focused on people in need of assistance by framing the issues of sovereignty and intervention in terms of the responsibility to protect. It identified a series of core principles that connected state sovereignty, obligations under the UN Charter, existing legal obligations under international law, and the developing practice of states, regional organizations and the Security Council. It extended the responsibility to protect to include the responsibility to prevent, to react, and to rebuild when faced with human protection claims in states that are either unable or unwilling to discharge their responsibility. It also provided a precise definition of the just cause threshold, as well as precautionary principles, right authority, and operational principles.

The R2P report makes a direct connection between the responsibility to protect and the broader conception of human security (defined as 'the security of people – their physical safety, their economic and social well being, respect for their dignity and worth as human beings, and the protection of human rights and fundamental freedoms').[9] Treating human security as 'indivisible', the report contends that:

> ... issues of sovereignty and intervention are not just matters affecting the rights or prerogatives of states, but they deeply affect and involve individual human beings in fundamental ways. One of the virtues of expressing the key issue in this debate as 'the responsibility to protect' is that it focuses attention where it should be most concentrated, on the human needs of those seeking protection or assistance ... The fundamental components of human security – the security of *people* against threats to life, health, livelihood, personalsafety and human dignity – can be put at risk by external aggression but also by factors within a country, including 'security' forces. Being wedded still to too narrow a concept of 'national security' may be one reason why many governments spend more to protect their citizens against undefined external military attack than to guard them against the omnipresent enemies of good health and other real threats to human security on a daily basis.[10]

The list of insecurities from which states should protect their citizens includes hunger, inadequate shelter, disease, crime, unemployment, social conflict and environmental hazards, as well as rape as an instrument of war, ethnic cleansing, genocide, and citizens killed by their security forces.[11] R2P is innovative in its move from the broad conception of threats and 'indivisibility' to a specific focus on two types of threat that might warrant outside military intervention: large-scale loss of life and ethnic cleansing.

The real focus of the narrower view is protection of individuals and communities in situations of violent conflict. Sometimes labelled the 'freedom-from-fear' approach, the focus is human security *in extremis*, often in the context of intrastate war. Adherents do not deny that there are multiple threats to human wellbeing but, for reasons of analytical clarity and operational focus, want to concentrate on one species of threat. Analytically, Andrew Mack, the progenitor of the Human Security Report, argues that:

> Conflating a very broad range of disparate harms under the rubric of 'insecurity' is an exercise in re-labelling that serves no apparent analytic purpose. If the term 'insecurity' embraces almost all forms of harm – from affronts to dignity to genocide – its descriptive power is extremely low ... To examine relationships between – say – poverty and violence requires that, for the purpose of analysis, each be treated separately. Any definition that has the consequence of conflating dependent and independent variables makes causal analysis virtually impossible.[12]

Operationally, its proponents claim that there already exist a variety of institutions and networks for addressing issues of economic development, and that what is needed is a concentration on a specific set of threats to human life and the creation of political will and practical instruments for addressing them. Human security, they contend, can make the biggest difference if it keeps squarely focused on protection of refugees, women and children in conflict zones, humanitarian intervention, peacekeeping and postconflict peacebuilding, as well as conflict management, prevention and resolution.

The narrow approach to human security based on the idea of R2P, however, has been more popular outside Asia than inside it. Very quickly, the Japanese government distanced itself from the leading protagonists of the narrow approach to human security, especially the Canadian efforts led by Foreign Minister Lloyd Axworthy. As noted in the introduction to this volume, Japan displayed 'discomfort' and 'unhappiness' with the seemingly interventionist stance taken by Western states, especially Canada.

The most developed variant of the broad approach can be found in the work of the Commission on Human Security, which conceives of human security in a comprehensive sense of dealing with both situations of violence and deprivation. Its final report states that:

> The aim of human security is to protect the vital core of all human lives in ways that enhance human freedoms and human fulfilment. Human security means protecting fundamental freedoms – freedoms that are the essence of life. It means protecting people from critical (severe) and pervasive (widespread) threats and situations. It means using processes that build on people's strengths and aspirations. It means creating political, social, environmental, economic, military and cultural systems that together give people the building blocks of survival, livelihood and dignity.... . The vital core of life is a

set of elementary rights and freedoms people enjoy. What people consider to be 'vital' – what they consider to be 'of the essence of life' and 'crucially important' – varies across individuals and societies. That is why any concept of human security must be dynamic. And that is why we refrain from proposing an itemized list of what makes up human security.[13]

The substantive chapters deal with situations of violent conflict, refugees and internally displaced persons, recovery from violent conflict, economic security, health and human security, knowledge, skills, and values for human security. The report explicitly aims to connect issues of protection, rights, development and governance.

Although the broad approach has a significant Asian pedigree – the initial UNDP report was written by a Pakistani with an Asian audience in mind – it initially appeared to be seeds scattered on barren rock in East Asia. Human security, as Amitav Acharya correctly notes, is 'a distinctive notion, which goes well beyond all earlier attempts by Asian governments to "redefine" and broaden their own traditional understanding of security as protection of sovereignty and territory against military threats'.[14] Few governments or intellectuals in East Asia showed immediate interest in human security, and several commentators immediately concluded that its fundamental premises and action agenda would not find support in a region where governments felt that states were the best (and perhaps only) providers of security, and where they ferociously guarded the principles of absolute state sovereignty and non-interference in domestic affairs. The first reactions were, in the phrase of a Taiwanese academic, 'hesitant, sceptical and cautious'.[15]

In the context of regional governmental institutions, human security has been used intermittently by political leaders and bureaucrats and is slowly entering the vocabulary of regional institutions, albeit with several different formulations of what the phrase means. The senior officials in the East Asia Study Group and the Association of Southeast Asian Nations' ASEAN+3 heads of government have used it since 2001, mainly in the context of the need to address a range of 'non-traditional' security issues including environmental degradation, illegal migration, piracy, communicable diseases and transnational crime. After considerable debate, the term was used in the Asia-Pacific Economic Cooperation (APEC), first in official meetings in 2002 and then as part of the Leaders' Declaration on 21 October 2003, which pledged APEC 'not only to advancing the prosperity of our economies, but also to the complementary mission of ensuring the security of our people'. APEC's prescriptions for 'enhancing human security' concentrated on dismantling terrorist groups, eliminating the danger of weapons of mass destruction, and confronting other direct threats to security including communicable diseases (especially SARS), protection of air travellers, and energy security. The use of the term merged conventional understandings of human security in its broadest sense and the American-promoted antiterrorist agenda, producing a politically compelling, if conceptually confusing, new variant.

Proclivity toward the broad approach and prospects for the narrow approach to human security

What explains the Asian proclivity toward the broad approach, and what can it tell us about the prospects of targeted ideas such as R2P? To answer this question, we must first explain why states in East Asia have leaned more heavily toward the broad approach, and then account for the fact that their resistance to the narrow approach has weakened.

The broad approach is attractive to Asians in general, for several reasons. First and foremost is the skepticism about motives reinforced by the interventionist thrust of US foreign policy in the Bush era after the terrorist attacks of 11 September 2001. The antiterrorism agenda has produced an expanded level of state-to-state cooperation, seen in the constructive interactions of the USA, China, and the other major powers. The current antiterrorism agenda has also complicated the discussion about human security. At one level, the fight against terror has focused new attention on the root causes of violence and the intrastate conflicts that have regional and global consequences. The postinvasion efforts at nation building and reconstruction in Afghanistan and Iraq have already involved the direct participation of Japan and South Korea and, if the United Nations plays a larger role, will probably involve several other East Asian countries in the future. At the same time, the strategies for responding to terrorism have generally been framed as strengthening states and regimes and using traditional coercive instruments (the military, police and intelligence agencies) as the main means for achieving the objective. Many Asians remain wary of western-style international humanitarianism, largely because they still regard it as promoting or condoning neo-imperialism, vigilantism and double standards.[16] The fear of great power intrusion into domestic affairs is palpable.

Second, the broader conception has been easier for scholars and public figures to embrace, if only as an aspiration, because of their support for the idea of the developmental state. This can be seen in a range of publications since 1995,[17] many of which aim to connect human security to developmental issues such as poverty and inequality, and a new brand of 'transnational' issues such as climate change.

Combining sensitivity to the developmental and transnational issues, the idea of 'non-traditional security' has been a growth industry in regional security studies. As a result, the resistance to connecting non-traditional security to human security is declining, even as some worry that at least the narrow conception of human security is either inappropriate to Asia, or will slow progress in achieving state action in addressing the non-traditional security agenda. What is distinctive about many of the approaches to non-traditional security is that they are ambiguous about whether the referent of security is the state or the individual and do not dwell on tensions between the two, and that its advocates normally emphasize the state and state-centric means as the best ways of responding to these threats, normally preferring to address these issues within their own states rather than on a regional basis. The transnational sources of threat to security may be new, but the instruments prescribed for dealing with them usually are not.[18]

Third, human security seems to connect fairly well to local conditions. As Acharya argues, it is compatible with most formulations of comprehensive security, resonates with the needs-oriented approach of many Asian governments, is flexible in including both individuals and communities as the referent of security, connects well to developmental issues, and is easily adapted to indigenous traditions of human dignity. The shift from ideological or nationalist foundations for regime legitimacy to performance-based legitimacy in the past two decades also put more pressure on governments to meet basic human needs and protection.[19] The fall of Suharto in the aftermath of the economic crisis was emblematic of the costs of not doing so. As argued by Rizal Sukma, 'While it might be presumptuous to argue that the emphasis on human security will automatically ensure political and economic stability, one can make a reasonably strong claim that ignoring it will definitely serve as a recipe for disaster'.[20] The economic crisis attracted attention in East Asia to the broader concept of human security.[21]

Fourth, the constituency for human security in East Asia also remains limited, centred initially on government officials involved in multilateral diplomacy, then including academics, and only recently civil society organizations. Very few advocates of human security have argued that its application in East Asia should go beyond wellbeing and protection to demand democratization as the logical extension of human security. R2P itself does not comment on the form of governance within a state, only that it provides protection of a narrow range of basic human rights pertaining to physical safety. Although there are a few academics and NGO activists who feel that the real issues are widening the scope of human rights and creating democracies, most of the advocates of the broad and narrow approaches to human security have restricted themselves to basic protection issues, and have not tried to use the concept to make the case for new forms of intervention against undemocratic regimes or to argue for regime transformation.[22] In crude terms, the first generation of human security thinking in East Asia has taken a Hobbesian turn, much more focused on the dangers posed by chaos and the breakdown of social order than by tyranny. Beyond being a nice-sounding phrase, human security provides a tool for acknowledging that even two decades of economic growth and statebuilding had not eliminated severe vulnerabilities for large numbers of Asians. And it at least hinted at the growing role of non-state actors as alternative service providers when states were unable to provide social welfare and protection for their own citizens, and as participants in the policy process.

Democracy seems to offer an additional explanation for the acceptance of human security in East Asia. It is an interesting question why Japan and Thailand have been more receptive to human security thinking than many of their neighbors. It may largely be the product of specific individuals in the right place at the right time, especially Surin Pitsuwan, the Thai Foreign Minister between 1998 and 2002, and Keizo Obuchi, the Japanese Foreign Minister, then Prime Minister from 1996 to 2000. Looking more structurally, in the case of Thailand, the democratic transition brought to power an elected government closely connected to liberally minded NGOs and academics, and very nervous about repeated border incidents and the stream of refugees and illegal drugs flowing out of Myanmar. In the case of Japan, human security opened up a more proactive role in international security that was independent of the USA, but not threatening to the alliance or the Japanese constitution. It provided a foreign policy tool that permitted Tokyo to put a more compassionate face on its aid programs and to address humanitarian issues that were on the global and regional agenda, especially in the wake of the Asian economic crisis. It is not surprising at all that interest in human security has been strongest in some of the new democracies in East Asia (especially Thailand, South Korea and the Philippines), and that the most negative reactions have come from North Korea and Myanmar.

The correlation with regime type, however, is far from perfect. In Taiwan, where there is a strong civil society and functioning democratic institutions, the concept is only just beginning to get attention and faces some serious constraints, considering Taiwan's exclusion from most of the international institutions where human security is being discussed in a multilateral forum.[23] Also, some of the most vehement criticisms of human security, at least in its narrower formulations, have come from Indian officials.

The role of civil society has proved crucial in the growing interest in human security. Deep-seated differences in doctrine, instruments and discourse continue to distinguish Southeast Asia from Northeast Asia. Despite the efforts of individuals in Japan, South Korea and China to open the discussion on human security, even ideas about regional responses to non-traditional security issues are making very slow progress. The level of discussion and tentative governmental and NGO action in Southeast Asia is somewhat stronger. NGOs and activists in Southeast Asia have begun to use human security in such settings as the ASEAN People's Assembly and other track III meetings. Pierre Lizée argues that it is emerging as 'something of a rallying cry for civil society organizations in Southeast Asia because it provides them with a powerful arguments against the state-centred model of economic and political development at the heart of the region in recent decades'.[24]

By delinking state and society, the concept 'leads quite immediately to the contention that groups and individuals ... could well want to define their hopes and priorities in terms of human rights or social welfare, and not in terms set by the states, but through closer reference to global standards ... it invites the idea that the state might be called upon to account for its actions on the basis of these supranational standards'.[25]

These differences between Southeast and Northeast Asia appear to be narrowing, in part because of the emergence of East Asian multilateral institutions, and they appear to be narrowing in the direction of increased support for at least the rhetoric of human security. A variety of track II regional processes, including the ASEAN Institutes of Strategic and International Studies and the Council for Security Cooperation in the Asia Pacific, have used human security in both its narrower and broader formulations. The East Asia Vision Group (EAVG) introduced it into several sections of its final report in 2001 (the EAVG has since been disbanded). In all, there were some 30 track II meetings between 1998 and 2002 that had human security as the principal focus or a major theme.[26]

The underlying issues and principles are so significant and complex that they have been an increasingly frequent topic at academic and track II policy discussions. R2P has been a featured subject topic at meetings including the Asia Pacific Roundtable and the ASEAN People's Assembly. It has also been the principal focus of conferences and workshops in Beijing, Shanghai and Nanjing (January 2002), Tokyo (December 2002), Bangkok (March 2003), Singapore (March 2003), Jakarta (April 2003) and Manila (July 2003). The discussions at these meetings have been lively, constructive and generally supportive of at least the intentions of the Report. With leadership from Australia and Thailand, an Asia-Pacific Center for the Responsibility to Protect was launched in Bangkok in February 2008 as part of a global network.

In the long run, it may be that citizen participation in addressing non-traditional issues will be the most powerful factor in widening support for human security in East Asia. In any formulation, the human security perspectives raise significant questions about the relationship between citizens and states. Even the softest prescriptions for dealing with non-traditional security make new demands on governments to protect citizens from an increasingly large number of threats. Some of the more robust ones call for the broader participation of civil society groups in priority-setting and action to deal with a myriad of transnational issues. Civil society actors – domestic and transnational – can thus play a useful advocacy role. The emphasis on the agency of non-state actors fits very well with the idea of the 'new diplomacy' that connects international institutions, sympathetic governments, and networks of NGOs and policy experts in advancing initiatives such as the International Campaign to Ban Landmines and the creation of the International Criminal Court (ICC).[27]

Regional responses to R2P and the case of China

One of the remarkable changes in East Asia in the past 25 years has been the dramatic reduction in battle deaths and war-related deaths resulting from civil conflicts. According to figures collected for the Human Security Report by the University of Uppsala and the International Peace Research Institute in Oslo, from 1946 until 1980 East Asia was the site of the three largest internal conflicts in the world (the Chinese civil war, the Korea War and the Vietnam war), with battle deaths of more than 4.5 million and war-related deaths somewhere in the vicinity of two and a half times that number. But since 1980, the number of battle deaths has been considerably fewer than 5000 annually for the entire region. Yet memories of the killing fields in Cambodia in the 1970s, East Timor in the late 1990s, and recurring armed conflicts inside Myanmar, the Philippines and Indonesia indicate that intrastate conflict is still part of the regional situation, albeit on a substantially lower scale than 25 years earlier.

Support of East Asian governments for the main global initiatives directly tied to the narrow approach to human security – the campaign to ban antipersonnel landmines, the ICC, humanitarian interventions in Kosovo, Haiti, Rwanda, Somalia and East Timor – has been mixed. In the context of the UN, some states have declared support for the principles and recommendations of the R2P. The last two secretaries general of the UN, Kofi Annan and Ban Ki Moon, have been strong supporters of the concept of human security and R2P. The report of the High-level Panel on Threats, Challenges and Change commissioned by Annan in 2003 identified six clusters of threats, two of which were closely connected to human security.[28] At the UN-organized World Summit in 2005, leaders of 150 countries, many of them in Asia, endorsed a statement in which 'human security' appeared several times, and adopted the concept of the responsibility to protect.[29] And in April 2006 the UN Security Council adopted Resolution 1674, reaffirming 'the provisions of paragraphs 138 and 139 of the 2005 World Summit Outcome Document regarding the responsibility to protect populations from genocide, war crimes, ethnic cleansing and crimes against humanity'.[30]

While some major states have now backed away from the commitments they made in 2005–06, their reasons have less to do with principle than with the practicalities of mobilizing political will and resources in difficult situations, such as Darfur in Sudan.[31] Some Asian countries, including Myanmar, North Korea and India, have also encouraged the Group of 77 to reject R2P on the grounds that it provides a pretext for developed countries to meddle in the domestic affairs of states in the developing world.[32] As noted elsewhere in this volume, none of the regional governmental institutions (including ASEAN, ASEAN+3, APEC, the ASEAN Regional Forum or the Asia–Europe Meeting) has so far made any official comments on the Report, reflecting the internal debate within them and their formal, if softening, commitment to non-interference principles.

In the short run, it is the issue of humanitarian intervention that is the most pointed and vexed aspect of the human security agenda. Even phrased as a 'responsibility to protect', the call for viewing security issues through the lenses of individuals and victims, and establishing rights and duties that justify and compel states and citizens to intervene in the affairs of neighbors, is a hard sell in many parts of the world. Although two of the ten commissioners on the ICISS were from Asia (Fidel Ramos and Ramesh Thakur), and the Commission held two of its ten consultative meetings in Asia (Delhi and Beijing) while preparing the draft, Asian reactions to the report have been mixed.

While there is some evidence of change in regional norms related to sovereignty, non-interference and institution-building, most East Asian states have been very reluctant to focus regional and global attention on the dynamics of intrastate war. Concepts such as preventive diplomacy have been slow to find acceptance. What has been accepted is that domestic instabilities and vulnerabilities need special attention by the states in which they are occurring. For many analysts, even a bad government can do this better than no government or a government imposed through outside intervention.

Critics of R2P have made several arguments: it is an insidious new form of interventionist doctrine that misunderstands and erodes the concept of sovereignty; military intervention under any circumstances is not the best option; it is too dependent on the Security Council as the preferred mechanism for action; the threshold criteria are too narrow and too demanding, ruling out action against a country such as Myanmar, where the level of killing is low on an annual basis but persistent; it may give false hopes to those suffering death and injury that external forces will come to their rescue when this is in fact an unlikely prospect; and, in the end, R2P depends on the powerful being willing to act and this will only occur when it suits their specific national interests in ways that no guidelines or moral principles can affect, reducing a debate about humanitarian obligations to an exercise in power politics.

Most commentators read R2P as state-enhancing rather than state-threatening. After looking carefully at the just cause threshold and the precautionary principles, they conclude that the R2P framework actually makes military intervention less likely and provides safeguards for developing countries against unilateral intervention.[33]

Those supportive of the basic aspects of the Report are aware that the American-led invasion of Iraq has produced a backlash against even well intentioned efforts to delineate the proper grounds for humanitarian intervention. Despite the fact that the Bush administration did not endorse the Report, and that Gareth Evans, the chair of the ICISS, has adamantly denied that the Iraq case meets the conditions for intervention outlined in the Report, it is seen by many as the slippery slope to legitimating great power intervention and doctrines of pre-emption. These anxieties will be hard to assuage. Ironically, it may be that the Bush administration's muscular neoconservative policies on regime change and nation-building in Iraq will do more to harm the case for multilateral efforts to promote human security than have direct administration criticisms of initiatives such as the ban on antipersonnel landmines or the ICC.

Governmental institutions may be unready to accept the narrower approach, but one indicator of changing attitudes about intervention is clear when comparing regional reactions to the Cambodian genocide in the 1970s with those to the large-scale killings in East Timor in 1998–99. In the context of Cambodia, there was virtually no discussion within ASEAN of the need for external intervention, and virtually no sympathy for occasional Vietnamese pretexts that its intervention was motivated by humanitarian impulses. In the context of East Timor, while Indonesia and ASEAN insisted on Indonesian consent before authorizing a military intervention, there were frequent demands for swift international action, including the use of military force, by citizens and top political leaders in several Southeast Asian capitals. While formal institutional responses and doctrinal principles have remained relatively rigid, the normative framework has clearly shifted on humanitarian intervention. As East Asian countries respond to the growing challenges of modernization and globalization by liberalizing their economies, opening their societies and deepening their interconnections, issues of interactions with neighbors are more numerous, more public and more complex than in the past.

Overall, the discussion about various forms of intervention for protection purposes, sovereignty and non-interference is becoming more complex and pragmatic in East Asia. In almost every capital, there has been a shift from an argument based on first principles and philosophy to a much more contingent one that takes account of specific situations, circumstances and instruments. In the context of

Southeast Asia, the primacy of norms of sovereignty and non-interference has been challenged by the deepening interest in a more intrusive 'flexible engagement' and 'enhanced interaction'.

Using the criteria set out in the R2P, it is difficult to imagine any scenarios in which outside intervention is conceivable in Northeast Asia. Asian leaders are not likely to lead the discussion or specific interventions, at least in the short term, but are likely to become more deeply involved in prevention and reconstruction activities, and to support externally led and endorsed multilateral interventions in conflict situations that meet ICISS-recommended thresholds inside Southeast Asia and in other parts of the world. In Acharya's words, 'a regional capacity for military prevention would be difficult to operationalize due to concerns about sovereignty. For Asian regional institutions, the key task would thus be to engage in conflict prevention or responsibility to prevent, while leaving it to the UN to undertake military protection'.[34] It is now at least imaginable that in the near future, East Asian countries would join in a regionally built coalition if the leadership came from outside the region but was not mandated by the UN.

Perhaps the most complex evolution in thinking about human security has occurred in China, which is still protective of the traditional concept of state sovereignty and the norm of non-intervention. Preferring the idea of 'non-traditional security' to 'human security', Chinese officials in November 2002 co-signed 'The Joint Declaration of ASEAN and China on Cooperation in the Field of Non-Traditional Security Issues' relating to illegal drugs, people smuggling, trafficking in women and children, piracy, terrorism, arms smuggling, money laundering, international economic crime and cyber-crime.[35]

Although Chinese scholars and officials still hold on to the concept of non-traditional security, the concept of human security has now penetrated academic and policy-related discussions in China. Until the late 1990s, the phrase 'human security' remained virtually unknown to Chinese academics, and is still used only rarely by government officials in formal meetings or by the media. As Chinese leaders began to get more familiar with the concept of human security, they showed resistance to the idea of intervention. At the Round Table Discussion in Beijing on 14 June 2001, for instance, the Chinese did not reject humanitarianism (viewing it as good), but regarded interventionism as bad, and further characterized 'humanitarian intervention' as 'tantamount to marrying evil to good'.[36]

The situation is now changing in two respects. First, some of the domestic aspects of human security – the threats from within – are receiving government and academic attention. These include environmental concerns, poverty and social security. Second, human security overlaps with some of the key elements of China's new security concept, especially the emphasis on cooperative action to address pressing transnational security concerns.[37] China and ASEAN have held joint conferences on poverty reduction and health crises such as avian influenza and SARS. A growing number of Chinese scholars have adopted a more liberal approach to security, emphasizing spiritual growth and human rights.[38]

Over the past six years or so, Chinese responses have evidently been more fluid than often portrayed. There remain vocal proponents of a strict interpretation of the principles of sovereignty and non-interference, stressing the Five Principles of Peaceful Co-existence, emphasizing Article 3(4) of the UN Charter, preferring humanitarian assistance to humanitarian intervention, advocating strict neutrality in peacekeeping, and seeing ulterior motives in the practice of intervention. They echo deeply embedded views in China about past humiliations, fears of potential interventions into Taiwan, Tibet and Xinjiang, and a political philosophy that focuses on the nation rather than the individual and that separates human safety from what now is called human security.[39] It did not come as a real surprise to observers when Chinese at the Beijing roundtable reacted to the R2P with little enthusiasm. They argued that 'Theoretically, the conceptualization of humanitarian intervention is a total fallacy. Practically, actions of humanitarian intervention posed grave problems for international law and international relations'. They added that, 'the assertion of "human rights transcending sovereignty" has serious fallacies in theory and lends no help to the legalization of humanitarian intervention'.[40]

Yet it would be shortsighted to see these views as static. Beijing has now professed a strong commitment to the enforcement of the Nuclear Non-proliferation Treaty. The Chinese government took an unprecedented step to support a UN resolution imposing sanctions on North Korea (one of its traditional socialist allies in East Asia) for having tested nuclear weapons in 2006. Chu Shulong further points out that 'the Chinese leadership will continue to defend fundamental national sovereignty rights, but at the same time, the pressure of global trends means they will become more flexible and accepting toward relative new concepts of security, including human security', adding that 'the Chinese recognize that in times of integration and globalization, nations and peoples around the world will gain more than they will lose from changing their traditional positions on national security'.[41]

Allen Carlson's report on discussions in China in January 2002, *after* the release of R2P, offers an insightful assessment of the historical evolution of Chinese thinking and practice on sovereignty and intervention issues. Demonstrating that thinking has changed over the past decade, he points to a 'heterogeneity' of approaches and narratives in policy circles. Despite 'deeply embedded misgivings', a combination of rational calculation of interests, concern about image and reputation, and an embrace of new normative principles has produced a more diverse debate. He concludes that 'many Chinese elites have now come to accept the general legitimacy of multilateral intervention to resolve particularly prominent humanitarian crises' and that 'China has become a reluctant participant in the international trend toward questioning the sanctity of state sovereignty and expanding the international community's right to intervene'.[42]

Since 1989, China has emerged as a major player in peace operations, beginning with the initial UN mission in Namibia. In Southeast Asia, China sent its first peacekeeping force to Cambodia in 1992. In another instance, in 2000 it supported the peace operations in East Timor by sending some 15 peacekeepers, emerging for the first time as a participant in a UN civilian police force and a donor involved in the process of postwar reconstruction. China's commitment to UN peace operations has now been extended around the world. Outside East Asia, China has joined peace operations such as those in the Democratic Republic of Congo, Liberia (where it sent 550 troops in 2003), Kosovo, Haiti, Afghanistan, and Bosnia and Herzegovina. After the Israeli bombardments of Lebanon in 2006, Beijing agreed to send more than 1,000 troops to the UN operation in Lebanon, its first in the Middle East. According to Michael Fullilove, 'China today deploys more military and civilian personnel to UN peacekeeping operations than any other of the five permanent members of the Security Council'.[43]

This change of behavior has coincided with changes in declaratory policy. China's position paper in 2005 on UN reform stated that 'Each state shoulders the primary responsibility to protect its own population [but] when a massive human-itarian crisis occurs, it is the legitimate concern of the international community to ease and defuse the crisis'.[44] At the opening ceremony of the China–Norway Peacekeeping Workshop on 26 March 2007, China's Assistant Foreign Minister, Cui Tiankai, made a statement that took pride in the Chinese role in UN peace operations. In his words, 'Asia is … the most active continent to take part in the UN peacekeeping operations. Asia has made remarkable contributions to enrich-ing the connotation of peacekeeping operations and strengthening its influence'. More specifically, 'China actively supports and takes part in the UN peacekeeping operations. Since 1989, China has participated in 16 UN peacekeeping operations and sent an accumulative total of over 7,000 peacekeeping soldiers and police-men. Currently there are over 1,800 Chinese peacekeepers serving in 12 mission areas, making China on the top of the permanent members of UNSC'.[45] As a per-manent member of the UN Security Council with veto power, China maintains the traditional position to defend the need for UNSC authorization.

Darfur still indicates the limits to China's support for R2P. The widely cited accusation of China's indifference to the plight of the people in this Sudanese region, and its opposition to harsh measures against the Sudanese government, is that Beijing is a major supplier of weapons to this African state and keeps an eye on its oil. But this public criticism has now caused Chinese officials to become increasingly defensive of their policy toward the humanitarian crisis in Darfur. In June 2007, for instance, Chinese Special Envoy on the Darfur issue Liu Guijin responded that China had helped to bring calm to Darfur, and played a positive role in persuading the Sudanese government to accept a major force of UN and African Union peacekeepers deployed in this region. Beijing had already commit-ted 275 military engineers to the current UN force in the region, had 'tried [its] best', and would consider sending its troops to join the planned 19,000-strong UN peacekeeping mission if a formal request to China were made.[46]

Conclusion

The policy debate on human security in the past decade is still at a formative stage. Underpinning ideas such as the responsibility to protect is a purportedly universal approach to conflict resolution and the management of violence. Despite the Hobbesian turn and the state-enhancing thrust of much of thinking about non-traditional and human security, the main ideas about conflict prevention, intervention and postconflict reconstruction are based on ideas about governance, democracy and the control of violence that grow out of Western experience.

By and large, postcolonial proclivities for statebuilding, resistance to external interference, and adherence to nineteenth-century conceptions of hard-shell sovereignty are deeply entrenched in East Asia. However, such growing forces as deepening interdependence, regional integration, the opening of Asian societies and economies, and new information and communication technologies have now combined to make a retreat into ossified Westphalianism tempting for some, but unrealistic in the long run. As this chapter shows, the new and growing complexity, sophistication and nuance in Chinese thinking and policy underline the fluidity of the current situation.

Looking to the decade ahead, the future of human security is promising. The reframing of issues related to humanitarian intervention, non-traditional security and transnational problems already has opened a new chapter in regional discussions. Rather than undermining acceptance for the broader notion of human security and non-traditional security, the narrower and broader concepts are a double helix inextricably bound to each other. In tandem, they are opening up a range of issues previously seen as too sensitive and intrusive. The question remains whether they can capture the imagination and support of more political leaders in the region and a new generation of civil society-based actors.

6 East Asian states' collaborative action in UN peace operations for East Timor

Maiko Ichihara

This chapter examines regional collaboration for human security in Timor-East – an important case study because of the incredible suffering the people of this land have endured from at least 1975 to now. Fortunately, since 1999 the world has not turned a blind eye to their plight as it had done before, as members of the United Nations began an intervention to end the ongoing atrocities. There have now been five peacekeeping operations: the UN Mission in East Timor (UNAMET); International Force for East Timor (INTERFET); UN Transitional Administration in East Timor (UNTAET); UN Mission of Support in East Timor (UNMISET); and UN Integrated Mission in Timor-Leste (UNMIT). Among these operations, UNAMET, INTERFET and UNTAET were peacekeeping missions that operated while East Timor was still a *de facto* province of Indonesia. These were the first-ever international peace operations to take place in a member state of ASEAN.

To date, surprisingly little ink has been spilled to shed light on East Asian states' policy responses concerning the personal security of the East Timorese. This is in clear contrast to a large number of works on Australian policy on this issue.[1] While some writers have analyzed Japanese policy behavior as well,[2] not much has been written on ASEAN countries.[3] More surprisingly, there is no substantial scholarly work comparing East Asian states' contribution to East Timor with that of extraregional states. This chapter provides an analysis of East Asian states' policy toward human security in East Timor, in comparison with two extraregional states – the USA and Australia.

This chapter makes four arguments. First, both East Asian and extraregional states were indifferent to the suffering of East Timorese throughout the 1970s and 1980s. Second, although East Asian states and the two extraregional states changed their policy in the 1990s and started taking action on East Timor, the timing of the change was different – while the extraregional states had started taking some action in the early 1990s for the sake of East Timorese, it was only in September 1999 that states in East Asia started to get their acts together. Third, East Asian states' actions were only reactive to the pressure and actions taken by extraregional actors such as the UN and Australia, and requests from Indonesia. Fourth, the East Asian states' policy responses toward the worsening security situation in East Timor after 1999 were still based on cooperation with Indonesia, and driven by their own interests.

Human insecurity in East Timor

East Timor was a Portuguese colony from the sixteenth century to 1974, except for three-and-a-half years of Japanese occupation during the World War II. After the Carnation Revolution in April 1974 in Portugal, the newly established government announced that it was going to give independence to Portuguese colonies.[4] Indonesia was afraid that independence and democratic governance in East Timor, if it occurred, would further precipitate Indonesia's domestic separatist movements (such as those in Papua, Ache and Maluku) and anti-authoritarian movements. In mid-September 1975, Indonesia began its border invasion into East Timor, then on 7 December it sent 10,000 soldiers in a full-scale invasion into the capital city, Dili. In April 1976 some 35,000 Indonesian soldiers, one-tenth of the Indonesian Armed Forces (*Tentara Nasional Indonesia*, TNI), occupied the Portuguese colony and further subjected it to Indonesian rule.

The military threat to the security of East Timorese continued unabated as TNI soldiers committed indiscriminate killings, theft, looting, rape and torture. Some 60,000 East Timorese, 10 per cent of the population, died during the first year of Indonesian occupation alone. Indonesia's genocidal violence against the East Timorese is one of the most costly losses of human life in modern conflict to date. The overall number of East Timorese killed by the TNI during Indonesian occupation is said to be between 100,000 and 250,000, which constitutes 14 to 30 per cent of the population (676,582 in 1974) at the time of the invasion.[5] People were killed even after they had surrendered; others were tortured in various cruel ways. Women were raped in front of their husbands and then killed. Indonesian soldiers also cut open pregnant women, took out their babies and killed them in front of their mothers. The TNI forced the sterilization of some women by removing their uterus without consent and by giving injections to schoolgirls under false pretences that it was for tetanus. The TNI forced Timorese to march in front of them when it fought with the Armed Forces of National Liberation of East Timor (*Forças Armadas da Libertação Nacional de Timor-Leste*, FALINTIL), using them as a human shield. Jakarta did not allow any humanitarian organizations to send representatives to East Timor until the mid-1980s.[6]

TNI personnel sent to East Timor were often lower- to middle-ranking officers without any prospects. Aware of this, they tried to find their own ways to enrich themselves on the occupied territory by monopolizing the economic sector.[7] They occupied most of the land in Dili (East Timor's most fertile area) and required East Timorese to register their land, fully aware that they could not afford to do so.[8] Coffee and sandalwood, the major products in East Timor, were monopolized by companies owned by TNI officials. In 1979 there were only 24,000 buffaloes, 15,000 horses, 27,000 pigs and 36,000 sheep/goats, a reduction by 83–91 per cent of the numbers from 1973.[9] Agriculture was ruined by TNI napalm bombs, and people died of famine. Indonesia also claimed jurisdiction over the Timor Sea, where oil and gas reserves exist. Jakarta signed the Timor Gap Treaty with Australia in 1989 to make sure that the oil and gas reserves would fall under Indonesian jurisdiction. The Suharto government also signed contracts with 12 multinational corporations for oil and gas exploration.[10]

Late in the 1990s, a dramatic political change in Indonesia opened up a new possibility for human security in East Timor. B. J. Habibie succeeded Suharto as President, and announced in June 1998 that his government would grant East Timor autonomy. The new president sought to lend the Indonesian government an air of international legitimacy with regard to East Timor by providing the option of deciding its political future.[11] Indonesia, suffering from the Asian Financial Crisis, hoped to secure funding from international relief agencies, particularly the International Monetary Fund (IMF).[12] The East Timorese rejected the offer, demanding instead a national referendum to be supervised by the UN. Their youths rallied in large numbers across the land, demanding independence.[13]

After reviewing the options for East Timor, in a move that surprised even his own cabinet members, Habibie announced on 27 January 1999 that East Timor would be granted full independence if it rejected the autonomy offer. A tripartite talk between the UN, Indonesia and Portugal reached a conclusion on 11 March 1999 that Indonesia should use a direct ballot as the method to determine the future of the East Timorese. UNAMET was thus formed to organize and oversee the ballot. The East Timorese finally gained an opportunity to put an end to Indonesian rule and to enjoy better security.

After Habibie's announcement of the referendum for independence, however, the security situation in East Timor worsened considerably. Pro-integration, pro-Indonesia militia conducted kidnappings and torture, destroyed houses, and killed on an even larger scale in order to intimidate the pro-independence forces. For its part, the TNI provided the militia with weapons and funding.[14] The killing caused thousands of East Timorese to become refugees.[15] In April 1999, on the increase in the number of militia killings, Xanana Gusmao, the then-jailed leader of FALINTIL, called on the pro-independence side to protect the East Timorese by any means possible, and this led to an open armed conflict between pro-independence and pro-integration factions. Arranging for a UN presence in East Timor became crucial for East Timorese security. The pro-independence side requested UN peacekeepers to restore order in East Timor, but Indonesia rejected any form of external intervention and insisted it had responsibility for security.

Although Indonesia accepted, on 22 April 1999, the UN proposal of unarmed Civilian Police (CIVPOL) and military liaison officers to play an advisory role for the Indonesian military as a part of UNAMET, the country insisted on being in charge of security in East Timor. Indonesia deployed 8,000 policemen and 10,000 TNI personnel in East Timor, which made it impossible for the UN forces to disarm pro-Indonesian militias. Although FALINTIL agreed to unilateral cantonment and laid down arms by 12 August, the pro-Indonesian militias did not end their campaign of violence and intimidation. Militia killings and destructive activities became rampant as the day of the referendum approached, twice causing delays in the planned vote.[16]

Even under such a volatile security situation, UNAMET pressed ahead with the planned independence referendum on 30 August 1999, because Megawati Sukarnoputri, a female politician who was then expected to become the next president of Indonesia after Habibie's term expired, was unlikely to allow such a referendum.[17] The referendum took place without much disturbance or intimidation, and the turnout was 98.6 per cent. Around 78.5 per cent of the voters voted for independence, and East Timor was thus expected to become an independent, sovereign state. But pro-Indonesia militia killings increased significantly after the results were released on 4 September 1999. A newspaper report from *The Evening Post* stated that militias were 'ready to "burn everything" if the territory's independence vote was not held again'.[18] More than 145 people were killed and about 20,000 people were displaced on 5 September alone.[19] Overall, about 1,400 East Timorese were killed; as many as 500,000 were displaced.[20] In addition, militias repeatedly raped East Timorese women, and the number of rape cases was said to be in the hundreds. About 70 per cent of the infrastructure was also destroyed.[21] International intervention to stop the violence was necessary.

Indonesia then insisted that it would not accept any international intervention unless the Indonesian People's Consultative Assembly, MPR (*Majelis Permusyawaratan Rakyator*) agreed to grant East Timor independence and ratified the use of an international force. However, it was unclear whether the MPR would grant independence to East Timor and agree to the deployment of an international peacekeeping force. In addition, the MPR was not scheduled to convene until October or November, by which time the East Timorese could potentially have been killed on a large scale. Kofi Annan, the Secretary-General of the UN, conducted personal diplomacy to Indonesia in order to obtain Indonesian consent to let the UN take over the responsibility of restoring security in East Timor. The Security Council also sent a mission to both Jakarta and East Timor to acquire consent for a UN peacekeeping operation in the distressed province.

Indonesia finally announced on 13 September 1999 that it would accept an international peacekeeping operation in East Timor. Financial factors seem to have had a decisive influence: Indonesia needed funding from international organizations to recover from the devastating Asian Financial Crisis, for which Indonesia needed to accept the will of the international society. Also, the humanitarian situation in East Timor was affecting Indonesia's financial markets, causing a notable drop in the Jakarta Stock Exchange and other indexes. Habibie then concluded that the acceptance of international intervention in East Timor and Indonesia's economic recovery must be tied together.[22] As a result, INTERFET was allowed to be established on 20 September 1999.

Once INTERFET was deployed in East Timor, the pro-Indonesia militias quickly faded away to Indonesia's West Timor, and the security situation in East Timor rapidly stabilized.[23] Although some skirmishes continued between militias and INTERFET along East Timor's borders, it was on a much smaller scale: 50 East Timorese were killed by the TNI and militias; six militiamen and one Indonesian police officer died; Sander Thoenes, a journalist for the *Financial Times*, was killed by the TNI during the five months of INTERFET's operations.[24] One crucial reason for the decrease of violence was that the TNI stopped supporting the militias. Leaving only 1,000 troops to guard Indonesian assets, the TNI completed its withdrawal from East Timor by 27 September. The security situation was restored to the extent that Bishop Belo, Nobel Prize winner and spiritual leader of East Timor, thanked INTERFET for getting rid of the militia threat.[25]

The remaining issue was that the pro-Indonesia militias continued terrorizing and preventing 100,000 East Timorese refugees in Indonesia's West Timor from going back to East Timor.[26] Although a series of militia attacks occurred sporadically, especially along the border of West Timor, the security situation became more stable.[27] A more pressing issue was a threat of violence, rape and arson from East Timorese police and gangs, as well as conflict between Easterners and Westerners among the Timorese.[28]

In sum, the TNI's and pro-Indonesia militias' violation of East Timorese security has long been serious, not only in military terms, but also in criminal, political and economic terms. What was done during the Suharto era was nothing short of genocide, and the TNI members and militias severely destroyed the economic capacity of the territory. Even after the East Timorese saw the beacon of hope in Habibie's independence offer, militia violence escalated. However, the situation drastically changed for the better after the arrival of INTERFET and the other subsequent international operations.

The East Asian states' responses to East Timor: from policy indifference to reaction

Regional responses during the Suharto era to the atrocities committed against the East Timorese were quite weak. Although the UN General Assembly passed resolutions called 'Question of East Timor' every year between 1975 and 1982 to demand Indonesia to withdraw from East Timor, the East Asian countries continued to support Indonesia by voting in favor of its annexation of East Timor.[29] Singapore started voting for the support of Indonesia consecutively from 1977, although it abstained in the resolutions of 1975 and 1976. The Philippines, Thailand, Malaysia and Japan continuously voted in support of the Indonesian annexation.[30] ASEAN countries became even more vocal in supporting Indonesia in its attempt to remove the East Timor issue from discussions in international scenes throughout the 1990s.[31] *The Straits Times* of Singapore published series of articles on East Timor and justified the Indonesian annexation.[32] ASEAN states occasionally conveyed a strong message to the European Union (EU), saying that EU–ASEAN relations would deteriorate if the EU linked the East Timor issue with its economic relations with ASEAN.[33] The Thai government deported foreign NGO personnel who came to Thailand to attend conferences on the East Timor issue. The Malaysian government banned conferences on the East Timor issue. The Philippines even refused the entry of Jose Ramos-Horta into its territory in October 1996.[34] When the arrangement of a UN presence in East Timor for the provision of security became crucial, no Asian country tried to persuade Indonesia to accept UN responsibility over security; they were simply unwilling to do what Indonesia did not want to see done.

Once Indonesia agreed to accept UN CIVPOL and military officers for advisory roles in UNAMET with the condition that Indonesia was to take control over the security, other East Asian countries contributed CIVPOL and military personnel. However, the number of these officers was largely symbolic: among the total number of 271 UNAMET CIVPOL, Japan sent three, South Korea five, Thailand seven and the Philippines six, together constituting just under 8 per cent of the total. Among 50 UNAMET military officers, Malaysia sent seven and Thailand two. Compared with 8,000 Indonesian policemen and 10,000 TNI personnel in East Timor, the number of CIVPOL and military officers from East Asia was insignificant. Japan contributed $10.11 million to the UN Trust Fund to help UNAMET take quick action without waiting for UN funding, and privately pressured Habibie to take direct control of the militias.[35]

Once the referendum was conducted on 30 August 1999 and the result was released on 4 September, the militia violence increased drastically. But ASEAN states did not take any initiative to end the violence. East Asian countries were generally reluctant to push Indonesia into accepting a peacekeeping mission to take control over the militia violence.[36] Thailand's Deputy Prime Minister, Supachai Panitchpakdi, said that the ASEAN countries should stick to the principle of non-interference and should not speak up on the East Timor issue. Even if ASEAN member states wanted to take action on this issue, he said ASEAN 'would have to seek advice from Indonesia first'.[37]

Although Japan was one of the major players in persuading Indonesia to stop the violence in East Timor during this period, it did not pressure Indonesia to accept a peacekeeping operation, either.[38] When Takeo Kawakami, then-Japanese Ambassador to Indonesia, met with Habibie on 8 September and told him that Indonesia should 'fulfill its responsibility in maintaining security and safety' in East Timor, no mention was made of the need for an international peacekeeping force.[39] Japan also opposed the idea of increasing economic pressure on Indonesia over the East Timor issue; Yutaka Iimura, the Director of the International Cooperation Bureau of the Ministry of Foreign Affairs, commented on 9 September that the Ministry of Foreign Affairs was not thinking about changing its Official Development Assistance (ODA) policy toward Indonesia. Given the fact that Japan's ODA comprised 60 per cent of all aid Indonesia received at that time, suspension of ODA would have had a significant impact on Indonesia, a country that was suffering from the devastating effects of the Asian Financial Crisis of 1997–98.

When INTERFET was established on 20 September 1999, it was Australia (not an East Asian state) that proved willing and able to lead a multinational peacekeeping force. Most ASEAN countries remained hesitant to participate in INTERFET, worrying that it might go against Jakarta's wishes.[40] Indonesia was unhappy about the Australian leadership, and demanded as a condition for accepting the INTERFET that Asian countries participate in and lead INTERFET.[41] It was only after Indonesia announced these requirements that most East Asian countries started seriously considering participating in INTERFET. Kofi Annan and Australian Prime Minister John Howard also played a significant role in persuading them to participate in INTERFET.

Upon the Indonesian request, Thailand persuaded other ASEAN countries to participate.[42] During the APEC summit in September 1999, representatives from the Philippines, Malaysia and Singapore agreed to take part in the international force in some way.[43] South Korea announced its willingness to participate in INTERFET on 30 September, and offered 500 ground troops.[44] Japan was reluctant to send its citizens to an area of conflict, because two Japanese peacekeepers were killed in the peacekeeping operation in Cambodia in 1992, which resulted in low domestic support for sending Japanese troops into dangerous conflict zones.[45] Instead, Japan offered $100 million for the Trust Fund, to support developing countries willing to contribute their military personnel to INTERFET and to help cover almost half of the expected operational cost of the operation.[46] This decision was also influenced by Thailand and the Philippines, because they could not finance their own troops being dispatched to East Timor.[47]

With Japan's financial contribution, Thailand managed to contribute 1,580 military, engineering, medical and technical personnel in addition to Major-General Songkitti Jaggabatara as INTERFET's deputy commander. The Philippines offered 600 military, engineering and medical personnel. Malaysia offered only 30 personnel, because Jose Ramos-Horta considered Malaysia to be sympathetic toward Indonesia, which angered Malaysia.[48] Singapore contributed 250 medical and logistics experts.

The total number of East Asian troops did not match the 4,500 Australian troops, however, and this allowed Australia to play the leading role in INTERFET. In addition, due to a lack of experience in peacekeeping operations, it was clear even in the eyes of ASEAN governments that ASEAN alone would be unable to lead such a force – only Malaysia had any significant experience in peacekeeping operations.[49] In addition, most military forces in ASEAN countries were trained to deal with internal, not external security.[50] Although the East Asian states played only a supportive role in INTERFET, it would have been difficult to persuade Indonesia to accept the operation if no East Asian state was willing to participate: the participation of East Asian states was thus critical for the establishment of this operation.

INTERFET was taken over by UNTAET's peacekeeping force in February 2000, which was to have up to 9,150 military personnel (70 per cent of whom were to be transferred from INTERFET). The UN sought to give the East Asian, especially ASEAN, countries a greater role, given Indonesian and other Asian countries' criticisms on Australian-led INTERFET. UNTAET's administrator, Sergio Vieira de Mello, asked Surin Pitsuwan to secure ASEAN countries' participation. East Asian countries, namely Malaysia, Thailand, the Philippines, South Korea and Bangladesh, were raised as candidates for the commander position of the UNTAET force. Indonesia also made diplomatic moves to secure Asian participation. While Japan was discussing whether it should dispatch peacekeepers, Indonesia's new President, Abdurrahman Wahid, said publicly that Japan's dispatch was no problem for Indonesia. Wiranto also told Japan that Indonesia welcomed an Asian-led UNTAET and welcomed Japan's participation.[51] He also asked Thailand in October 1999 to keep its peacekeepers under UNTAET.[52]

A number of states in East Asia were committed to UNTAET. Although it did not participate in the UNTAET peacekeeping force, China endorsed the peace operation at the time of its establishment (For more Chinese peacekeeping, see Chapter 5).[53] Other countries named as candidates for the commander position, especially Malaysia, also showed willingness to take up the role: Malaysian Defense Minister Abang Abu Bakar said that Malaysia was willing to dispatch up to 1,700 peacekeepers.[54] Foreign Minister Datuk Sri Syed Hamid Albar said that Malaysia had an excellent record in peacekeeping operations and human rights, and thus was appropriate for the commander position.[55] But Malaysia ended up dispatching only 20 military observers to UNTAET. Malaysia was upset that it was not chosen for the UNTAET peacekeeping commander position.[56]

The Nation commented that Thailand and the Philippines were good candidates for the position because they were democracies,[57] and a Filipino, General Jaime de los Santos, was chosen for the commander position of UNTAET's peacekeeping force. Other Asian countries were also assigned to the top positions: Malaysian former Ambassador to Vietnam, N. Parameswaran, was appointed UNTAET chief of staff, and Thai General Boonsrang Niumpradit was chosen for the Force Commander after the term of General Jaime de los Santos expired. These appointments secured the involvement of ASEAN countries: the Philippines announced that it would send 400 peacekeepers in addition to those serving under INTER-FET, which would increase the number of Filipino soldiers in East Timor to 1,000. Singapore announced the dispatch of 185 personnel, a landing ship and a cargo aircraft. Thailand kept its 1,581 peacekeepers serving INTERFET for UNTAET. Japan dispatched 680 peacekeepers in February 2002, making this the first dispatch of its troops to a peacekeeping operation. South Korea maintained its 419 INTERFET peacekeepers for UNTAET.

These East Asian countries also demonstrated collaborative action. Japanese peacekeepers worked in collaboration with South Korean peacekeepers in Okusi by providing logistical support for the latter. Singapore and Japan jointly trained East Timorese police through the Japan–Singapore Partnership Program for the 21st Century. Japan also sponsored a conference on UNTAET in September 2002 in order to analyze the UNTAET experience and turn it to practical use for future peace missions.

However, the East Asian states' participation in the peacekeeping operations remained cautious: they participated only after Indonesia requested they do so, and sent Jakarta messages of support for Indonesia. Thailand suggested Indonesia play a role in UNTAET.[58] Japanese Foreign Minister Yohei Kono and Singaporean Prime Minister Goh Chok Tong and Foreign Minister Shanmugam Jayakumar called for international support for Wahid on reconciliation with East Timor.[59] Malaysian Prime Minister Mahathir Mohamad commented that Indonesia was entitled to integrate East Timor. When Japan gave a grant of $5.9 million for East Timor, $5.4 million of it was directed for the Indonesian government, while the remainder was directed for UNTAET.[60]

After UNTAET completed its mission on the day of East Timor's independence, UNMISET was established to take over the job of nationbuilding and to provide security for East Timor. UNMISET also secured East Asians for top positions. Suke-hiro Hasegawa of Japan was appointed the UN Deputy Representative in East Timor on 14 June 2002. The Force Commander's position was rotated among ASEAN countries; Thailand's Lieutenant-General Winai Phattiyakul served from May to August 2002, Major General Tan Huck Gim of Singapore Armed Forces served from August 2002 to August 2003, and Malaysian Lieutenant-General Khairuddin Mat Yusof served from August 2003 to the end of the UNMISET operation. Sin-gapore increased the number of its peacekeepers in East Timor threefold and also sent four helicopters and 72 pilots. Japan maintained its 680 peacekeepers working under UNTAET as peacekeepers for UNMISET, and pledged financial assistance of $60 million for East Timor. Thailand dispatched an additional 123 peacekeep-ers to UNMISET. When the UN started discussing the pullout of UNMISET, the Philippines supported the idea of maintaining some peacekeepers to avoid leaving a security vacuum in East Timor. Currently, UNMIT is under operation in East Timor, and it also has East Asians in top positions: Rodolfo Asel Tor of the Philippines as the Police Commissioner, and Tan Huck Gim of Singapore as the Deputy Special Representative of the Secretary-General for Security Sector Support and Rule of Law. The East Asian states continue to play important roles in UNMIT's functions.

Explaining East Asian states' policy shift after 1999

There were at least four major reasons for the reluctance of East Asian states to take action. First is the political and economic importance of Indonesia, which caused reluctance of taking action not only for East Asian countries but also for extraregional states. Indonesia's political importance arose from the fact that the largest state of ASEAN was a strong anticommunist pillar in Southeast Asia from the birth of the Suharto regime. Suharto exterminated members of the Communist Party of Indonesia (*Partai Komunis Indonesia*, PKI), which had grown largely under Sukarno, the former president of Indonesia, and posed a serious threat for the Suharto regime. Being only several years after the American withdrawal from Vietnam, and facing the expansion of communism in Indochina, the USA, Australia and Japan regarded Suharto's Indonesia as the stable anticommunist cen-ter of Southeast Asia in the 1970s. The political importance of Suharto's Indonesia remained until the end of the Cold War.

ASEAN members also regarded Indonesia as their important anticommunist friend. Although the founding members of ASEAN were part of non-alignment force in the international scene, they were all combating communism domesti-cally in the 1970s. Communists in Southeast Asia were backed by China, and the domestic growth of communists was a serious threat for the small Southeast Asian countries that shared borders with giant China. Because Indonesian annexation was framed as the country's combat against the communist-inclined Revolution-ary Front for an Independent East Timor (*Frente Revolucionária de Timor-Leste Independente*, FRETILIN), ASEAN countries supported Indonesian annexation of East Timor.[61] Obviously, China was an exception: being unhappy about Suhar-to's mopping-up of Chinese-backed PKI, China did not support Indonesia's claim of annexation of East Timor, and kept voting in favor of Indonesia's withdrawal from East Timor in the UN General Assembly from 1975 to 1982.[62]

Indonesia was important in an economic sense for both the East Asian and the extraregional states as well. Indonesia was an important source of imports, one of the largest exporters of oil outside the Middle East, and an attractive market for foreign countries. Indonesia was the sixth largest source of imports for Japan and the eighth largest for Australia in 1999.[63] Such economic importance caused domestic opposition to taking action against Indonesia on the East Timor issue. In the USA, the American Indonesian Chamber of Commerce opposed any aid cut-off to Indonesia, afraid of possible damage to their business in Indonesia. The US Department of Defense also opposed it because it had an interest in maintaining good relations with Indonesia, a major importer of American weapons.[64] When Seoul announced its willingness to participate in peacekeeping operations in East Timor, Korean business community worried that its business in Indonesia might be damaged.[65]

Second, there was an even greater fear in the late 1990s that inhibited East Asian countries from taking collaborative action on the East Timor issue: they were wary of destabilizing Indonesia, which was suffering both economically and politically. The Indonesian economy took a substantial downturn after the Asian Financial Crisis; the GDP dropped drastically to the 1989 level. This severe economic setback undermined the legitimacy of the Suharto regime, resulting in its breakdown and a transition to democracy. For Habibie, whose domestic support was precariously low during the early period of political transition, gaining domestic support was significant for his policy decisions. Domestic criticisms leveled against his autonomy offer were strong, especially from the TNI. It was thus important for him to placate the TNI in order to maintain a civilian presidency.[66] With such a fragile domestic situation in Indonesia, other East Asian governments reasoned that pressuring Indonesia from outside could further weaken the legitimacy of the new government and destabilize the country, which might eventually destabilize the regional economy as a whole.[67]

Third, the East Asian states worried about setting a precedent of international intervention in their own region. Having separatist movements within their national boundaries, they, particularly Thailand, the Philippines and China, had concerns for the integrity of their territorial and national sovereignty: the Moro Islamic Liberation Front of the Philippines, the Pattani United Liberation Organization of Thailand, and Xinjiang, Inner Mongolia and Tibet of China were all seeking independence. The governments of these countries feared that allowing the UN to interfere in Indonesia's *de facto* 'domestic affair' might allow future international intervention in their own territories.[68] Filipino President Fidel Ramos stated in May 1994 that 'respect for one another's territorial integrity, non-interference in one another's internal affairs and the ASEAN practice of quiet bilateral and regional dialogue are tried and tested tools that have helped us maintain the stability we now enjoy in South-east Asia'.[69] Prime Minister Chuan Leekpai of Thailand also stated on 20 July 1994 that Thailand should not interfere in the East Timor issue because ASEAN members had consensus on non-interference.

Although China showed its willingness to participate in a UN peacekeeping operation in East Timor before its establishment, it maintained the stance that the international community should not intervene in Indonesian domestic issues unless Indonesia was first willing to accept an international role.[70]

Last, but not least, most East Asian states were either semidemocratic or authoritarian: South Korea democratized only in the mid-1980s, and Thailand and the Philippines became democracies only in the 1990s. China, Singapore and Malaysia were, and still are, authoritarian countries. Although Thailand and the Philippines allowed NGO activities, they controlled public opinion if it conflicted with their national interests. NGO activities were oppressed; here was little political space in which ordinary people could exert influence on politics. Although Japan had much more experience with democracy, the end result was not so different: although some Diet members acted to gain attention on the East Timor issue and to make policy changes in Japan and Indonesia, their voices were not strong enough to be heard.

The biggest force of change came from two states outside the region: Australia and the USA. Until the late 1980s, they had given Indonesia a green light to invade East Timor: Suharto met Gerald Ford and Henry Kissinger several hours before the invasion on 7 December 1975 and obtained approval from them.[71] The USA further lent support to the Indonesian annexation of East Timor by increasing the sales of weapons and voting against the UN General Assembly 'Question of East Timor' resolutions.[72] Several days before the invasion, Australian Prime Minister Gough Whitlam said Indonesia should incorporate East Timor and that he would do nothing to prevent an annexation. Australia was afraid that East Timor might become a communist outpost in the power vacuum after Portugal's departure; such an occurrence would also pose a direct threat to Australia's security interests, as it was the closest neighbor of East Timor. This concern prompted Australia to become the first country officially to acknowledge Indonesian sovereignty over East Timor in 1978.[73]

From the early 1990s, however, a political change on the East Timor issue took place in both the USA and Australia, despite the governments' support for Indonesia; public opinion drove the reluctant governments slowly into action. They changed their policies after the Santa Cruz Massacre of 1991. In October 1993, despite opposition from the US Departments of Defense and State, the US Congress passed a bill prohibiting the USA from providing international military education and training to Indonesia.[74] This bill was re-enacted the following year because Indonesia had not improved the situation in East Timor.[75] Starting in 1994, and in large part due to Congressional pressure, the State Department prohibited the export of small arms to Indonesia.[76] Congress also passed the Omnibus Consolidated and Emergency Appropriations Act on 21 October 1998, which prohibited Indonesia from using US-supplied weapons in East Timor.[77] This act was passed while the East Timorese were rallying for political independence in response to President Habibie's autonomy offer. Although these American policy measures might not have been direct triggers for his offer, they did apply tangible pressure to Jakarta. During this time, the East Asian states still explicitly supported Indonesia on the East Timor issue.

Australia also started to place importance on a moral obligation towards the East Timorese.[78] While still reluctant to put pressure on Jakarta, Howard sent a letter to Habibie on 19 December 1998, suggesting that giving independence to East Timor might be one option, especially if East Timor did not take the autonomy package.[79] Although the letter at first appeared to have angered Habibie, it seemed to have a growing influence on his decisions on East Timor. Reviewing options for East Timor, he announced on 27 January 1999 that East Timor would be granted full independence if it rejected the autonomy offer. UNAMET was thus established to administer the referendum.

The USA and Australia then publicly called for Indonesia to disarm the pro-Indonesian militias.[80] Indonesia accepted the UN proposal of unarmed CIVPOL and military liaison officers to take an advisory role for the Indonesian military as a part of UNAMET, and agreed that the number of CIVPOL officers would be 50. Given the worsened human security condition in East Timor after Habibie's announcement of a referendum in January 1999, the number was too small. Howard put pressure on him to accept an increase in the CIVPOL number up to 300, which Indonesia accepted.[81] Due to the fact that the Indonesian policemen and the TNI were still in charge of security of East Timor, the militias could not be disarmed, and their violence continued.[82]

The USA requested, along with European countries, that international organizations pressure Indonesia: the IMF stated on 6 September that it would suspend $450 million of financial aid if Indonesia did not restore security in East Timor;[83] the World Bank conveyed a message on 7 September that it might stop its financial aid as well.[84] President Bill Clinton announced in a speech on 9 September that Indonesia would face a cut in economic and military assistance from the USA if it failed either to restore order in East Timor or to accept international involvement.[85]

The Asia-Pacific Economic Cooperation (APEC) members also conveyed their hope that Indonesia would accept international intervention for the purpose of restoring security in East Timor, in the Special Ministerial Meeting on East Timor at the APEC Summit held in Brunei. ASEAN countries initially refused to participate in this meeting, and Australia, along with Canada and New Zealand, conducted intensive lobbying to persuade ASEAN members to participate.[86] All the East Asian states eventually agreed to participate in the meeting under the condition that it not be considered an official part of the summit.[87] Facing such a growing pressure from the international community, Indonesia agreed to accept INTERFET in the end.

Despite the above mention causes for reluctance, however, there occurred a change in the East Asian states behaviours on the East Timor issue in September 1999. First, as external pressure on Indonesia from outside the region intensified, states in East Asia reached some consensus on the need to prevent Australian intervention in their own region. When Australia showed its readiness to lead INTERFET in September 1999, Indonesia regarded the Australian leadership role as intervention in an Asian matter, and called for Asian participation. There were mainly two interrelated reasons for their distrust of Australia. Second, Australia's recognition of itself as a 'deputy sheriff' for the USA in the region bothered Asian countries, as this view revealed that Australia looked down on Asian countries. Ever since *The Bulletin* magazine used the phrase 'deputy sheriff' in 1999 in reporting an interview with Howard, ASEAN countries had been criticizing Australia. Malaysian opposition leader Lim Kit Siang commented that 'the role as US deputy international policeman for Asia is not only the height of arrogance but also completely misplaced and unwelcome to Asians'. Third, and related to the first point, the Howard government had close ties with the USA at the cost of sacrificing its ties with Asian countries; Southeast Asians speculated that Australia's real incentive for leading INTERFET might be in obtaining economic gains, such as oil in the Timor Gap, and breaking down Indonesia.[88]

Such distrust of Australia's motives, shared among East Asian states, strengthened their will to participate in INTERFET and subsequent operations. They now wanted to solve Asian problems on their own. Officials from the Thai foreign ministry said that 'ASEAN must play the primary role in Southeast Asia', and Malaysian deputy Prime Minister Abdullah Ahmad Badawi said that 'Asian countries are capable of looking after the region themselves and cherish peace for the region more than others'.[89]

While there was such immediate incentive for the East Asian states' attitude-change, the basis for their participation in the peacekeeping operations in a *de facto* Indonesian territory was also facilitated by the policy shift in ASEAN from non-interference to some form of engagement. ASEAN state leaders had a growing realization in the 1990s that the regional organization lacked the political will and capacity to respond to a variety of emerging global issues and threats, most notably the Asian Financial Crisis. ASEAN's inability to respond to emerging transborder issues caused increased international criticisms against the 'ASEAN Way', which placed importance on consensus-building and left member countries' domestic issues untouched.[90]

In order to maintain ASEAN's value as an organization, ASEAN member states were trying to relax the ASEAN Way in an attempt at overcoming such criticisms. For ASEAN, whose members are relatively small powers in international politics, maintenance of the *raison d'etre* of this grouping was useful in combining the member states' power and gaining leverage in international negotiations. Malaysia proposed 'constructive intervention' in 1997 to enhance interaction among member countries and to accept voluntarily member countries' intervention in one another's domestic problems. Thailand proposed 'flexible engagement' in 1998, and encouraged the ASEAN states to discuss their domestic issues frankly. ASEAN established the 'ASEAN Surveillance Process' in 1998, which would allow its members to share information on economic policies with the aim of enhancing regional economic coordination.

Conclusion

The people of East Timor suffered from extreme human insecurity during Indonesia's occupation after 1975. Not only did the TNI carry out massacres against them, but they also engaged in numerous criminal activities and economic plundering. East Timor was a case where action for human security was tested. No East Asian state took action on behalf of the East Timorese during the occupation era. First, they did not want to set a precedent of international interference in Asian states' domestic affairs, because other East Asian states also faced internal separatist movements. Second, the East Asian states did not want to see growing instability in Indonesia, which was still suffering from the financial and political crises after 1997. The inaction on East Timor was not unique to the East Asian states, however: the USA and Australia also did not take any action throughout the 1970s and 1980s. They placed greater importance on Indonesia's economic growth and regarded it as a major anticommunist pillar in Southeast Asia.

The change first occurred in 1991: the Santa Cruz Massacre helped mobilize public opinion in Australia and the USA. Public opinion pressured the Australian government into action against Indonesia when Canberra urged Jakarta to consider giving East Timor full independence. Once President Habibie accepted the idea and allowed a referendum for East Timor's independence to take place, the USA and Australia made various efforts to provide security for the East Timorese. East Asian governments continued to move in the opposite direction: they became more vocal in supporting Indonesia and justifying Indonesian annexation of East Timor. Nevertheless, change occurred when they started participating in INTER-FET from September 1999. Their participation was motivated by their intention into Asian affairs and by their willingness to change ASEAN into a more engaging organisation. But their participation in the peacekeeping operation was basically reactive and cautious; they became involved only after Indonesia asked them to do so, and kept checking with the Indonesian government to ensure their participation did not offend Jakarta. Although the East Asian governments were no doubt concerned about the security of the East Timorese, they placed greater importance on their relations with Indonesia. In other words, their participation in the peace operations in East Timor was a form of cooperation with Indonesia, based on the pursuit of their national interests.

7 The limits of collaborative action on criminal justice in East Asia

Sorpong Peou

International criminal justice as a 'public good' has now become an essential component of recent global efforts to promote human security around the world.[1] Important progress has been made, especially with the establishment of *ad hoc* international criminal tribunals (such as the International Criminal Tribunal in Yugoslavia, ICTY in 1991, and the International Criminal Tribunal in Rwanda, ICTR in 1994) and the creation of the International Criminal Court (ICC) in July 2002. The ICC marked a new era in world politics, as its founding members succeeded for the first time in history in establishing a permanent international institution of criminal justice not associated with any particular conflict. Another innovative effort to promote this type of justice is the more recent establishment of hybrid (domestic–international) criminal courts for crimes committed in wartorn countries such as Sierra Leone, Timor-Leste and Cambodia.[2]

As a legal mechanism for the promotion of human security, international criminal justice is worth examining for several reasons. It is now believed to have more potential than military intervention in terms of terminating war and building peace. There also appears to be a growing international fatigue with military actions taken to protect victims of human rights violations: 'Recent history has … bolstered arguments for criminalization over intervention. The American and European left, despite humanitarian impulses, have grown increasingly uneasy with the use of military force'.[3] Many UN officials also 'view the resort to force as a diplomatic and legal failure'.[4] Moreover, the pursuit of criminal justice has a relatively low cost; UN peacekeeping missions, for instance, cost somewhere between \$2–3 billion per year, whereas the ICC would cost only \$10 million annually when 'at rest' and approximately \$100 million when 'in action'.[5] Because the ICC is funded mostly by state party assessments, states would find such modest costs more bearable and would thus be willing to support its actions.

In reality, global support for criminal justice remains limited. This study seeks to shed more light on critical challenges to collaborative action in the international legal field. This chapter argues that, although challenges to global criminal justice remain powerful in the sense that states, regional organizations and non-state actors in East Asia have not been forthcoming in giving their full support for this legalistic approach to human security, prospects for their collaboration are not as grim as they appear.

The promise and limits of collaborative action in international criminal justice: a historical review

Attempts at promoting and executing criminal justice can be traced back to the fifteenth century, when in 1474 the Court of the Holy Roman Empire tried Peter von Hagenbach (in Bresiach, Germany) for 'Crimes Against God and Humanity'. Subsequent actions in this direction were taken, but not until the end of World War I did states 'seriously attempt ... to investigate and prosecute international crimes'.[6] The Allies sought to establish a tribunal to prosecute Kaiser Wilhelm II and other German officials, but did not proceed because of their explicit concern about political instability. After World War II, the USA took the lead in the establishment of the International Military Tribunal at Nuremburg and the International Military Tribunal for the Far East, yet it turned out to be just another classic case of 'victors' justice', executed against national criminals in defeated states; 'there was no clear triumph of law over politics; political imperatives remained pervasive'.[7] The execution of justice was also largely selective.

The history of international criminal justice further shows that past actions taken against perpetrators were not intended to build peace within states. Military and political leaders who were brought to justice after World War II were tried for war crimes, crimes against humanity, and crimes against peace, but the concept of peace at the time was of an international nature. Even though the International Law Commission worked on a Draft Code of Offenses against the Peace and Security of Mankind, approved by the UN General Assembly in 1954,[8] it was not until the Cold War was over that the international community began to link violations of international humanitarian law and international, as well as domestic, peace. Domestic violent conflict came to be seen as a threat to international and domestic security. The establishment of the ICTR marked the first attempt by the UN Security Council to deal with domestic conflict and promote international criminal justice in an essentially non-international situation.

Legalists in general now regard criminal justice as a beacon of hope for peace and security. Cherif Bassiouni asserts that 'the vast tragedies of the 20th century are also due to the absence of a permanent system of international criminal justice'.[9] Criminal justice is generally viewed as a potentially effective method for both conflict termination and war prevention. The ICTY 'was meant to end a real war'.[10] War ends when criminal leaders are arrested, convicted, sentenced and put away.[11] *Ad hoc* international criminal tribunals 'have significantly contributed to peace building in postwar societies'.[12] Criminal justice has now been regarded as 'part of an integrated peacebuilding'.[13]

International criminal justice helps prevent threats to human security in several ways. First, criminal justice 'will contribute to the reduction of social harm and to the preservation or restoration and maintenance of peace'.[14] Without any recourse to justice, victims of violence may take matters into their own hands,[15] but the cycle of revenge can be broken by the pursuit of criminal justice, which further helps 'restore peace and stability, respect for the rule of law, and reconciliation'.[16] Payam Akhavan contends that 'A postconflict culture of justice ... makes moral credibility a valuable political asset for victim groups, rendering vengeance less tempting and more costly'.[17] Persecution of individual leaders furthers the process of individualizing guilt and 'can help defuse the animosities and mistrust among formerly warring communities'. Armed factions are no longer subject to collective punishment for crimes committed by individuals, 'thus contributing to social and political healing and reconstruction'.[18] More specifically, the ICC rests on the hopes that it can help end impunity, contribute to the prevention of the most serious crimes, and ultimately aid in the maintenance of peace and security.

Second, according to David Wippman, 'for many [proponents of criminal justice], deterrence is the most important justification [for pursuing criminal justice], and the most important goal'.[19] In preconflict situations, political oppressors may be discouraged or prevented from making fateful decisions that foment ethnic hatred and violence. Optimists may now count on the fact that tyrants can no longer 'feel confident of escaping international justice' because '[t]he certainty of impunity is gone'.[20] Those in favor of the need to put Cambodia's Khmer Rouge leaders on trial, for instance, base their logic on the importance of prevention. Even before the signing of the Peace Agreements in October 1991, lawmakers, scholars and human rights activists pressed for legal action against them with the aim of preventing the resurgence of genocide.[21]

Third, international criminal justice helps promote democracy. According to some legalists, 'the continuing legacy of impunity proved a serious impediment to democratization'.[22] They view the norm of accountability as capable of addressing the problem of impunity if peace is to be built and sustained. Peace comes when dictators and torturers are excluded from positions of political power and influence or put away, and when politicians come to power through peaceful and legitimate means, such as free and fair elections. The idea of 'peace through justice' further rests on the growing belief that impunity has not prevented human rights violations from recurring.[23]

Fourth, some proponents of international criminal justice further make the case that, even if this method produces no immediate results, it would provide an important learning process that could introduce new judicial norms to help locals establish new legal institutions, based on a new political culture that rejects atrocities.[24] New moral force can be established through 'unconscious inhibiting against crime' or 'a condition of habitual lawfulness' within society.[25] In other words, leaders' rational calculations are important, but society can play a role in constraining them through 'the progressive entrenchment of a more moral self-conception [that] can occur among a wider public, which could stiffen resistance to the blandishments of a leader seeking to exploit ethnic enmity and thereby reduce the prospect of renewed violence after a conflict'.[26]

The next question is whether criminal justice can achieve these objectives without effective collaborative action among various relevant actors, such as states, international organizations and civil society. There has been no shortage of attempts by various actors to promote international collaboration. Article 1 of the UN Charter emphasizes the need for 'collective measures', 'international cooperation', and 'harmonizing' actions among nations. The General Framework

Agreement for Peace in Bosnia and Herzegovina, initialed at Dayton on 20 November 1995, for instance, mentioned 'the obligation of all Parties to cooperate in the investigation and prosecution of war crimes and other violations of international humanitarian law'.[27] Since the 1990s, the pursuit of criminal justice has required further global collaboration among actors including states, international organizations and non-state actors (such as academics and NGOs).

This requirement is seen as 'the first step toward the emergence of a new post-Westphalian normative standard of international criminal justice'.[28] States and other actors have now shown a greater degree of willingness and ability to promote criminal justice. There has been 'an increase in states' willingness to allow national-level prosecutions under loose international supervision'.[29] In July 1998, some 120 nations 'played an important role in the outcome of the talks' concerning the ICC in Rome.[30]

NGOs also played a positive role. According to the 1999 world report of Human Rights Watch, 'the NGOs were seen as an important contributing force in the negotiations. The extent of "partnering" with governments and the degree of consultation with the UN Secretariat provided a model for future multilateral negotiations'.[31] The ICC negotiating process was successful partly because the non-governmental Coalition for the International Criminal Court played a positive role throughout. Made up of more than 1000 civil society groups, the Coalition coordinated civil society involvement in the three Preparatory Commissions in 2000 and brought activists from Latin America, Africa, the Middle East, Europe and Asia to the meetings. Prior to the Conference in Rome, NGOs played a supportive role in developing substantive positions and providing strategic assessments. During the Conference, they enjoyed access to government delegations and were able to share with the latter their perspectives, which were taken into account. For instance, they contributed to the agreement in the Rome Statute that the ICC Prosecutor should have the power to initiate proceedings on his or her own initiative, without having to wait for UN Security Council referrals or state complaints. Although the ICC Statute grants the right of initiation to only the state parties, the Prosecutor and the UN Security Council (all of whom are entitled to 'trigger the mechanism'), NGOs and pressure groups can also approach any of them by presenting 'a case for the indictment and prosecution of a suspected criminal'.[32] Some observers continue to believe that international criminal justice can be further promoted if survivors' long memories are kept, and NGOs play an active role in this effort.[33]

The pursuit of international criminal justice now looks more promising, but evidence shows the limits of this legalistic approach to human security. The atrocities committed against the Timorese are well known (see Chapter 6 in this volume), but few perpetrators have been indicted and fewer still have been brought to justice.[34] Since the trials began in 2001, only a relatively small number of defendants have been punished. When it ceased its investigations in November 2004, the Serious Crimes Unit (SCU) had filed 95 indictments against 391 persons, and 84 were convicted to prison terms in Timor-Leste, but 290 of those indicted remain at large in Indonesia today.[35] The promise of justice remained unfulfilled.

In a report issued in November 2004, the Open Society Justice Initiative and the Coalition for International Justice point out that the commitment based on the principle that the perpetrators of the atrocities in East Timor would not go unpunished 'has not been fulfilled'. It states specifically that, 'Despite the energy and resources that have been invested, both trial processes established after the 1999 atrocities ... have failed fundamentally to bring to account those most responsible for the atrocities in East Timor'.[36] The Security Council passed resolution 1704 (2006) to resume the SCU, but Dili and Jakarta took a different approach; they extended their bilateral Commission of Truth and Friendship, established on 1 August 2005, to address human rights violations in 1999, but committed to not prosecuting perpetrators. This was boycotted by the UN, which has so far refused to endorse or condone amnesties for genocide, war crimes, crimes against humanity, or gross violations of human rights.

The recent and ongoing trials in Cambodia have also been under stress. The Khmer Rouge leadership has been held responsible for the death of more than 1 million Cambodians during 1975–78, and charged with war crimes, crimes against humanity, and genocide. But it took a long time before a formal agreement was finally reached between the UN and the Cambodian government to bring Khmer Rouge leaders to justice. On 13 May 2003, the UN General Assembly adopted a resolution approving the Agreement between the Cambodian government and the UN to establish the Extraordinary Chambers in the Courts of Cambodia (ECCC), which was mandated to put Khmer Rouge leaders on trial. On 6 June, the UN and Cambodia officially signed the Agreement. But the Extraordinary Chambers are far from ideal, and can be considered a major setback for the pursuit of international criminal justice. The criminal system for this purpose would consist of three separate institutional bodies: the Trial Chamber, the Appeals Chamber and the Supreme Court. The Chambers would be dominated by Cambodian judges and would thus be less subject to international control than the Special Panels in East Timor, each of which has one local judge and two international judges. According to the Agreement, the Trial Chamber would have three Cambodian judges and two international judges; the Appeals Chamber would have four Cambodian judges and three international judges; and the Supreme Court would have five Cambodian judges and four international judges. The decisions on guilt and innocence would be made on a 'supermajority rule' based on the consent of at least one international judge. The Chambers have no real international character in that they are basically considered 'national courts' established under Cambodian law, and they operate within the country's existing national judicial system. Moreover, the Chambers seek to prosecute only those Khmer Rouge leaders 'most responsible' for 'the most serious crimes' committed under their regime. Human Rights Watch criticized the draft agreement on the trials as 'deeply flawed' and urged the General Assembly and its Third Committee not to approve it, as it would only prosecute 'senior leaders of Democratic Kampuchea and those who were most responsible'.[37] By late 2007, only six Khmer Rouge leaders had been arrested and detained (one of whom died and three others, aged between 75 and 82, were unwell). Meanwhile, the UN underestimated the three-year costs of the ECCC (estimated at $56.3 million, of which $43 million had been received by late 2007), which has already faced 'significant shortfalls' in staffing and budgeting and is still struggling to find additional donors willing and able to help the Extraordinary Chambers meet their mandate.[38]

In short, there has been a lack of almost everything necessary for hybrid criminal courts to function effectively. Recent criminal courts have been hampered by underfunding and logistical difficulties.[39] They badly need resources and capacity (there is an insufficient number of trial judges and a non-functioning court of appeals), support staff services and material resources for judges (such as inadequate trial transcripts and translation services), adequate professional training for the judiciary, and so on.[40] The lack of professional judges posed a serious challenge to international criminal justice.[41]

The question of collaborative action among actors in the field of international criminal justice thus requires more empirical investigation: without effective collaboration among relevant actors, especially state leaders, the pursuit of criminal justice will always remain limited. Without active support from powerful states like the USA and China, little will be achieved. We can draw some lessons from our experience with peacekeeping: without their support and contributions, the 'current level of peacekeeping operations will be difficult or even impossible to sustain'.[42]

The limits of collaborative action among non-government and regional organizations in East Asia

There exists a sense of optimism that non-state actors, such as members of civil society, can help ensure success in the pursuit of international criminal justice. According to one observer, for instance, 'the ICC will continue to garner widespread support from NGOS and civil society … ; indeed, continued NGO support will be essential if the Court is to succeed'.[43] Non-state actors in East Asia, however, appear to be less active and supportive of international criminal justice than those in North America and Europe.

Academic and professional activists in East Asia have, in general, been far from enthusiastic about, or wholeheartedly supportive of, international criminal justice. In Cambodia, for instance, those who have been the most vocal about Khmer Rouge trial issues live in the west.[44] The most important professional group that initially guided the UN efforts in its pursuit of international criminal justice was the 'Group of Experts' made up of three foreign legal scholars from outside East Asia: Ninian Stephen from Australia, Rajsoomer Lallah from Mauritius, and Steven Ratner from the USA. There is little evidence showing that many academics in East Asia have taken keen interest in the ICC. Public seminars were held in few places, such as the Asian Experts Study Session in Thailand in 2003, and those organized by the Chinese Society of International Law on 15 October 2003 and the National University of Singapore on 24 August 2004. Moreover, these public conferences and seminars were mostly funded by foreign organizations.

Regional NGOs took part in the ICC negotiating process and formed the Coalition for the ICC, but the efforts of those from East Asia appear to have been comparatively less vigorous when compared with those in other regions. Representatives from Latin American, African and Asian NGOs, for instance, formed the 'Three Continents Alliance', but the NGO community in East Asia has been far from active. Some 19 NGOs from 13 countries established the Asian Network for the International Criminal Court (ANICC), but only six of the 13 countries were from East Asia. Other involved groups include the Asian Forum for Human Rights and Development and Forum Asia, but they have held few public seminars advocating or promoting the ICC.

Regarding Timor-Leste, international NGOs have been particularly active in providing support for criminal justice. The Coalition for International Justice and the Open Society Justice Initiative joined other NGOs in calling for international action to execute justice. The NGO Forum of Timor-Leste, concerned with the slow progress of prosecutions in the pursuit of criminal justice, called for the establishment of an international *ad hoc* criminal tribunal, and urged donors to fund an independent Judicial System Monitoring System capable of monitoring judicial proceedings in the Special Panels and other district court matters. The Judicial System Monitoring Program (JSMP) was then established (as an NGO based in Dili) to monitor the operation of the Special Panels for Serious Crimes (SPSC) and Timor-Leste's broader judicial system. But it has been the only independent organization that has monitored more than 90 per cent of all serious crimes. It has also taken a stance against impunity and urged donors to fund the SCU.[45] As it puts it, 'JSMP ... believes that it is the responsibility of all states to assure the effective functioning of the SCU through adequate and sustainable findings'.[46] Together with Amnesty International, the JSMP sought to promote criminal justice in Timor-Leste.[47]

In Cambodia, non-state actors in East Asia also have played a growing but still limited role. Leading local and international NGOs have provided moral support to the UN. In November 1998, for instance, a group of leading Cambodian NGOs issued a statement calling for action to try Khmer Rouge leaders 'both for the reconciliation and healing of the Cambodian people, and as a warning to those who violate human rights that they will not escape the punishment they deserve'.[48] On 22 October 1999, the Cambodian Bar Association, Cambodian Defenders Project, and Legal Aid of Cambodia issued a joint statement supporting the position that all judges and a prosecutor should be appointed by the UN. Non-Cambodians should also play the role of investigators, and a Chief Administrator of the tribunal should be foreign and appointed by the UN.[49]

The Documentation Center of Cambodia, the best known center in Cambodia, which has worked tirelessly to bring Khmer Rouge leaders to justice, also rejected a Cambodian-run trial, seeing it as one not having 'the full support of the people' or providing 'full justice to its citizens'. The Center has extensively documented evidence of crimes committed by the Khmer Rouge regime, having mapped 19,440 mass graves, 167 extermination centers and 77 genocide memorials, collected more than 600,000 pages of Khmer Rouge documents, and assembled dossiers on 18,000 Khmer Rouge cadres.[50]

Overall, NGOs in East Asia remain politically less influential than could be desired. When international and national NGOs, for instance, expressed their readiness to assist the Cambodian government in drafting the tribunal legislation and requested that the latter provide them with an opportunity to review it prior to its presentation to the National Assembly, 'the Cambodian government denied their requests'.[51] Although civil society organizations such as human rights NGOs have been at the forefront associated with the efforts to promote criminal justice, their role remains limited.

NGOs in the ASEAN countries remain far from influential. In November 2002, for instance, when Cambodia hosted the ASEAN Summit for the first time since it became a member in 1999, civil society groups sought to meet with ASEAN leaders. Cambodian officials at first agreed to facilitate this, but made no efforts to make it happen. This was the first time in four years that ASEAN officials refused to meet with them. During a peaceful march in Phnom Penh, some 35 human-rights activists (belonging to the ASEAN People's Forum) from eight ASEAN countries made efforts to deliver their joint statements to the ASEAN leaders at the Summit, but 'were physically pushed away in a very intimidating manner'.[52] The ASEAN Charter, signed by the ten heads of state on 20 November 2007, had been drafted by the Eminent Persons Group and High-level Task Force, but was kept away from public scrutiny during its development. A few social groups, especially those in the Solidarity for Asian Peoples Advocates, tried to influence the drafting process, but the Charter remains state-centric.

Regional organizations in East Asia have been less active in promoting criminal justice when compared with those in Europe, Latin America and Africa. ASEAN has proved unwilling to exert its influence on its members regarding human rights. Throughout the 1980s, several of its members provided active support to the Coalition Government of Democratic Kampuchea (CGDK) that included the Khmer Rouge, and ASEAN admitted Cambodia into the regional group as a member in 1999, after its government had violated human rights during the violent incident in July 1997 that ousted Prime Minister Ranariddh from power. Until the early 1990s, ASEAN countries had little to say about human rights and made no real attempts to help promote them, either within their national boundaries or within the region. Malaysia, for instance, did not favor intervention in the affairs of other states, even if they violated human rights. When asked if his country would intervene in another country controlled by someone like Pol Pot, former Prime Minister Mahathir Mohamad replied, 'There will be ways of intervening that don't amount to actually interfering with their administration'.[53] Singapore was even less enthusiastic about the case against Khmer Rouge leaders. When asked if his country would intervene in a country controlled by a leader like Pol Pot, Singapore's Prime Minister Goh Chok Tong said that 'The principal idea is not to comment or interfere in someone else's domestic affairs'.[54] Even the most democratic state in ASEAN, the Philippines, would not impose liberal values on another country.[55]

The regional organizations supportive of efforts to establish the ICC and listed in Human Rights Watch's *World Report 2002* included none of those inside East

Asia: the European Union (EU), the Council of Europe, the Organization of the American States (OAS), the Rio Group, the Economic Community of African States (ECOWAS), and the Southern African Development Cooperation.[56] Regional organizations within the EU have played an essential role in the ICC negotiating process. At the February and August 1998 Preparatory Commission sessions in New York, the German and then the Finish presidency of the EU issued statements on its behalf in support of the Court, and in June emphasized the importance of ICC ratification. The European Parliament, the Council of Europe's Parliamentary Assembly, the Common Wealth Law Ministers and *La Francophonie* also adopted strongly worded resolutions expressing their commitment to the treaty's early entry into force. On 26 May 1998, the Standing Committee of the Council of Europe's Parliamentary Assembly adopted Recommendation 1408 urging all member and associate states to ratify the Rome Treaty as soon as possible, and to adopt necessary legislation that would make national laws consistent with the Rome Treaty. The Public International Law Working Group of the European Commission was also active. The OAS General Assembly Summit in Guatemala City in June 1998 issued a final communiqué making reference to the ICC as part of a resolution on the enforcement of international humanitarian law.[57] In June 2000, the OAS members called for ICC signature and ratification. In Africa, regional organizations have given more consideration to issues related to criminal justice. After the Accra Workshop on War Affected Children in West Africa, held in 2000, for instance, ECOWAS issued a final declaration stating that its member states were committed to ratifying the ICC Statute.

Regional organizations in East Asia, however, have not formulated a common position on the ICC.[58] ASEAN has not discussed the ICC in any meaningful way. According to one scholar, 'the opportunity to appraise the ICC at a regional level does exist for Southeast Asia, namely through ASEAN, but somehow the Statute has never been tabled for formal discussions'. The most promising declaration by ASEAN up until 2004 was the Joint Co-Chairmen Statement, issued at the EU-ASEAN Ministerial Meeting on 28 January 2003, that the two regions viewed the Court as a 'positive development in the fight against impunity for crimes against humanity, war crimes and genocide'.[59] On 30 July 2007, the ten ASEAN foreign ministers finally agreed to establish a landmark human rights commission, but few expect the regional commission to play a credible role in Southeast Asia. The historic ASEAN Charter devotes a few paragraphs to democracy and human rights issues, but these are still subject to interpretation by the member states. The Charter does not even mention internationally recognized treaties such as the Universal Declaration of Human Rights, and maintains traditional norms such as state sovereignty and non-interference in states' domestic affairs.

The limits of collaborative action among East Asian States

More needs to be said about the varying levels of East Asian states' show of support for international criminal justice. Without active support from states, the ICC will not function effectively, because 'decisions, orders and requests of the ICC can only be enforced through national authorities'. The Court has no 'enforcement agencies, cannot execute arrest warrants, cannot seize evidentiary material, nor compel witnesses to give testimony, nor search the scenes where crimes have been allegedly committed'.[60]

Prior to the Rome Conference in 1998, states in other regions – particularly Latin America and Africa – appeared to be far more active than those in East Asia. Along with NGOs and international governments, African governments cosponsored a series of regional conferences discussing substantive issues raised by the draft text. In early February 1998, Senegalese civil servants took part in a conference discussing substantive issues on criminal justice. In another conference, Senegal's President Diop gave an opening address to representatives from 20 African governments. African states further showed a great deal of interest in the ICC negotiating process at the March 1998 Preparatory Commission and the Rome Conference. In 2000, the Accra Workshop on War Affected Children in West Africa included a session on the ICC with government officials from the 16 members of ECOWAS. In Latin America, states showed a similar interest in criminal justice. In mid-February 1998 (along with other a number of domestic, regional and international NGOs), representatives from 20 governments met in Guatemala City to discuss the ICC draft text.

Fewer steps have been taken in East Asia. By 2007, only Cambodia, Timor-Leste, South Korea and Japan had ratified it. Cambodia signed it on 23 October 2000 and ratified on 11 April 2002; Timor-Leste ratified on 6 September 2002; South Korea signed it on 8 March 2000 and ratified it on 13 November 2002. Seoul also contributed one ICC judge, Sang-Hyun Song, elected twice in 2003 and 2006. Japan was the last to ratify the Statute, but it has since been taking the lead on criminal justice issues. In June 1998, when the UN Diplomatic Conference of Plenipotentiaries on the Establishment of an International Criminal Court was held in Rome, the Japanese delegation was still reluctant, but made its opinion clear with regard to the norm of 'state consent': namely, if a state ratified the Statute establishing the court, it would have to accept the ICC's authority over cases involving its citizens. This position was then hailed as 'bringing the world one step closer to a truly effective ICC', and was seen as having the potential to help 'end impunity for the most heinous crimes'.[61] Japan has since taken positive steps toward helping the ICC realize its institutional potential. On 17 July 2007, the World Day for International Justice in commemoration of the date on which the Rome Statute was adopted in 1998, Tokyo made a concrete policy commitment by depositing the instrument of accession to the Rome Statute, making it clear that it would join the other 104 State Parties and finally became the 105th member on 1 October. Tokyo also nominated its Ambassador in Charge of Human Rights and a member of the Committee on the Elimination of All Forms of Discrimination against Women, Fumiko Saiga, as a candidate for the election of ICC judges. She was elected as an ICC judge on 30 November 2007, filling one of the three vacant judge seats and serving as the first woman ICC judge from East Asia, having received 82 of the 105 votes cast. Tokyo further pledged to send more nationals to the ICC and to cover 22 per cent of the Court's annual budget of $124 million, making Japan the largest contributor.

Japan has made a policy commitment to the administration of international criminal justice in Timor-Leste and Cambodia, and has made financial contributions. While still Prime Minister, Keizo Obuchi said he supported a tribunal that would meet international standards, and this was viewed as 'rebuffing attempts by Hun Sen to negotiate Japanese involvement on a bilateral basis'.[62] On 19 April 2000, Japan submitted a resolution to the UN Human Rights Commission urging the Cambodian government to resolve its differences with the UN. One year later, on 25 April 2001, a Japan-sponsored resolution urging the Cambodian government to set up a criminal tribunal was adopted by the UN Human Rights Commission. After the UN pulled out of the negotiation process in February 2002, Japan again took the initiative to re-establish direct communications between the UN and the Cambodian government. Tokyo also contributed a judge to the ECCC and pledged $21 million to help cover the UN's $43 million commitment.

Beside Japan, other states in the region have been lukewarm in terms of policy commitment to international criminal justice. Cambodia has been accused of dragging its feet and playing hardball with the international community. Disputes between the Cambodian and international judges over several sticky issues, such as the Internal Rules of the ECCC, slowed down the process. Critics charged that the draft Internal Rules (first introduced in November 2006) did not meet the highest standards of international justice. It was not until mid-2007 that the Internal Rules were finally adopted. Other disputes included the Cambodian judges' threat not to attend a plenary session to adopt the draft Internal Rules because their international colleagues proposed to exclude the Bar Association of the Kingdom of Cambodia (BAKC) from the ECCC process. The BAKC apparently felt that the international judges sought to control the whole process and take advantage of Cambodia's weak legal profession. Prime Minister Hun Sen continues to take issue with UN Special Envoy for human rights to Cambodia Yash Ghai, who has been critical of the country's human rights situation. On 12 December 2007, *Television Kampuchea* reported his speech attacking Ghai and asserting that 'Every time he comes, he causes trouble to other people. If his country is talked about, it is 100 times worse than ours. You should go and improve your country. He is a Kenyan'.

So far Timor-Leste has also proved to be far from cooperative with the SPSC and the SCU. When, in May 2004, a US judge of the Special Panel issued the arrest warrant for former Indonesian armed forces commander General Wiranto for his chain-of-command responsibility for the crimes committed in 1999, the East Timorese President said that his government would do nothing to 'carry it out', even though it had no authority to annul the warrant, and that it 'does not always follow or recognize the SCU's decisions'.[63] Kofi Annan acknowledged the necessity of positive bilateral relations between Timor-Leste and Jakarta, saying that 'It is important that Timor-Leste has good relations with Indonesia, with Australia and all the neighbors in the region'.[64] The new political leadership in Dili remains uncommitted or unwilling 'to even request that Indonesia extradite indictees to the Special Panels in East Timor'.[65] As of August 2007, Timor-Leste's National Parliament had yet to discuss the final report submitted to it in October 2005 by the Commission for Reception, Truth, and Reconciliation, established by the UN Transitional Authority in Timor-Leste (UNTAET) on 13 July 2001 to investigate the human rights violations committed from April 1974 to October 1999. Instead of lending active support to the SCU, Timor-Leste has chosen to cooperate with Indonesia on the Commission on Truth and Friendship (CTF). The UN has not supported this bilateral Commission because its terms of reference 'allow for recommending amnesty for serious crimes such as war crimes and crimes against humanity'.[66]

Although an accession party to the ICC, Indonesia (which has also made a policy commitment to ratifying it in 2008) has failed to collaborate effectively on matters regarding criminal justice in Timor-Leste. Jakarta remains intransigent 'in shielding its officers from accountability'.[67] In July 2007, its Foreign Minister, Hassan Wirayuda, made it clear that his government supported the CTF (still boycotted by the UN). He urged the world organization to be realistic about the limits of its prosecutorial approach. In his words, 'The UN has to realize this is a reconciliation process and not a prosecutorial one ... we are committed to not prosecuting perpetrators'.[68] Before this, Jakarta had signed in April 2000 a Memorandum of Understanding with UNTAET, which established the two Special Panels. Indonesia's Parliament then passed legislation authorizing the establishment of a Human Rights Court, as a special chamber within the existing Indonesian court system. Not much has been done since, however. In reality, 'Indonesia has signally failed to keep its commitments'; it did not have the political will to prosecute its civil and military officials responsible for the serious crimes committed in 1999.[69] Moreover, Indonesia has ignored the work of the SPSC and SCU, and even considered unofficial and irrelevant the SCU's arrest warrant for its top military commander, Wiranto.[70] As the majority of those indicted for serious crimes live in Indonesia, progress in criminal justice has been limited and required international collaboration from other states.[71]

Other states in East Asia have also done poorly relative to states in other regions, and the region remains underrepresented at the ICC. By November 2001, only 46 states had ratified the Rome Statute: 21 from Europe, ten from the Americas, ten from Africa, and only five from the Asia–Pacific. By the end of 2001, Thailand (2000) and the Philippines (2001) had signed the Statute. None of the East Asian states ratified it then, although the Philippines and Thailand had at the time signaled interest in examining the implications of ratification. As of July 2007, Brunei, China, North Korea, Laos, Malaysia, Myanmar, Singapore and Vietnam had yet to sign or accede to the Statute. According to Human Rights Watch, states 'in the Asia/Pacific region continue to be the most wary of the ICC and this was reflected in the low numbers of ratifications in the region'.[72]

The largest state in East Asia, China, also took part in the Conference in Rome, but its government has not signed it, stating from early on that the ICC should be involved only when the national judiciaries become dysfunctional or when target states give consent. In October 2003, Beijing's position on the ICC was that it would support 'the establishment of an independent, impartial, effective and universal international criminal court'. As a matter of principle, it did not reject the need for making 'the individuals who perpetrate the gravest crimes receive due punishment', but viewed this action as helping 'people to establish confidence in the international community' and as 'conducive to international peace and security at long last'. China voted against the Rome Statute, however, because some of its articles did not address its own concerns.

From Beijing's perspective, the ICC should first respect the principle of state sovereignty to the extent that the Court would adhere to the principle of complementarity: namely, it should help 'improve' all states' domestic judicial systems and guarantee that all states 'exercise jurisdiction over perpetrators of grave crimes according to their domestic judicial systems'. Second, Beijing took the position that the crimes under the ICC's jurisdiction should be limited to only 'the gravest international crimes as provided by the Statute'. Third, Beijing further raised concern with regard to the type of crime consistent with the UN Charter, namely 'crimes of aggression'. Fourth, the ICC 'should execute its duties objectively and impartially, make best efforts to avoid political bias and prevent the Court from becoming a place for political misuse of litigation'.[73]

As the main patron of the Khmer Rouge regime, China also emerged as the main opponent of an international criminal tribunal for Cambodia, saying that such an attempt would infringe upon its sovereignty. When the letter from the two Prime Ministers of Cambodia sent to the UN in June 1997 was circulated to the UN Security Council, the 'Chinese delegation made it clear that it did not want to put the topic on the Security Council agenda'.[74] The Chinese communist leadership was 'unwilling to support a Security Council resolution under Chapter VII of the UN Charter'[75] to bring surviving Khmer Rouge leaders to justice. When the UN Secretary-General submitted a letter with the Group of Experts' report to the Security Council and the General Assembly on 15 March 1999, '[t]he Chinese were actively working against any further UN initiative'. Hammarberg was told in a meeting with the Chinese Ambassador in Phnom Penh 'that the issue of the Khmer Rouge was an "internal" matter and should not be dealt with by the UN – not even on a Cambodian invitation'.[76] Beijing is believed to have interfered in the process of legislation through personal connections inside Cambodia. The Chinese embassy there also played an active role in thwarting any attempts to set up an international criminal tribunal. On 18 February 2002, for instance, Chinese ambassador Ning Fukui met with Sok An and issued a statement that 'A Khmer Rouge trial is an internal affair of Cambodia, and the Chinese government supports such a decision'.[77]

China remains the biggest ally of the junta government in Myanmar, and did its part to defend it when the latter launched a series of crackdowns on protestors, including Buddhist monks, in September 2007. Before the ASEAN Summit in November, Singapore proposed the idea of inviting a UN Special Envoy to Myanmar to brief members on the situation in Myanmar, but only the Philippines and Thailand supported the proposal. China was alleged to have sent other ASEAN states letters of its objection, which may have had an impact on their decision to reject Singapore's initiative.[78]

In short, most states, non-state actors and regional organizations in East Asia still hesitate to embrace international criminal justice. China in particular, and other lesser powers in general, regard this global effort with suspicion. Few academics have lent active public support for this effort. The next section explains this has been the case.

Future prospects for collaboration on international criminal justice in East Asia

Power remains a key obstacle to the adoption of new legal norms. The USA – the world's only superpower after the Cold War – has been most effective in preventing any attempts to make the ICC autonomous from the UN Security Council, whose permanent members (including the USA) have veto power, and in putting pressure on other states to agree that they would not send US nationals to the ICC. Without the support of China, UN attempts to get a resolution from the Security Council to bring Khmer Rouge to justice remain limited. The biggest power in Southeast Asia, Indonesia has proved successful in putting pressure on Timor-Leste to turn against its people's calls for justice against Indonesian military leaders. Timor-Leste depends on Indonesia for trade and transportation links, and has found it futile to go against its large neighbor.

However, material power alone does not explain why some great powers have chosen to support efforts to promote global criminal justice. Since the Labor Government came to power in 1997, for instance, Britain became 'a strong supporter of a strong ICC'.[79] Furthermore, power also does not explain why middle-powers or small states such as Israel, Iran, Iraq and Syria have neither signed nor ratified the Rome Statute.

One may argue that national legal traditional norms within certain states remain incompatible with the international criminal justice's new legal norms. East Asians have non-legalistic traditions that offer alternatives to the pursuit of peace. Even Japanese in general remain uncomfortable with legalistic means as the way to promote peace and security. According to Yasuaki Onuma, 'legalistic thinking has been rather foreign to many Japanese ... to resort to juridical measures and to enforce one's rights is not appreciated'. He adds: 'Rather, one is expected to reach the same goal by resorting to less forceful measures such as patient negotiations, mediation, and other reconciliatory measures'.[80] According to Motoo Noguchi, a Japanese judge at the ECCC, the majority of citizens often do not support the criminal justice system. Asian countries do not have a strong legal tradition, tend to have weak domestic laws, and settle disputes in an unofficial way outside court, or they use it only as a last resort and are uncomfortable with outside interference because of their colonial past and recent history of independence.[81] The norm of state sovereignty has been viewed as a challenge to international criminal justice. Fen Osler Hampson and his associates, for instance, raise this point in their work: 'Normative barriers were a function of the fact that the rights of states, based on traditional conceptions of sovereignty, and the rights of people, based on conceptions of human security, are not always congruent'.[82]

But the norm of state sovereignty should not be treated as an eternal hindrance to international criminal justice. The ICC now has 105 party member states. States in East Asia will not forever reject universal values. Cambodia, Timor-Leste, Japan and South Korea have already joined the ICC. Other liberal democracies in the region, such as the Philippines and Thailand, have not yet ratified the Rome Treaty, but the reasons for their delay have little to do with permanent objections to the universal values of criminal justice. The Philippines' department of foreign affairs acknowledged that the ICC was consistent with the country's obligations to other associated conventions.[83] The Thai government shared the same attitude: it agreed in principle to the ICC.[84] While some autocratic states, notably Burma, have strongly rejected the intrusive nature of international criminal justice,[85] other non-democracies, such as Laos and Vietnam, do not say they will never join the ICC. Vietnamese officials admitted that their country would at some point accede to the Rome Statute. On 1 November 2007, for instance, the Representative of Vietnam, Nguyen Thi Thanh Ha, stated that 'We have many times stated our support for an independent and objective international criminal court, which complements the national juridical system and operates in accordance with the fundamental principles of international law'.[86] She emphasized the need to include the crime of aggression and for the court to exercise jurisdiction over this crime.

State leaders in the region remain insecure and tend to take the position that security takes precedence over criminal justice.[87] They tend to reject western-style interventionism, not in defense of Asian values *per se*, but because of their 'more fundamental concern for their own regime security'.[88] The Cambodian government, for instance, resisted the idea of an effective international criminal tribunal controlled by the UN, largely because its leaders felt insecure. By not acting swiftly against Khmer Rouge leaders, the subsequent governments hoped to gain more security for themselves. First, the incumbent leaders were afraid that any genuine trials would pose a threat to their political legitimacy and personal security. Many of them were former Khmer Rouge officials and highly sensitive to any charges of their involvement in the atrocities. For instance, Foreign Minister Hor Namhong sued three journalists over allegations that he was put in charge of prisoners in a camp where innocent people were tortured and executed. The journalists were found guilty; the judge ordered them to pay the Minister $6,500 in compensation and a $1,280 fine to the state.[89] The Group of Experts correctly identifies the perceived threat of an international tribunal to regime security. The Group wrote that 'both of the principal political parties have over the years had strong connections with the Khmer Rouge and include former Khmer Rouge among their members, including some who might be targets of any investigation into atrocities in the 1970s'. They go on to say that 'The current Prime Minister [Hun Sen] and many of his colleagues in the Cambodian People's Party (CPP) were once members of the Khmer Rouge before defecting to Vietnam'. As well, 'FUNCINPEC and other parties were closely allied with the Khmer Rouge in the struggle against Vietnam and the PRK/SOC'.[90] There is no criminal evidence against Hun Sen, but files compiled by the Documentation Center of Cambodia provided 'enough evidence to indict CPP President and Senate Speaker Chea Sim and CPP Honorary President and National Assembly

Deputy Speaker Heng Samrin for crimes against humanity and/or war crimes'. Chea Sim was a district chief under the Khmer Rouge regime and 'could be accused of mass killings'. Heng, an army commander under the Khmer Rouge regime and now President of the Samrin Assembly, 'could be held responsible for gruesome massacres of civilians', as his 'unit was engaged in fierce battles against the Vietnamese along the border'.[91]

Domestic or regime insecurity in other states remains a powerful hindrance to international criminal justice. Although they are signatories of the ICC, Thailand and the Philippines face security challenges at home. In November 2006, for instance, former Senator Kraisak Choonhavan called on Thailand to ratify the Rome Statute, but he had his eye on former Prime Minister Thanksin Shinawatra, who was alleged to have committed crimes against humanity in connection to 2,500 extrajudicial killings of suspected drug dealers in 2003.[92] Some lawmakers in the Philippines have shown keen interest in joining the ICC, but faced domestic resistance from the military and security apparatus still deeply involved in armed conflict with insurgent groups, such as *Abu Sayyaf*, the New People's Army, and the Moro Islamic Liberation Front.[93] Both Singapore and Malaysia have relied on their longstanding Internal Security Act to arrest and detain individuals suspected of terrorism without trial, and have tightened restrictions on freedom of expression. China remains deeply weary of foreign interference in its domestic issues such as Tibet and Taiwan. After the terrorist attacks inside the USA on 11 September 2001, China stepped up its military campaign against separatists in Xinjiang Province.

Last, but not least, the lack of East Asian actors' political will or support for international criminal justice appears to be rooted in the empirical fact that criminal justice does not necessarily bring about immediate peace. Few scholars in East Asia are staunch legalists, nor are they cultural determinists, not because they see or hear no evil or because their cultural values ignore evil, but because they fail to see the real effectiveness of judicial means. From Tokyo to East Timor, political leaders also appear to be less keen on the pursuit of international criminal justice than their immediate quest for economic reconstruction and development. Japan contributed 690 peacekeepers to East Timor, but much of its assistance ($120 million pledged in 2002) was for economic and humanitarian purposes. Tokyo has helped cover the budget for Khmer Rouge trials more than any other state, but this is only a fraction of the total amount of aid it has delivered to Cambodia. Former Prime Minister of Singapore Lee Kuan Yew and former Malaysian Prime Minister Mohamad Mahathir were champions of the idea that democratic development or the eradication of poverty stands over and above other priorities, such as democracy and human rights. Lee found receptive audiences in China, Japan, Vietnam and the Philippines.[94] Timor-Leste has claimed from the beginning to have other priorities in mind, such as economic reconstruction and good relations with Indonesia and other states in the region.[95] President Xanana Gusmao defended the need for development and social justice to come before criminal justice: 'We fought, we suffered, we died for what? ... To try other people or to receive benefits from independence?'[96]

Conclusion

This chapter shows that the regional prospects for international criminal justice are not completely bleak; however, there are several reasons why East Asians hesitate to jump on the legal bandwagon of western globalists. The limits of normative convergence between East and West have much to do with the selective nature of universal justice in practice, as do fears of western neo-imperialism (seen as posing a threat to national and regime security) and the lack of evidence that criminal justice effectively promotes human security. Recent international criminal tribunals often practice selective justice that politically suits or serves the interests of powerful states bent on bullying others, especially their enemies. The ICTY offers a good example of such biased or selective justice. Ramesh Thakur, for instance, points to the fact that 'the supposedly independent ICTY prosecutes only those whom Washington wants prosecuted; Washington in turn uses the threat of ICTY prosecution to secure compliance from political actors in the Balkans; and it has shown a lack of interest in investigating prosecutorial misconduct'.[97] Leaders in developing countries further tend to view 'the US refusal to join the universal justice of the ICC' as 'the moral imperialism of human rights as the handmaiden to judicial colonialism in the form of *ad hoc* tribunals that leave the process of international criminal law vulnerable to the pursuit of power politics'.[98] Unless legal globalists can also prove that international criminal justice has become an effective instrument for the promotion of human security, and not at the expense of national and regime security, the legal norms will not soon be fully accepted and institutionalized by most Asian states.

8 The neoliberalization of security and violence in Cambodia's transition

Simon Springer

Security should mean freedom from the fear of direct and indirect physical harm, defined in military, criminal, political and economic terms. This chapter differs from these conventional interpretations in adding that it also means more than the preservation of the market, a position reflected in the actions of Cambodia's donor community, in particular the World Bank and the International Monetary Fund (IMF). While drawing on postmodernist concerns for governmentality, the theoretical edifice here is rooted in a Marxian political economy approach,[1] offering a skeptical perspective on calls for security from the international financial institutions and powerful bilateral donors. In examining the political economy of Cambodia's recent triple transition – from war to peace, from command economy to free market economics, and from authoritarianism to democracy – I argue that donor-promoted notions of security have been rhetorical in terms of concern for humanitarianism. Instead, Cambodia's donor community has focused on security as it relates to the preservation of market principles.

Complementing the preceding chapters, I offer an opportunity for critical reflection on the theory and praxis of the human security agenda. In particular, for collaborative action to retain the emancipatory potential of a freedom-from-violence agenda in pushing the human security doctrine forward, a cynical vigilance is required of both the actors involved, and their degree of involvement in any collaborative effort. As the discourse of human security has been inundated by the neoliberal fervor of governments, international financial institutions, and non-governmental organizations (NGOs) alike, it has been rendered nearly hollow by the inherent tensions of neoliberal ideology. Cutting to the crux of the security discourse promoted by Cambodia's donor community reveals it as deceptive, having little to do with the prevention of violence, a defining feature of human security. Rather, what I have termed the 'security pretext' effectively translates into acceptance and promotion of the political *status quo*, as secured hegemony for the reigning political party means a stabilized marketplace. Members of the international community, including donors, are viewed as somewhat complacent to state violence in transitional settings, so long as the state remains committed to a type of governmentality based on market reforms.

The authoritarian actions of transitional governments can be understood as resulting from their inability to respond to the demands of the citizenry in meaningful ways, a position fostered by prescribed 'rollbacks' that remove the state from the workings of the economy. The rolling back of the state is a ratio-nale of neoliberal governance, not an informed choice of the autonomous agents that comprise the nation. Thus, we find those marginalized by neoliberal reform in continuous struggle to have their voices heard, which is frequently met with state violence when expressed as dissent. As inequality sharpens under neoliber-alism, citizens are more likely to express dismay with particular characteristics of neoliberalization, most prominently the privatization of essential social pro-visions such as education and healthcare. Recourse to violence thus becomes one of the few available options to governments weakened by neoliberal reform as they attempt to retain legitimacy. Approval of such violence is never given explicitly by international donors, yet violence is implicitly accepted as neces-sary for maintaining the 'hollowed-out' shell of the neoliberalized state, which in turn preserves the market.[2]

I challenge this dominant discourse of security, recognizing unscripted and embodied individual representation – something the security pretext seeks to marginalize when manifested in a form other than 'consumer' – as essential for empowering the people, furthering democratization and enhancing human security.

The chapter begins with a critical examination of the human security dis-course, illuminating the potential danger involved in sharing some theoretical imperatives with neoliberalism. I emphasize collaboration as having more than one context, and if inattentive to the question of who is actually collaborating, the potential for collaborative action may be subsumed by neoliberal orthodoxy becoming partiality-based, leaving the honourable cause and fundamental ele-ments of human security unaddressed. I then turn to the empirical experience of Cambodia's transitional political economy, where I explain authoritarian tendencies in Cambodia as a reality of maintaining both domestic and interna-tional political motivations. Domestically, security is premised on maintaining the hegemony of the incumbent regime, a concern that shapes the extraneous imperative, which has a stake in preserving such hegemony inasmuch as main-taining security is crucial for the free flow of capital and a functioning market economy.

I make no allusions to the enormous and politically complex tasks of identify-ing concrete alternatives to neoliberalism and Cambodia's current predicament of aid dependency, as each is beyond the scope of a single chapter. My main purpose instead is to question the potential of neoliberalism to ensnare the human secu-rity discourse. The task of (re)imagining and (re)constructing Cambodian society should rightfully be an ongoing, protean and democratic process, enacted through collective will and empowered by the unanimity of Cambodians themselves. It is this type of solidarity-based collaborative action, founded on struggle and pro-test, that may open pathways toward change that will be meaningful, and hence lasting, for Cambodians. Such a positive incarnation of collaboration as grass-roots, radical democracy has the potential to undo Cambodia's 'actually existing' version of neoliberalism-as-kleptocracy.[3]

Neoliberalizing human security

The human security doctrine has emerged as a response to the problems presented by failed states, where the United Nations Development Program's (UNDP) 1994 *Human Development Report* is credited with introducing the term into the vernacular of academic and policy discourses (see other chapters in this volume).[4] The basic argument presented by the report is that human emancipation is concomitant to international security, whereby ensuring the protection of the individual requires mitigating the inequalities and social tensions that might later erupt into conflict. The Commission on Human Security (CHS) has adopted a similar definition.[5]

The concept of human security embraces an expansive agenda, one that William Bain contends 'enlarges significantly the scope and substance of the word security – that includes issues such as environmental degradation, human rights, equity, human potential, health, children, labour standards, narcotic trafficking, organised crime, small arms proliferation, religion, ethnicity, gender, identity, governance, civil society, and internal conflict'.[6] Compiling a list of this sort provides a useful initial step, but may be criticized for not providing a conceptual definition, failing to offer a method of evaluating the components of the list, and attempting to do too much.[7] In spite of such critiques, and in accepting a conceptual definition of human security as broadly concerned with reducing the potential for conflict and existing inequalities – social, political and, importantly, economic – we need to allow for a significant degree of flexibility. Human security represents a complex picture, one that is as protean as the human experience itself, and consequently it can be assured only through the adaptability and continuous negotiation of democratic means. Democracy is the crux of human security.

While disagreements about the meaning of human security are frequent, questions of timing have not been problematized to the same degree. Advocates point to the post-Cold War security environment, where the deepening of globalization has been said to produce 'new information networks and media capacity, which have exacerbated the problems faced by failed and failing states, and which have produced new forces for democratisation'.[8] What such accounts fail to identify is the potential for globalization in the form of neoliberal economics to aggravate the difficulties facing states in terms of their ability to respond to the demands of the citizenry due to privatization, deregulation and withdrawal from most areas of social provision.[9] Such prescribed rollbacks undermine human security, as neoliberalism's much touted assumption of the 'trickle-down effect' – which holds that poverty can be eliminated through secured free markets and free trade – has failed to materialize. According to the UNDP, 'the income gap between the fifth of the world's people living in the richest countries and the fifth in the poorest was 74 to 1 in 1997, up from 60 to 1 in 1990 and 30 to 1 in 1960'.[10] Importunate inequality is such a persistent feature of neoliberalization as to be regarded as structural to the whole project. Thus neoliberalism is a doctrine concerned with the restoration of class power where it exists, and its creation where it does not.[11]

In some ways, the timing of the emergent human security agenda is not surprising in that it coincides with the post-Cold War global 'triumph' of capitalism and the associated drive toward its current neoliberal incarnation. This is because neoliberalism's exacerbation of inequality runs counter to the notion of human security ascribed to it here, where only a society free from extreme socioeconomic and political hierarchy, guaranteeing a decent livelihood and living standard for all, can ensure sustained human security. How the agenda is operationalized is still very questionable given its related interests with neoliberalism over reconfiguring the relationship between state and citizen, the associated push for individualism, and the shared potential for atomization. Invoking political slogans to mask specific strategies beneath vague rhetorical devices is commonplace *realpolitik*, and thus '[a]ny political movement that holds individual freedoms to be sacrosanct is vulnerable to incorporation into the neoliberal fold'.[12] This is the precarious position the human security doctrine now finds itself in, as questionable global initiatives are increasingly justified by the ethics of human security.[13] Submergence to the neoliberal tide is made clear in the World Bank's working paper that links human security to poverty levels in four Asian countries, including Cambodia, where continued structural adjustment is the order of the day.[14] Neoliberal pragmatism is also evident in the CHS manifesto, which states, 'Markets and trade are basic to economic growth and ... use of markets will be required to generate the kinds of growth and human security measures that an expanding human population needs.'[15]

The human security doctrine underscores how the state has marginalized and oppressed many groups, thus allowing its proponents to bring greater force to arguments about the need to lessen the influence of entrenched state elites in the processes of development.[16] Herein rests a potentially problematic feature of human security, insofar as 'it raises the moral claims of individual human beings above those of the communities in which they live'.[17] This is precisely why human security is emerging as a rallying cry for neoliberals everywhere, because neoliberalism rests on the idea of rejecting both direct state control and all forms of social solidarity. Through freedom in the marketplace, each individual is held responsible for her or his own actions and wellbeing, leaving little room for shared aims and the collectivism required by democracy. In this sense, human security and neoliberalism both pose questions of governmentality, and both envision a similar solution as they make the same fundamental arguments regarding the role the state should play in guaranteeing freedom and development.

While much of the existing literature tends to interpret neoliberal orthodoxy as a political and economic philosophy, there is relatively little understanding of neoliberalism as a political–economic practice relying on a new construction of citizen-subjects.[18] Thus we must come to grips with the tension between neoliberalism as a theory and the actual pragmatics of neoliberalization.[19] Following Michel Foucault's concept of governmentality offers considerable insight in this regard, as power is de-centered and the rationalities of governance take place at a distance where 'the conduct of conduct' is not dependent on juridical or administrative apparatuses of the state.[20] Instead, the 'art of governance' takes place at numerous sites, through an array of 'techniques of power' designed to observe, shape and control the behavior of individuals situated in a range of institutional domains such as the prison, factory or school.[21] Accordingly, neoliberalism is governmentality *par excellence*, as the shift from government (state power on its own) to governance (a broader configuration of state and central elements of civil society) has been marked under neoliberalism.[22]

In the neoliberal art of governance, it is the newly atomized and now fiercely individualistic citizen-subjects to whom the theory must pander in order to allow governance at a distance to continue to operate. The rhetorical employment of the human security discourse by entrenched powerful state actors and international institutions works hard to accomplish the task, as few would question the benevolence of an agenda that espouses freedom from want, freedom from fear, and freedom to take action on one's own behalf as its primary tenets,[23] especially in a post-Cold War context where leviathan fears continue to show much resilience. Neoliberalism is, by definition, a global governmentality, and it is therefore unsurprising that the UN represents the originator and primary practitioner of the human security discourse. Given the ever-increasing cries for help born of exponentially growing inequality, the UN has actively sought collaboration on human security with the World Bank and IMF, as well as national governments, NGOs and regional institutions.[24]

In East Asia, few governments or scholars showed immediate interest in human security, concluding that the agenda and its premises were inconsistent with the region's strong notions of government (as opposed to governance) where states continued to be viewed as the best providers of security, and absolute sovereignty and non-interference are ferociously guarded principles.[25] In contrast, civil society has been quick to respond to this call, as the human security agenda provides a powerful argument against the state-centered model of development that has dominated the region in recent decades.

Amid such calls for a new division of responsibility between state and non-state actors in political and economic development are arguments for more international accountability in procuring human security, whether or not individual states agree with this situation.[26] The potential for new modes of imperialist intervention is apparent. While typically collaboration is referred to as the notion of working jointly with others, the term has another, more sinister context. *Merriam-Webster's Collegiate Dictionary* provides the following two alternative definitions for collaboration: 1) 'to cooperate with or willingly assist an enemy of one's country and especially an occupying force'; and 2) 'to cooperate with an agency or instrumentality with which one is not immediately connected'.[27] These connotations make perfect sense in the context of how the human security discourse is currently deployed in feeding into a neoliberal mode of governance.

Accordingly, we can identify two visions of collaborative action. The first is a solidarity-based version, which is a grassroots attempt to radicalize democracy through visible struggles and protests launched in public space. Such an approach implies a significant amount of uncertainty, and there will inevitably be innumerable mistakes, hiccups and setbacks along the way to improving human security, but the frame of democracy advocated here – a radicalized and processual one, where democracy is a grassroots and incomplete project, always in a process of becoming – sees this as the only legitimate form of democratic action inasmuch as all other forms remove those most affected, through representation or other-wise, from direct ownership of the democratic process. My position, following critical scholars such as Chantal Mouffe and C. Douglas Lummis,[28] is that if we really believe in democracy – the gateway to lasting human security – then the merging of *demos* (the people) and *kratia* (power), or radical democracy, is the only genuine incarnation. The underlying concern of solidarity-based collabora-tive action is empowerment, emancipation from tyranny (whether of the state or the market), and improved human security through tangible democratic means. This is the collective establishing their own terms, on their own terms.

Contrasting this democratically virtuous conception of collaborative action is a more authoritarian version, where a bias for any actions that will preserve, enhance or deepen the penetration of the market is adopted in a one-size-fits-all-styled pre-scriptive approach. Neoliberalism is the lynchpin upon which a partiality-based notion of collaborative action turns. In this context, we should rightly ask to what extent the now orthodox neoliberal governmentality and its associated economic reforms have been successful in increasing meaningful employment, distribut-ing resources evenly, and ensuring equal access to fundamental provisions such as healthcare and education, which each lay at the heart of conflict alleviation. The answer is bleak, yet such questioning is mandatory if we are to conceive of human security as the reduction of socioeconomic inequalities and poverty as is commonly understood.[29]

Opening for business and the renewal of patron–client politics

In response to the *de facto* privatization that crept across Cambodia since the early 1980s, and coinciding with the emerging sea change in global geopolitics, the government in Phnom Penh introduced a number of economic reforms in 1989. These reforms, consisting of changes in land tenure, tax and marketing policies, a new investment law designed to attract foreign capital, and a separation of the state from production through the reduction of subsidies and the privatization of state-owned businesses,[30] were not incidental, as the fall of the Soviet Union that same year signalled to Cambodian political elites that the communist era had ended, leaving them with little option but to embrace the free market economics of the West. Such economic liberalization also coincided with renewed interest from state leaders in the West in ending Cambodia's three decades of civil war after ten years of indifference throughout the 1980s.

Humanitarian intervention is the most arduous aspect of the human security agenda, suggesting that even when phrased as a 'responsibility to protect', the call for states and citizens to intervene in the affairs of neighbors has been poorly received in many parts of the world.[31] The termination of the Cold War, however, reinvigorated the UN, and the newfound unity of the Security Council gave the organization the moral certitude 'to act in a relatively large number of conflicts, and in the process raised expectations with regard to its primary responsibility for maintaining international peace and security'.[32] In this respect, although the human security doctrine was yet to be officially defined, the UN intervention in Cambodia can be understood as a litmus test of instituting human security at a global level. Through the dispatch of the UN Transitional Authority in Cambodia (UNTAC) to settle the ongoing conflict, Cambodia became the proverbial guinea pig to a rejuvenated UN. What is particularly salient here is the association between neoliberalism and what would soon become formally defined as the human security agenda, as the UN mission had as much to do with securing a footing for marketization as it did for bolstering human rights in Cambodia.

With foreign capital poised at the door, awaiting conditions that would guarantee security on investments,[33] economic reform became a major factor in the timing of the UN's attempt to settle Cambodia's ongoing civil conflict. One of the principal aspects of the proposed UN intervention was the establishment of a (neo)liberal order via Cambodia's reconnection to the international economy.[34] The demise of the Soviet Union and the 27 September 1989 exit of the Vietnamese client government meant the USA could end its policy of covert subversion in backing the Khmer Rouge, and begin engaging openly with the Phnom Penh government.[35] Cambodian markets were now open for business, where logging, fishing, petroleum and tourism ventures were among the many enterprises that stood to profit. Equally, the UN proposal was an opportunity to jettison some of the guilt that surely lingered after the decade of international apathy that followed in the wake of the Khmer Rouge atrocities.[36]

With at least somewhat dubious motives, in 1991 the UN negotiated a settlement to the long-running civil war between the Coalition Government of Democratic Kampuchea (CGDK), consisting of Cambodian resistance groups including remnants of the Khmer Rouge, and Vietnam's former clients, the Cambodian People's Party (CPP).[37] The signing of the Paris Peace Agreements on 23 October 1991 marked the official beginning of Cambodia's triple transition, a process initially overseen by UNTAC, which was charged with disarming the warring factions and creating a 'neutral political environment' for future 'free and fair' elections, laying the groundwork in which a new constitution would be ratified to included human rights and basic freedoms.[38] In early 1992, Sophal Ear suggests Cambodia began 'normalising relations with the developed world and accepting large amounts of aid in the form of grants and loans from bilateral and multilateral sources ... with the idea of becoming fully reintegrated into the global economy'.[39] Conferring the attribute of 'normal' to such a relationship is a problematic rendering, and can only refer to the procurement of the *status quo* with respect to aid dependency and debt that encumbers much of the third world. The UN's subsequent articulation of the human security concept immediately following the UNTAC mission in the 1994 UNDP *Human Development Report* is neither inconsequential nor mere coincidence in this regard, as it retroactively provided the necessary language to justify intervention in the Cambodian conflict as an exclusively humanitarian concern, effectively diffusing attention away from the mission's neoliberal imperative of opening the Cambodian marketplace to global capital.

Despite signing the Paris Peace Agreements, it was not long before Cambodian authorities violated the 'democratic' spirit of the agreements when faced with opposition to their newly realized neoliberal mode of governance. On 17 December 1991, for instance, demonstrators consisting of both government employees and students gathered in Phnom Penh to protest privatization and high-level government corruption related to this process.[40] In an early appearance of the 'shadow state' at work,[41] government staff accused their superiors of appropriating money made from selling or leasing factories and official residences to private foreign entrepreneurs.[42] The demonstrations proceeded without incident until 21 December 1991, when police beat two students.[43] Over the next two days police stepped up their aggression, assaulting protesters with batons and firing their weapons into the crowds.[44] By 24 December 1991, the demonstrations were dispersed, but not without bloodshed, as eight civilians had been left dead, with another 26 injured. In the days following the protests, the government imposed a curfew in Phnom Penh and passed legislation restricting permission for demonstrations it believed could lead to violence.[45] This response represents both a temporal and spatial strategy to deny democracy, thus undermining human security, and ultimately functioning to preserve the social, political and economic *status quo*.

Contrary to the prevailing perceptions of Cambodia's donor community, the participation of government employees in the demonstrations indicated that the patronage system in the country is in fact not monolithic, and holds its own tensions and contradictions that evidently can cause public condemnation.[46] The government response to such discontent, however, conveyed a strong message to Cambodians that it would not budge on its agenda of economic liberalization, presumably because those in high positions quickly realized that, via shadow state politics, they could amass extraordinary wealth whereby their position of political power was guaranteed by their rising economic power as patron–client networks were reinforced. The former communists had recognized the utility of neoliberal governmentality to the maintenance of their own elite status, and the politics of patronage were retooled to accommodate this ideological shift.

For Cambodian economic and political elites, the move to free market economics seemed to offer 'a matrix of resources that could shore up exclusionary loyalties within the weak state apparatus, and reduce the field of action for resistance in rural villages, as a means to strengthen the state militarily and politically'.[47] In other words, economic liberalization transformed patron–clientelism, which effectively translated into the attenuation of villagers' individual and collective freedoms, and in direct contrast to the language of the human security discourse, market principles intensified the oppression and marginalization of poor Cambodians at the hands of elites. Illustrating the contradictions between neoliberal theory and practice, marketization in Cambodia offered increased opportunities for the ruling elites to solidify their economic and political power, where neoliberalism-as-governmentality blinded citizens to the source of their domination as they came to accept the supposed virtues of neoliberal policy.

That many of CPP's high-ranking officials received education in the economically liberal West should not be overlooked,[48] and the move toward free market economics, and particularly its timing, suggests that Cambodia's political elites were shrewd planners who intended this transformation as a strategic manoeuvre to ensure their position of power into the future, albeit requiring a new *modus operandi*. This was to be found in building their personal wealth, and since a Marxian political economy recognizes capitalism as an exploitative system that allows for very few 'winners', the newfound embracement of neoliberalism allowed elites to harden their political power *vis-á-vis* society. Despite rapid economic liberalization after 1991, the benefits were mostly limited to the urban areas and the elite, as Cambodian leaders seized every opportunity to enrich themselves and fortify their power bases.[49] Such entrenchment was effected principally through their ability to control privatization schemes prescribed by international financial institutions, where many state-owned enterprises were either purchased by members of the ruling class themselves, or corruption and bribery were used to negotiate the purchase or lease of public land and enterprise. In the context of human security, as elites accumulated ever more of the country's resources and land for themselves, this lent itself to a future of heightened conflict, where the contemporary situation of rampant land grabbing, numerous land-swap deals, and widespread dispossession of the poor serves as a dire testament.[50]

The ongoing plunder of Cambodian forests provides another example of such rampant corruption and refurbished patronage, as public lands are leased to foreign companies not only with the typical neoliberal practices of allowing tax holidays and renewable leases, but also under circumstances of bribery, where government royalties fail to reflect the value of the timber.[51] Many private companies have gained access to concessions through hostile takeovers and intimidation of locals through payoffs to local military personnel, and by forming alliances with Cambodian elites enabling them to skirt laws, manipulate judicial processes and influence national legislation.[52] Global Witness, Cambodia's former official forest-crime monitor, which in 2003 was sacked under dubious circumstances of government intimidation and the complicity with international financial institutions,[53] have argued that Cambodia's kleptocratic elite generates much of its wealth via the seizure of public assets and natural resources, particularly forests, with the most powerful logging syndicate led by relatives of Prime Minister Hun Sen.[54] The poor, who have become increasingly militant towards such siphoning of public resources into private hands, attempt to erect their own version of solidarity-based collaborative action by frequently mobilizing protests in hope of stemming the activities directly responsible for threatening their human security via a decline in their ability to sustain their own livelihoods. Such wholesale privatization of public resources increases the likelihood of conflict by reducing collective, democratic control, and thus serves as an example of how the partiality-based collaborative action of elites, logging companies, and those donors promoting privatization and deregulation of the economy runs counter to the stated goals of the human security agenda. The only way to reconcile these practices of pillage with the human security discourse is to mask the systemic inequality fostered by an elitist project under a wash of rhetoric stressing benevolence and equal benefit to all.

Subverting democracy in the name of market security

The first indication that democratization would not be as smooth as envisioned by the Paris Peace Agreements came when the CGDK's Khmer Rouge element destroyed the prospect of moving from war to peace soon after UNTAC arrived in Cambodia. Although signatories to the Paris Peace Agreements, the Khmer Rouge ultimately rejected the plan and resumed guerrilla activities from Cambodia's periphery when they realized that they would be unable to attain political power through democratic means as their support base had all but evaporated following years of abuse.[55] This withdrawal threatened the entire UNTAC mission by throwing the disarmament proposal into disarray when other factions refused to hand over their weapons as the Khmer Rouge ignored the ceasefire. Failed disarmament subsequently had detrimental effects on the creation of a neutral political environment, as the continued strength of the military, and its control by CPP, made it impossible to disentangle CPP from the state apparatus.[56] Despite the obvious threats to human security posed by resumed insurgency, the UN mission was successful in terms of the election proceeding in May 1993. Three major parties competed: CPP, headed by Hun Sen; and the two remaining CGDK elements, the Royalist Party National United Front for an Independent, Neutral, Peaceful, and Co-operative Cambodia (FUNCINPEC), headed by Prince Norodom Ranariddh; and the Buddhist Liberal Democratic Party (BLDP), headed by former Prime Minister Son Sann, who ran independently of each other.[57]

Regardless of one's position on the utility of UNTAC, it is important to recognize that the UN-sponsored transition did not end the violence. The predominant characteristics of the run-up to the 1993 elections were threats, intimidation and bloodshed. Although scholars such as Michael Vickery and David Roberts deny any pattern to CPP violence during the elections,[58] both have reputations as CPP apologists. More balanced analyses suggest that CPP acted with extreme brutality, killing more than 100 opposition members, and subjecting the population at large to arbitrary violence and intimidation,[59] implicitly informing voters that that democracy was not attainable.

CPP did everything it could to sabotage the attempt to enforce democratic political and judicial norms, reinforcing its grasp on the population by reorienting state administrative structures to party-building tasks.[60] CPP appeared monolithic insofar as it maintained tight control over the bureaucracy, military, police, civil service, media and judiciary.[61] While the Paris Peace Agreements stipulated there must be a separation of party and state, in reality the two moved closer together during the UNTAC period, meaning that the UN failed to implement its primary mandate of creating a neutral political environment through disentanglement of CPP and the State of Cambodia (SOC). This failure struck a blow to human security, and on the surface appeared to be detrimental to the larger project of neoliberalization as well. However, in recognizing the contradictions between the declared goals of neoliberal theory – the wellbeing of all – and its actual pragmatics – the consolidation of elite power and the procurement of markets regardless of the social consequences,[62] the continued CPP/SOC nexus could provide the necessary hegemony for securing market principles should they win the forth-coming elections. That this entire situation clearly defies the logic of the human security agenda in terms of the freedom-from-violence imperative speaks to the security pretext.

For their part, the Khmer Rouge rebels terrorized the countryside using random violence, arbitrary detention, execution of SOC officials, and propaganda all aimed at preventing the elections from taking place.[63] The prospect of a neutral political environment was clearly in tatters, and given the potential for political catastrophe and personal danger, voter turnout was remarkable, as UNTAC managed to persuade 95 per cent of the population to register to vote, and 90 per cent of those registered showed up at the polls.[64] The turnout sent a clear message to political parties and the world: peace and democracy were overwhelmingly desired, and violence and intimidation would not be a deterrent to the Cambodian people's realization of these goals. Yet despite this strong showing at the polls, controversy swirled over the outcome. FUNCINPEC won the election with 45.5 per cent of the votes, CPP placed second with 38.2 per cent, while the BLDP placed third with 3.8 per cent,[65] and although UNTAC quickly declared the elections 'free and fair', Hun Sen and CPP refused to accept the results. Claiming electoral fraud, CPP threatened secession of all the land to the east of the Mekong River if removed from power, an ultimatum to which UNTAC acquiesced.[66]

The most common explanation for UNTAC's acceptance of an outcome inconsistent with the 1993 election results was that it was not in a position to confront CPP militarily or to challenge the fundamental power dynamics in Cambodia.[67] This, however, does not answer why then the UN felt it was appropriate to get involved in the first place. Securing a neutral political environment, a key UNTAC mandate, is an objective that is manifestly involved in changing the underlying power arrangement, where UNTAC's failure to do so speaks to a lack of commitment. A slightly more skeptical view of the UNTAC's docility to CPP threats suggests that Cambodia was to become the model both for the subsequent articulation of the human security agenda, and for future UN peacekeeping interventions. The Cambodian mission was thus pre-ordained as the organization's biggest success story to date, and in order to avoid the whole operation blowing up in their face, the UN presided over the creation of an inauspicious coalition between CPP and FUNCINPEC.[68] Given the neo-liberal imperative of the UNTAC process, the mission can be interpreted as an exercise in *realpolitik*, intended to confer legitimacy upon Hun Sen's regime as CPP offered not only the best prospect for electoral victory, but also, more importantly, for market security. Indeed, the Paris Peace Agreements 'were not designed to undermine SOC's hegemonic status. In fact, one could argue that they weakened the resistance forces and could enhance SOC's political legitimacy by electoral means'.[69] This assessment fits neatly with the neoliberal focus on the prominence of market security, which can be viewed as the primary goal of the Paris Peace Agreements as the UN was looking for options that would bring political stability to Cambodia, regardless of the result of the vote.[70] In this respect, the UN took power out of the hands of the Cambodian electorate and gave it to the factional leaders. Reinforcing the powerful position of the CPP/SOC would increase security in the short term, and allow for an immediate influx of foreign companies eager to exploit Cambodia's natural resources and its newly opened markets following an early international financial institution prescription adopted by SOC, which called for the removal of barriers impeding the establishment of foreign firms.[71] The electoral victory of FUNCINPEC not only came as a shock to most observers,[72] but also posed a significant obstacle to the machinations of foreign enterprise insofar as CPP was still firmly in control of the military, and the change of government to a party without military hegemony threatened political and hence economic stability.

Moreover, UNTAC lent implicit support to the 'iron fist' of Hun Sen by sitting idle as he forced his way into a renewed position of power, thus complicitly allowing democracy to take a backseat to neoliberal pragmatism. While Prince Ranariddh and Hun Sen became co-Prime Ministers, with Ranariddh as the 'official' leader of the country, CPP never truly shared power, and dominated the new regime. This was easily predictable because of the continued entanglement of CPP and the state apparatus, the failure of disarmament and, as the following section will illustrate, civil service downsizing prescribed by international financial institutions. Thus, from the very beginning of the operation, the UN's preoccupation with the security pretext over the will of the people undermined the prospect of Cambodian democracy and hence the realization of non-rhetorical human security.

We can either recognize UNTAC as an unmitigated failure; acknowledge that its underlying goal was to deepen the economic stability offered by an entrenched regime that was already displaying an affinity for a neoliberal policy orientation via privatization schemes, or both. Economic stability would pave the way for neoliberalization, a task that could be accomplished through organizing supposedly democratic elections to confer legitimacy on CPP. The UN clearly has the ability to involve the powerful militaries of many first-world nations when necessary, and thus had the capacity to enforce the election results in Cambodia, which they appropriately should have been committed to after involving themselves at the outset. Instead, they simply lacked the political–economic motivation to do so. Thus, when CPP surprisingly lost an election where the fix was thought to be in, this jeopardized the potential future penetration of foreign capital. FUNCINPEC could not offer the same degree of political-*cum*-economic stability, and accordingly the will of the Cambodian people was disrespected in favor of an authoritarian regime seen as the best chance of both commitment to, and capacity for, neoliberalizing Cambodia. The repercussions of such a partiality-based version of collaborative action reflected by this decision would later come back to haunt Cambodia. Indeed, as the shocking *coup d'état* of July 1997 would subsequently illustrate when Hun Sen led a murderous campaign against FUNCINPEC officials, ousting Prince Ranariddh as first Prime Minister during two days of factional warfare in the streets of Phnom Penh,[73] human security is born not of submission to the whims of the powerful, but through the collective good of democracy and solidarity-based collaborative action.

The neo-authoritarianism of neoliberalism

Following the elections, a new constitution was promulgated, which reinstated the monarchy and renamed the country the Kingdom of Cambodia. Along with renewed pledges to ensure structural adjustment and continued privatization,[74] Cambodia's experiment with economic liberalization was also signed into law. Article 56 of the new constitution states 'The Kingdom of Cambodia shall adopt a market economy system',[75] which in effect pre-emptively silences any future democratic debate over the economic arrangement of the country, not that there had been any collective accountability in its choosing to begin with. The signing of a new constitution also officially ended UNTAC's mandate, and the entire operation left Cambodia before the end of 1993.[76]

Despite the presence of international peacekeepers until September 1993, armed clashes between factional groups lingered for several years,[77] meaning the imposed liberal peace was tenuous at best. Similarly, it was not long before cracks began to show in the new coalition government, attributable to international financial institutions' preoccupation with macroeconomic stabilization and structural adjustment, which undermined the potential of building political consensus and subverted other programs essential to the consolidation of peace, such as addressing humanitarian needs.[78] Neoliberalism was the order of the day, as immediately following the 1993 election the Ministry of Economy and Finance, under tutelage from the World Bank, IMF and the Asian Development Bank, was already promising that a stringent fiscal plan would be in place by 1995.[79] Furthermore, Cambodia was locked into a condition of dependency on foreign assistance as nearly half the country's budgetary allocations were being drawn from foreign aid, translating into a limited ability to challenge donor agendas and timetables.[80] Most technical assistance projects since 1993 have undermined government ownership and capacity in that they have been donor-driven in their identification, implementation and design.[81]

In a statement that appears emblematic of the entire UN operation's position, given its fixation on economic security, former Secretary-General of the UN for Human Rights in Cambodia Michael Kirby states, 'I have always made the point that an improvement in the economy, filtering down to the average citizen, is a vitally important step on the path of rebuilding human rights in Cambodia. It helps to give a sense of well-being, purpose and commitment to society'.[82] These comments echo the neoliberal theory of the trickle-down effect, as the focus is shifted from democracy to economics as the vehicle providing individuals with a sense of agency and a participatory stake in society. It is, however, hard to see the efficacy of the trickle-down effect when the gap between rich and poor has only increased in post-transition Cambodia.[83]

Even Ronald St John, a scholar who appears inspired by neoliberalism, recognizes that while 'some disparities existed before liberalization, social and economic inequalities are significantly greater now'.[84] Similarly, one has to wonder how those Cambodians whose political, civil and social liberties have been sacrificed to excesses of 'anarchic freedom as a consequence of rampant marketization and the weakening of state authority' view current conditions of human security.[85] The rapid and unreflective transition to a free-market economy drove a relatively weak state to financial crisis, raised inflation to three-digit levels, and weakened Cambodia's social and economic infrastructure, particularly in rural areas.[86] The poor, punished by nearly 15 years of international abandonment, were now forced via Structural Adjustment Programmes to pay the further costs of reintegration into the international mainstream.

Further neoliberal reforms were ordered in 1994, as donors emphasized downsizing the civil service – the traditional power base for CPP – in an effort to build administrative capacity. Prioritizing a reduction in the civil service is one example of 'rolling back' the state, and it derives from the international financial institutions' preoccupation with controlling public expenditure as a method of achieving macro-economic stability.[87] Such a focus is highly problematic in that it contributes to shadow-state politics by encouraging rent-seeking behavior and hardening patron–client relations, as civil service members become reliant on alternative means to supplement their incomes. Following the shift to the free market, many officials began making their living in the speculative underground economy.[88] The international financial institutions approached downsizing as an administrative exercise, while ignoring the social and political costs, and the negative ramifications this might have for human security. Furthermore, such a prescription was deleterious to the stability of the fragile power-sharing arrangement in Cambodia, as the new coalition government was originally premised on the integration of large numbers of FUNCINPEC and BLDP functionaries into the CPP-dominated administrative apparatus.[89] Thus a strengthening, not a weakening, of the Cambodian government's administrative capacity was required.

In what appears to be a self-interested and calculated response to downsizing efforts, the government enshrined impunity in the law in 1994 by prohibiting civil servants, including police and soldiers, from being charged or arrested without the permission of the relevant minister.[90] In this instance, CPP used downsizing of the civil service prescribed by international financial institutions to its advantage, as this amendment would further entrench its hold on power via the politics of patronage. Thus the so-called 'culture of impunity', a frequent Orientalist rendering of Cambodia by the donor community,[91] is not a cultural feature at all. Rather, impunity can be seen as another example of the shadow-state response to neoliberal reforms, again illustrating the contradictions between neoliberal theory and its 'actually existing' practice.

CPP's jovial mood following its commandeering of the 1993 election results, coupled with a renewed position of hegemony and what appears to be a pandering to Cambodia's new patrons in the West, led Hun Sen to proclaim 1994 as the year of the resurrection of the media.[92] This honeymoon period was short-lived, and by July 1994 the media were effectively muzzled after the government issued a list of instructions indicating what the press could and could not say.[93] Journalists became subject to the whims of the political leadership and confined to expressing the *status quo*. As a result, 1994 saw several attacks against the press, including the prosecution and imprisonment of several reporters, and the murder of three high-profile journalists who were particularly critical of the new coalition government.[94] In April 1995, action was extended to foreign journalists when the American editor of the *Phnom Penh Post*, Michael Hayes, was faced with charges of 'misinformation' and 'incitement'. King Sihanouk stepped in and assured Hayes of an official pardon if convicted, but Cambodian journalists were not so fortunate, as four editors of Khmer-language newspapers were either fined or imprisoned.[95]

In light of such developments and an ongoing pattern of repressive violence, long-time Cambodia observer Steve Heder refers to Cambodia's transition as one to neo-authoritarianism, where 'In the name of political stability and economic development, as well as in order to fight a lingering and murderous insurgency, the country's current 'multiparty' ruling elite coalition ... has been working to dampen open political contestation and to deliberalize the political atmosphere by co-opting, cowing, or marginalising contesting centers of power'.[96] While Heder recognizes that such restriction of political contestation is done in the name of economic security in order to see the 'integration of Cambodia into the world capitalist system',[97] he fails to make the connection that this neo-authoritarian behavior not only falls in line with the neoliberal canon, but also appears to be a direct outcome of this doctrine.[98] Although Cambodia's donor community is very vocal about democracy promotion, it generally accepts the perceived need for 'order' and 'security' at face value precisely because it shares the same concern with order as necessary for promoting economic liberalism. In contrast, democracy must be open and accommodating to all social groups, including 'unruly' elements, so that the public as a whole may define the public interest. Recognizing this may help us to realize that predetermining and enforcing an economic model on a country is not only undemocratic, but also an act of sedition with respect to the emergence of a democratic polity. In line with neoliberalism as a project seeking the (re)creation of class power,[99] it is not at all surprising that democracy is suppressed.

Democratic subversion is illuminated in the presupposed purpose that neoliberalism imposes on citizens, where individuals must define their social, political and economic relationships through the market mechanism. While this is not necessarily effected through juridical means, a market orientation to social relations is paramount to the canon of order, most often produced through governance at a distance, where citizen-subjects 'freely' conduct themselves as market agents (consumers and sellers). It is only when the neoliberal code of conduct breaks down that such 'freedom' is revealed as a chimera. Those engaging in solidarity-based collaborative action on human security through protesting privatization, land-grabbing, inflation, poverty, and other outcomes of the state's adherence to free market principles quickly learn this precept, as they are frequently subjected to authoritarian violence that enforces the neoliberal line. Here, again, the contradictions of neoliberalism are revealed. In theory the state is to be removed from market interference, yet in practice, if the market comes into question by citizens, the engagement of the state is required to go beyond governmentality to the realm of violence in enforcing the market's vaunted position.

That a people may freely choose the economic policies and practices that directly affect their lives, and articulate their opinions, concerns, desires and demands freely and openly, appears to be a frightening proposition to neoliberals. Capitalism is premised on inequality, and democracy threatens to reveal this truth by firing the collective imagination so that ordinary individuals without institutionalized power can mobilize to change the *status quo*, seize power from those refusing to share it, or exercise it justly for the benefit of all.[100] Such action represents the heart of solidarity-based collaborative action on human security, and is an affront to those who effect its partiality-based version. Thus, within the larger discursive practices of the human security agenda, the authoritarianism of third-world governments is, on the one hand, a symptom of the neoliberal doctrine they often subscribe to and abide by, and on the other, an easy and ideal scapegoat to deflect attention away from the profound socioeconomic injustices of capitalism. In essence, neoliberalism's partiality-based appropriation of the human security doctrine provides free-market ideology with the necessary language to veil its inherent hypocrisy, shrouding the frequent need for authoritarian responses behind a humanitarian discourse that supposedly aims to protect from this very circumstance.

Conclusion

This chapter's account of the human security agenda in the context of Cambodia's transition has shown the international donor community's interest to be far from altruistic in terms of genuine concern for grassroots democratic empowerment and its corollary, improved human security. Instead, partiality-based collaborative efforts have been a contradictory exercise in *realpolitik*. The Cambodian holocaust was followed by a decade of neglect, as those in the outside world turned a blind eye to the misery they had done much to create. The sudden renewed interest in Cambodia following the fall of the Iron Curtain is thus at least somewhat peculiar, insofar as concern expressed for the political, social and economic conditions in Cambodia could hardly be taken at face value as humanitarian. The situation of Cambodia tells a very different story, where most often, extraneous expressions of concern for democracy and human security were mere rhetoric serving an ulterior motive: to pry open the Cambodian economy. Any discussion about the prospects of human security in society is futile when the competitiveness of neoliberal economics leaves problems of poverty and inequality unaddressed.[101]

In this chapter, I have attempted to peel back the layers of lies that have been heaped on Cambodia's transition to capitalist democracy. The goals of security and order for the purpose of economic investment have been exposed as taking precedence over both the desire for democracy expressed by the Cambodian electorate, and any conception of human security as freedom from fear and violence. This security pretext was reaffirmed by UNTAC's failure to create a neutral political environment, and its subsequent haste in deeming the elections free and fair. While the victory of FUNCINPEC was definite, it could have been even more resounding had UNTAC been more diligent in its attempts to unravel CPP from the state apparatus. Such disentanglement may have avoided the need for a coalition government, and certainly would not have left CPP in the militarily strong position that has ultimately allowed the party to continue to intimidate and coerce the population to this day. UNTAC was not prepared for CPP's failure at the polls, and Hun Sen was accordingly allowed to force his way into a co-Prime Ministerial position. It would appear that the consolidation of CPP hegemony was the goal of the UN mission all along.[102] Hun Sen, given his economic inclinations throughout the late 1980s, was pre-ordained as the ideal candidate to bring the stability necessary for further economic liberalization in Cambodia. In this capacity, Cambodia's 'strongman' was more than willing to engage in a partiality-based collaboration with the global instrumentality of neoliberal reform, as such action would further entrench his socioeconomic and political position *vis-à-vis* Cambodian society, a prediction he made in the late 1980s when he started the liberalization process.

With CPP's implementation and institutionalization of neoliberal modes of governance, and its subsequent deeper penetration via governmentality in Cambodia, Hun Sen's continual subversion of democracy in the immediate post-UNTAC years was of little consequence to the donor community. In truth, such authoritarian action was often a feature and/or outcome of instituting neoliberal reforms, and represented a move toward greater market security in the country. Of course, donors would quickly call for Cambodia's political parties to respect the constitution and adhere to the principles of democracy whenever violence was employed, but such criticism was always little more than lip service. What donors really wanted was the restoration of the sociopolitical *status quo* so that the neoliberal agenda could be implemented and subsequently preserved, thus illustrating all too well the rhetorical nature of partiality-based collaborative action on human security.

Conclusion

Human security and policy implications for future collaborative action

Sorpong Peou

The policy debate on human security over the past decade has been at a formative stage. Although the concept of human security is generally regarded as universal, in that it means to apply to humans anywhere on Earth, and despite the fact that thinking about human security is now evident throughout East Asia, the main ideas grew out of Western liberal experience deeply rooted in the concept of individualism, rather than that of collectivism.

One of the critical challenges to this conceptual evolution in contemporary security studies is how to bring states and other actors in other regions of the world to share Western ideas about human security, and to contribute their own in a global collaborative effort to promote this type of security. We have sought to engage in both direct and indirect dialogue among scholars from different countries by adopting a general, eclectic approach to human security, but hope that the concept will become somewhat less amorphous.

This study clearly shows both the growth of collaboration in recent years among East Asian actors – state, non-state and international – and the limits of collaborative action. This volume reveals the growing complexity of collaborative action on human security (Chapter 1), largely because normative consensus on the concept's Western liberal roots, discussed in Chapter 2, finds resistance on Asian soil (Chapters 3–5). In recent years, however, the resistance has weakened, as actors in East Asia have tolerated norms of intervention (Chapter 6). Liberal institutionalism, in terms of its effort to spread such Western values as individualism, criminal justice and democracy, is still challenged by East Asia's cultural norms, such as collectivism, autocratic rule, and insecurity at various levels (Chapter 7). Actors in the region, especially states, have also adopted capitalism, yet the market forces do not necessarily serve the interests of democracy and justice for all individuals, especially the poor; in fact, they tend to promote, first and foremost, the interests of economic and political elites (Chapter 8).

Overall, we can say with confidence that normative convergence, policy coordination and material contribution, which form the basis for collaborative action in human security, have become more evident in East Asia; however, collaborative action in such areas as peace operations, democracy, international criminal justice and economic development may never become sufficiently effective. Nevertheless, there are still some important lessons that show how global collaborative action for human security can be enhanced.

In theoretical terms, realism has now been softened. Some realists no longer remain 'hard-nosed' in their way of looking at security, and do not object to the need for promoting security at the individual level. Others, such as complex realist institutionalists, help expose the lack of donors' collaborative action in their efforts to help democratize postwar societies. International donors prove unable to transform structural constraints on, and impediments to, the process of democratic regime consolidation.[1] Other realist-inclined scholars, such as Nicholas Thomas, William Tow and others,[2] have sought to reconcile the concept of national security with that of human security by taking nonmilitary challenges into account. Tow, for instance, took note of the financial crisis in 1997 that led to the fall of President Suharto in 1999, and warns that many Asian governments face similar pressures, which may well prove beyond their capacity to resolve or contain if they continue to adhere to more traditional security focuses and approaches. He contends that the very complexity of these [non-military] challenges defies their resolution through traditional and exclusive state-centric approaches.[3]

In recent decades, critical perspectives have offered healthy criticism of both realism and liberalism, especially with regard to socioeconomic injustices committed against the weak, the poor, or those excluded from the benefits of globalization. We must thus take into account useful criticisms by critical theorists. The extent to which we should follow in the footsteps of critical theorists, particularly postmodernists, is still a matter of intellectual judgment. Some of them want little or nothing to do with realism and liberalism, viewing these intellectual discourses as stifling to the idea of openness and creativity.[4] In my view, we may be unable to go down this path to the end for several reasons.

First, we must avoid the pitfall of producing a concept that seeks to meet everyone's needs on one's own terms, but leaves us unable to make critical judgments. If human security means what everybody thinks it means, then each individual ends up providing for their own security, thus going back to a self-help world. As Chapter 1 shows, even the concept of peacebuilding has now become so ambiguous that it 'camouflages divisions over how to handle postconflict challenges or to facilitate collective action among different actors'. Actors have found it useful to adopt a meaning of peacebuilding consistent with their existing mandates, worldviews and organizational interests. If human security means what every human being or actor says it means, the concept no longer has any analytical or policy merit. An extremely amorphous concept may do more harm than good by preventing us from promoting human security effectively. To be of any analytical use, the concept must be precise enough to help us observe a certain social phenomenon and make useful assessments. We need to focus, first and foremost, on only the most important sources of threat to human security, so that we will be able to deal with them urgently and effectively. On the question of agency, we cannot expect policymakers and other relevant actors to do everything for everyone, particularly according to all the security needs everyone has in mind. A reasonably restrictive concept of human security must never become an endless 'wish list' that includes anything from human-made destruction to natural disaster, from personal safety issues to social welfare, and from egalitarian economic development to human dignity. Most of these concepts are no doubt extremely important, but they should be left to stand on their own.

Second, while critical theorists are justified in questioning the state's traditional role in providing security for its people, a possible tension lies with the empirical fact that human security cannot be promoted by simply trashing the role of the modern state. Human security is not and should not be freedom from all state constraints, for without any constraints, humans may become insecure. If anarchy were indeed a better non-structural condition for human security, we would expect structurally weak or failed states to promote human security better than those with functioning state structures. In general, both realists and liberals have good reason not to demonize the state to the same extent as some critical theorists. Both Thomas and Tow, for instance, wisely argue that 'In order for human security to be advanced, at least in the short-term, it must be embodied by states that overwhelmingly remain the predominant agents of international relations in our time'.[5] In Tow's view, 'states remain critical agents in the role of implementing and enforcing standards and mechanisms designed to overcome functional challenges to human prosperity and welfare such as narcotics traffic, environmental degradation, and terrorism'.[6] The relatively just state is the key actor that plays a crucial role in exerting control over market forces, and ensuring more equitable economic policies and an element of justice in the distribution of wealth.[7]

Third, the most realistic, if not ideal, system of government (compared with radical democracy discussed in Chapter 8), with the most potential to enhance human security (as defined here) in many parts of the world, is liberal or social democracy. At the international level, liberal democratic states are less likely than autocratic ones to engage in warfare against one another. Democracies and their democratic leaders can build and maintain security communities, not because they stop balancing against each other, but because this balancing is unlikely to lead to war.[8] At the domestic level, democratic political leaders can be better kept in check and thus prevented from using power against their people. Humanitarian disasters tend to take place inside non-liberal democratic states, such as Cambodia under Pol Pot, Uganda under Idi Amin, Rwanda under the Hutu government, and Yugoslavia under Slobodan Milošević. Without an effective system of institutional checks and balances, basic human freedom cannot be guaranteed. Some leftist or radical scholars have now recognized the need for a certain degree of realism. Writing on Cambodia's ruthless Pol Pot regime, Yale historian Ben Kiernan, for instance, warns us of the need to caution against 'the dangers of unbridled lust for power'.[9] Gabriel Kolko, a leading pro-Soviet American scholar, wrote of the Vietnamese socialists as follows: 'all too many Vietnamese Communists were no different from people in successful parties everywhere: their overriding concern was power'.[10] Because of his antihegemonic political stance, his critical or revisionist perspective seems strangely sympathetic toward both the liberal system of institutional checks and balances at the domestic level, and the realist system of power-balancing at the international level. Concentration of power within the hands of the Communist Party's Politburo alone, in his view, 'removes any check on both its abuse and ... its ignorance that are highly dangerous'.[11] Internationally, unchecked power also has its own perils. Kolko shares his view on this: 'I have always deplored the hegemonic pretensions of the Soviet Union, China, the US, and all nations that aspire to dominate others'.[12]

Evidence further shows the limits of normative commitment to radical democracy and proves that past radical impulses tend to create and perpetuate human security problems instead of eliminating them. Classical Marxists advocated that the only way to dismantle unjust capitalist systems is to promote radical change through revolutionary warfare. Communist regimes around the world sought to achieve socioeconomic justice, but left at least 100 million people dead and caused much human suffering because of socialist totalitarianism. In the name of socialist uto-pianism, earlier radical scholars defended the Soviet Union regardless of what Moscow did to its citizens or others'; few questioned Soviet hegemony. With Cambodia, some apologists even blamed racialism, rather than communism, for the widespread atrocities. The problem with contemporary radical movements (including the post-Marxist social movements of 'identity politics') is that they remain far-fetched. Postmodernism, if ontologically defensible, is conservative in its normative commitment and provides no realistic remedies for human insecu-rity. The desire to transcend politics or the messy business of democratic disagree-ment through installing a solidaristic world society embodying human interests is profoundly apolitical and may lead to repression.[13] This does not mean liberal democracies should not address socioeconomic injustices, as discussed later, but rather that egalitarian development, even highly desirable, may not be possible.

Fourth, an effective system of democratic government may help prevent other non-military sources of threat to human security. Ramesh Thakur (along with others) notes that 'Terrorism flourishes amidst frustration with repressive, inept, unresponsive and dynastic regimes that spawn angry and twisted young men, and sometimes even women, taking recourse to lethal violence'.[14] Moreover, democ-racy helps prevent large-scale famine. Nobel Price laureate Amartya Sen argues famously that 'one of the remarkable facts in the terrible history of famines in the world is that no substantial famine has ever occurred in any country with a democratic form of government and a relatively free press'.[15] If this thesis is cor-rect, democracy is more likely to help political leaders to ensure more equitable economic development, especially in countries where the press is free to expose poor economic policies, and where civil societies can advocate justice.

It thus seems to me that the liberal democratic concept of human security, while not as ideal as the radical democratic one, is still the most realistic in terms of its ability to make the concept analytically restrictive, policy-relevant and practical. The intellectual ambitions shown by many critical theorists are helpful in terms of offering critiques and creative ideas about what human security ought to mean, but amorphous concepts will only leave the human security agenda unfulfilled. One recent 'casualty' in human security studies is the fact that the current gov-ernment of Canada (a country that stood at the forefront in the field, as pointed out throughout this volume) has already officially abandoned the concept. Even the term 'Responsibility to Protect' has now become largely dormant in official Canadian policy, used only in a descriptive fashion. Although Canada did not object to the Friends of Human Security Forum, as noted in Chapter 3, the concept of human security has not formed a global consensus. The Human Security Network has also lost steam, following the Netherlands' withdrawal.[16]

Human security should be defined in more restrictive military, political, criminal and economic terms in accordance with the MPCE framework. Just as states seek to protect themselves against military attack, and from being subject to political, cultural and economic domination by others, so also human beings are secure only if and when they are not subject to the fear of actual, perceived, or structural violence in military, political, criminal and economic terms, committed by individuals or groups rather than caused by nature. This definition calls for concessions from realism, liberalism and critical theory, as it incorporates insights from all these on human security.

The MPCE framework for human security is reasonably restrictive. In *military* terms, humans are insecure when directly subject to the actual use of armed force in such forms as military attack (external and domestic) and other brutal violent acts, such as genocide. In *political* terms, the use of threat to terrorize or threaten individuals or groups is distinguished from armed violence because it does not involve the actual use of force to kill or wound the human body. Global terrorism is still a form of political violence: it is primarily aimed at instilling fear in civilians for political rather than military purposes. Colonial powers, terrorists and dictators in general rule by fear, based on the perceived threat of punishment. In *criminal* terms, humans remain insecure as long as they are subject to physical violence for non-political purposes. Criminals create fear without seeking any political or policy gains. Individuals commit homicide or rape for personal reasons. Those who deliberately, unlawfully, directly or indirectly, commit murder or sexual violence are criminals, as they do not challenge the state, nor do they have any real military purpose. In *economic* terms, human security is at risk when individuals or groups are deprived of the means of survival, such as land-grabbing and forced eviction from property. The extreme poverty that kills 8 million people a year is a structural threat to human security, because the victims do not possess means to earn enough to live, and because extreme structural inequalities and poor or unjust policies by ruling elites are in operation.

In short, human security improves when the use of armed force ends, when the threat of terror or political tyranny declines, when criminal activities decrease, and when extreme poverty rooted in highly structural inequalities is reduced. Of these four types of violence against humans, the use of armed force should rank highest because it tends to produce ripple effects that create or exacerbate the other forms of violence. Military violence tends to result in political authoritarianism or totalitarianism, and thus fears of political terror, extreme poverty and criminal activities (such as homicide and rape). This can be seen, for example, in the atrocities that took place in Cambodia after the civil war and in East Timor after the Indonesian military invasion. These wars further caused severe destruction and impoverished the people in these two countries, which are endowed with rich natural resources. Killer diseases then prey on bodies weakened by extreme poverty, which further gives rise to criminal violence.

The next big questions are how to begin the collective journey to human security, and what methods should be used to help promote and sustain it. One of the most critical challenges in human security studies, in my view, is finding the most effective or optimal means to deal with the most urgent human security challenges, as described earlier, in such a way that generates the greatest possibility of effective collaborative action.

Positivism in a 'soft' form may not give us the best answer, but 'it is [still] better for us to be clear and (possibly) wrong than to be so impenetrable that other writers are obliged to debate the meaning of what has been written'.[17] In a world where old and new visions remain rivals and where all sorts of proposed methods for promoting these visions compete for limited policy attention and action, it would help if we could also state our propositions as clearly as possible and put them to empirical test, rather than defending untested wisdom, personal convictions or mere polemics. In the paragraphs that follow, I make a brief but important attempt to 'test' a number of propositions.

The first proposition is that coercive military intervention helps end violent threats to human security before democracy can be built, poverty can be reduced, or violent crimes can be minimized. This type of intervention can protect and save lives. When based on consent and support from various actors inside and outside the region, as the East Timor case study illustrates, coercive military intervention may serve a useful humanitarian purpose.

Unfortunately, recent empirical evidence still urges us to acknowledge that coercive military intervention has not proved the most effective (or the most frequently used) method for promoting human security, as its supporters believe. We have seen few effective humanitarian interventions in recent years, because they tend to face numerous complications. First, coercive interventions often prove too difficult to undertake. Powerful actors must exert considerable diplomatic pressure on the regimes that commit violence and, more often than not, powerful states must also have their own strategic interests at stake. When atrocities are committed within the national borders of powerful states, such as China and Russia, such interventions are effectively impossible. Coercive interventions also tend to come too late; by the time Australia and others intervened in East Timor, for instance, more than 200,000 people had perished.

Second, coercive interventions tend to perpetuate the militarist norms of conflict termination, rather than the democratic norms of conflict resolution. As one pacifist advocate puts it, 'humanitarian intervention tends to institutionalize military responses to political and social conflict and thus justifies the militarism that pervades our societies and political structures'.[18] The perils of military coercion also come when decision-makers are too quick to rule out other non-military options. They often prove too eager to call for aggressive or excessive military action without considering the possible negative consequences.

Third, even the use of massive force tends to be counterproductive, especially in wartorn countries or fragile or failing states, as it tends to work against peace.[19]

The brutal use of force in countries such as East Timor is 'likely to fail in the face of the non-violent movement of protest ... the transnational diplomacy and activism, the power of imagery, and changing domestic and international opinion'.[20] In another instance, the global war on terrorism in Afghanistan, one of the world's failed states, has proved far from successful, despite the fact that NATO members and other states (39 countries in total) have contributed a large number of national troops: 41,700 as of December 2007. Instead of improving the security of Afghans, the situation has deteriorated (when compared with 2005), as almost the entire southern part of the country was now characterized as an extreme risk/ hostile environment. The year 2007 saw violence soar to new heights, with no military victory in sight for NATO. As its collective forces made a greater push to defeat the Taliban, the number of violent incidents rose. The Southeast Asian experiences further show very clearly that military solutions to violent conflicts have not only failed miserably, but also have significantly exacerbated them.[21]

Last, but not least, international collaborative action in military operations is difficult to sustain for a long period of time. This helps explain why coercive interventions tend to be undertaken by one powerful state, such as the USA. If powerful states intervene unilaterally,[22] without any authorization from the UN Security Council, they run the risk of losing international political legitimacy. The US military invasion of Iraq illustrates this point. Unilateralism tends to diminish the possibility of collaborative action. When powerful states decide to go it alone, they also run the risk of being blamed for failure and having others unwilling or unable to lend them a helping hand at a later date.[23]

Coercive interventions tend to be prohibitively costly in political, human and financial terms. The cost in human life and misery can be a significant blow to democratic state leaders, because they tend to worry about the 'body-bag' syndrome, especially in election periods. The war in Iraq has claimed more than 4,000 American lives, tens of thousands of Iraqi lives, and has created at least 4,500,000 refugees. In material terms, most regional organizations lack the resources to undertake collective military action in urgent situations. Few states, therefore, are willing to commit themselves to coercive military intervention, and, if they are willing, they may be incapable of carrying out their long-term commitment to the causes they defend. Even NATO has had difficulty undertaking collective military action against the threat of terrorism. Right after 9/11, the world stood united with the USA and lent its military support against the Taliban in Afghanistan. Recently, the use of force against terrorism has resulted in frictions among allies. Supporters of counterterrorism became suspicious of violent actions. Kidnapping and abduction – carried out by terrorists against different nationals – have undermined the collective will of states contributing troops to the war on terrorism. Contributing states tend to see no military victory in sight, and may withdraw from this collaborative action. Washington has become increasingly worried about contributing countries' 'exit strategies' from Afghanistan. Tension between NATO member states has become increasingly evident as the war on terrorism drags on, without any end in sight; European and Canadian public opinion supporting the war has also declined since 2002.[24] In December 2007, Secretary of Defense Robert Gate called on NATO to redouble its efforts, but its allies have proved reluctant to supply more forces, to provide more money to rebuild Afghanistan, or to assume more responsibilities.

In financial terms, coercive military intervention tends to be prohibitively costly, thus making collaborative action extremely fragile. Between 11 September 2001 and the end of 2007, for instance, US Congress spent $691 billion to cover the wars in Afghanistan and Iraq. The amounts spent on the wars rose from an average of about $93 billion a year between 2003 and 2005 to $120 billion in 2006 and $171 billion in 2007.[25] According to the recent estimate by Nobel Peace Price winner Joseph Stiglitz, the overall cost of the US war in Iraq alone will be around $3 trillion.[26] Whether states can indefinitely maintain collaborative efforts in such expensive operations is highly questionable.

It should thus come as no surprise that discussion concerning the need for political solutions in Afghanistan includes the suggestion that NATO negotiate with the Taliban leadership.

International peacekeeping has proved much more effective as a strategy for military intervention on behalf of humanity. Armed conflicts in failing or failed states require political solutions that only the armed adversaries themselves can bring about. International peacekeeping operations are more likely to result in sustainable peace than humanitarian intervention or peace enforcement, largely because they are based on the principle of consent among adversaries and are more likely to receive contributions from various states and other actors. Peacekeeping may help ensure the process of disarmament, demobilization, and the reintegration of armed factions into national armed forces, because it operates on the basis of the former adversaries' consent and security.

Collaboration on peacekeeping is more sustainable than coercive intervention. Peacekeeping techniques and principles (consent, consensus and neutrality) were adopted in the first place because the permanent members of the UN Security Council could not agree on enforcement operations.[27] Since the early 1990s there have been far fewer humanitarian interventions than peacekeeping operations, because UN member states tend to be more willing and able to become involved. Between 1945 and 1990, only 16 peacekeeping operations were carried out, but the number rose to 41 from 1990 to 2003. More importantly, more states contributed to peacekeeping operations: by April 2004, 130 states had made their troops available to UN peacekeeping operations. In March 2005, 103 states contributed over 65,000 troops to UN peacekeeping operations.[28]

International peacekeeping operations led by the UN are more likely to maintain longer-term collaborative action among its member states and possibly other non-state actors, largely because they are less costly and pose fewer risks than coercive military intervention. Between 1948 and March 2005, for instance, peacekeeping resulted in only 1941 casualties. The annual budget of peacekeeping operations remains low (only $3.9 billion in 2005), and 'the accumulative cost from 1948 to 30 June 2004 was a surprisingly low $31.5 billion' compared with the $1 trillion governments spend on arms every year;[29] it is definitely far lower than the military interventions in both Iraq and Afghanistan.

The trouble with international peacekeeping operations is that observers are often impatient with the slow results and critical of the UN's inability to meet rising expectations due to respect for such principles as neutrality, impartiality, and non-use of force. Critics argue that such principles should be abandoned when aggression takes place, or when 'evildoers' or potential peace spoilers are included in the peace process.

The challenge for peacekeeping is that it must be made more effective if it is to enhance human security. Peacekeeping operations are likely to fail when they are unable to overcome the security dilemma that drives adversaries to arm and fight for their survival. While peacekeeping operations enjoy more legitimacy than humanitarian interventions, they are not free from collective action problems. States and their troops must be willing to work with local partners and institutions to create enduring structures of democratic governance, the rule of law, market economy and civil society.[30]

The second proposition is that economic sanctions work to promote human security. As a policy strategy, sanctions have been regarded as an attractive non-violent alternative to war, and remain popular among leaders of powerful states. This non-military strategy has also been accepted as an instrument for the promotion of human security: it advocates disarmament, punishes and deters terrorism, brings armed factions to peace negotiations, exerts influence on authoritarian and rogue regimes, and pressures them into complying with the world's collective will. More recently, the concept of 'smart' sanctions addresses their harmful impact on people, based on the assumption that targeted regimes or leaders rather than peoples, will come under international pressure.

Most academic studies, however, show that sanctions – both 'dumb' and 'smart' – tend to be ineffectual and even counterproductive or detrimental to human security.[31] First, sanctions work best when they serve the interests of major powers, not peoples.[32] Second, sanctions hurt humans, especially innocent civilians, as the case of Iraq clearly shows,[33] and exacerbate human suffering.[34] Third, sanctions do not serve as an effective strategy for the promotion of democracy. Sanctions work more effectively when imposed on democratic states than when imposed on authoritarian states: 'Sanctions against authoritarian states failed in more than 98 per cent of the hundred-plus cases'.[35] Moreover, sanctions can intensify corruption, weaken industrial and other economic infrastructures, criminalize economic activities (giving rise to black markets),[36] cause 'further violations of economic and social rights on a large scale',[37] undermine the economic independence of middle classes and civil society,[38] and 'sometimes strengthen the repressive capability of the targeted government and thus disempower the opposition',[39] thus ultimately preventing democratization from becoming consolidated. Sanctions may in fact strengthen undemocratic or rogue regimes, because they tend to result in human suffering and thus allow people to fall prey to statist propaganda against the international community. For instance, instead of 'dislodging [Fidel] Castro [of Cuba] from power, the [US] sanctions helped him to consolidate power by delegitimising domestic critics, scapegoating Washington for the disastrous consequences of bankrupt economic policies and acquiring the stature of a mystic hero throughout Latin America for repeated tweaking Uncle Sam's nose'. Above all else, sanctions do not enjoy a great deal of global legitimacy. Despite their appeal, they remain as 'contentious as ever'.[40] States adversely affected by sanctions against particular regimes choose to defect when the costs to their economic interests rise. Overall, sanctions remain an ineffective strategy for enhancing coordination and collaborative action among actors promoting human security.[41]

The third proposition is that international criminal justice promotes human security through bringing about peace to countries suffering from violent conflict and brutality. The extent to which this legal form of intervention can enhance human security is still a matter of debate. Chapter 7 contends that legal intervention has its own limits. The exercise of power in the pursuit of justice may help promote human security, but does not always succeed. There is no convincing evidence to suggest that this method can effectively terminate war or armed conflict. The Cambodian war ended in 1998, but it was not because the Khmer Rouge leaders had been prosecuted or put in jail, but rather from a political solution through a series of secret negotiations and deals between Khmer Rouge leaders and the government in Phnom Penh that produced a series of formal and informal amnesties. The pursuit of criminal justice was basically a byproduct of this negotiated peace, after the rebellious Khmer Rouge movement had finally disintegrated and reintegrated into the Cambodian national armed forces. Evidence shows that the pursuit of criminal justice may have even rendered the incumbent political leadership determined to stay in power, fearing that the process had become politicized and that some of its leaders (with Khmer Rouge backgrounds) may be subject to future prosecution.

Other empirical studies validate this point. First, criminal justice does not effectively prevent violent conflict, nor does it contribute to the building of peace in any noticeable way. Rachel Kerr argues that the establishment of the International Criminal Tribunal for the former Yugoslavia (ICTY) did not stop the war and did not deter further crimes during the last two years of the war – nor was it expected to do so. In fact, 'one of the worst crimes took place in Srebrenica in July 1995, even after indictments had been issued against the Bosnian Serb political and military leaders ... Nor did the existence of the ICTY deter or prevent the commission of crimes in Kosovo in 1988–89'.[42] Skeptics have offered other sobering assessments of the legalistic approach to peacebuilding or human security.[43] Some have ridiculed the belief that genocide is deterred through such legal arrangements.[44] War crime tribunals have a limited utility 'for stopping wars and making peace'. Moreover, 'the belief in war crimes tribunals as a magic-bullet technique for deterring and stopping wars and making peace is unfounded'.[45] The argument that the pursuit of criminal justice deters future atrocities, genocide, or crimes against humanity overlooks the fact such deterrence appears to be largely ineffective. These criminal activities tend to take place in failing or failed states, where political leaders become obsessed with their regime security. 'Ethnic cleansing' has taken place in structurally fragile states such as Sudan; and some regard the ongoing atrocities in Darfur to be the first instance of genocide of the twenty-first century. Caught in this desperate life-and-death situation, political and military leaders care little for what the International Criminal Court (ICC) or *ad hoc* international criminal tribunals would think of them, or might do to them. Jean-Marie Guéhenno, Under-Secretary-General of the UN Department of Peace-keeping Operations, wisely notes that 'non-state actors would not necessarily care about international opinion, or feel obliged to respect international convention and norms'.[46] The reason they do not care is not simply that they are 'evil', but rather that their national, regime or personal survival may be at stake.

Some historians, political scientists, and even lawyers remain unconvinced that the relentless pursuit of international criminal justice serves as the most effective way to build peace or help consolidate democracy in postconflict societies. A long time ago, E. H. Carr attacked the 'fallacy of legalism', for good reason.[47] John Bolton, who attended the Law School at Yale University and served as a former Assistant Secretary of State in the Bush Administration and a former US ambassador to the United Nations, criticizes 'the global prosecutors' who 'hunt war criminals in the name of utopia'.[48] According to Robert Tucker, 'Politics, which deal with issues of power and force, must precede law. Advocates of the court err in confusing law with politics and in expecting from a court results, whether remedial or deterrent, that at best can only be the consequences of a functioning political order.'[49] Jack Snyder and Leslie Vinjamuri also make a forceful argument that lends further support to the Cambodia case: 'Trials do little to deter further violence and are not highly correlated with the consolidation of peaceful democracy'.[50] Furthermore: 'Justice does not lead; it follows'. In their view, 'a norm-governed political order must be based on a political bargain among contending groups and on the creation of robust administrative institutions that can predictably enforce the law'.[51]

We should not, however, reject the idea of human security through criminal justice. When prospects for renewed violence or war diminish, as the case of Cambodia shows, actions should be taken to prosecute criminal leaders. However, greater attention must be placed on the need to reform national military, security, judicial and legal institutions than on the need to heal old wounds, which can be reopened and rendered more painful. How such efforts can contribute to institution-building is unclear. The ruling party in Cambodia, for instance, seems more determined than ever to consolidate power by preventing the judiciary from becoming highly institutionalized.

The fourth proposition is that democracy-building promotes human security. Democratic institutions are not ends in themselves; they are means to promote human security. Political intervention through democracy-building seems more promising than any of the other propositions discussed above, if actors can collectively engage in the process of democratic institution-building. Recent work lends support to my early thesis that liberal democracy helps bring peace to wartorn societies, but its seeds should not be planted in fragile states without being sensitive to the insecurity dilemma, or without adequate means of protection put in place. Edward Newman, Oliver Richmond and their associates get it right when they argue for the need for serious attention at the initial stage of the peace process,[52] where a just and inclusive process is a critical prerequisite 'to limit the power of spoiling and extremist violence'[53] and to reduce opportunities for spoilers to undermine peace,[54] 'neutralizing' the political environment to prevent aggression[55] and refraining from the use of force that tends to undermine confidence-building efforts.[56] They also correctly warn that third-party helpers may become spoilers themselves when allocating resources, offering recognition, or playing favorites among the antagonistic forces, and when they overlook the need to coordinate their peace activities. Roland Paris properly stresses the need to build institutions in extremely fragile states, but the 'institutionalization before liberalization' he proposes tends to threaten the security of those who rely on undemocratic institutions such as armed forces, militias, politicized judges and lawyers. Unless liberalization and institutionalization go hand in hand to enhance human security, little institution-building is possible.

The fifth proposition is that economic intervention helps promote human security in general, and democracy in particular. Economic development should not be confused with human security, but it should be recognized as an effective method for human security promotion. First, Japan demonstrates that capitalism need not result in excessive militarism.[57] Second, development can help prevent terrorism, which tends to flourish in impoverished conditions, as noted earlier. Economically developed countries may not be free from the threat of terrorism, but they can better afford the means to defend themselves and can enforce the law more effectively than poor states. Security doctrines and the current rules and structure of the global economy can still be reformed in such a way that they become less power-based and state-centric, and more people-centered.[58] Third, economic reconstruction helps normalize daily life in wartorn countries and reduce the extreme poverty that kills or damages those left without the means of survival. Timor-Leste remains politically unstable, as the assassination attempts on the lives of its leaders on 11 February 2008 have shown. It remains one of the world's poorest countries, with an unemployment rate of over 80 per cent. Other Southeast Asian experiences lend further empirical support to these three economic factors. Social exclusion or marginalization and extreme poverty in resource-rich but less-developed regions (such as Mindanao of the Philippines, Aceh of Indonesia, and southern Thailand) have perpetuated secessionist struggles, given rise to authoritarianism, and destabilized nascent democratic states (for example, Thailand and the Philippines).[59] Additional evidence shows that more equitable economic development helps sustain democratization and consolidate democratic gains, thus preventing armed conflict from recurring.[60]

How exactly economic development can be achieved in a more equitable manner is open to further debate. A welfare system, as some critical theorists strongly advocate, may prove helpful, and international actors should do more to provide support for this policy, but more attention must be paid toward economic institution-building. Economic institutions are not ends in themselves, but they are means for human security. Without effective institutions in the economic field, a national welfare system is impossible, adequate taxes cannot be collected, and more equitable distribution of wealth cannot be ensured. History provides little comfort to those who wish international donors would provide more welfare support to the poor anywhere. Even if they are willing, they may never be able to provide a sufficient amount for a sustainable period.

The next question is whether political democracy and more equitable economic development should be promoted in sequence or simultaneously. The East Asian way seems to prefer developmental statism, with little sympathy for democratization; however, without democratization, economic development tends to benefit only a minority of rich and powerful individuals. Without democratization, economic development is bound to stay fragile, as Indonesia showed in 1997. East Asians have been wise in recognizing the virtue of economic development as a method for human security, but would be wiser still if they were to recognize the limits of developmental statism. Westerners have been wise in recognizing the urgent need for coercive intervention on behalf of humanity, but would be wiser still if they also considered East Asian economic perspectives more often.

Effectively harnessing actors' interests to human security objectives remains a daunting task, but together peacekeeping, democratic institution-building and more equitable development may serve as the best recipe for human security, largely because they seem to encourage more global collaborative action.

Notes

Introduction

1 MacFarlane and Khong 2006: chapter 1, especially 26–27.
2 Thakur 2006: 75–76.
3 MacFarlane and Khong 2006: 59–60.
4 Waltz 2000: 5–41; Mearsheimer 1998b, 2001.
5 Human Security Centre 2005: 23.
6 Van Evera 1998: 92.
7 Kaufmann 1996; Mearsheimer and Van Evera 1995: 16–18, 21; Mearsheimer and Pape 1993: 22–25, 28.
8 Betts 1994.
9 *Christian Science Monitor*, 9 February 1993: 19; Mearsheimer 1998a.
10 Walt 2001/02: 69.
11 Morgenthau 1993: 120.
12 Human Security Centre 2005: 150–51.
13 *Ibid.*: 10.
14 Barnett *et al.* 2007: 35.
15 Morgenthau 1993: 122.
16 Nye 2003: 169.
17 McKenzie 2001; Alagappa 1997; MacFarlane and Weiss 1994; Peou 1998d.
18 Carey and Richmond 2003a.
19 Wheeler 2000.
20 Paris 2001b.
21 See Bell 1996; Bauer and Bell 1999.
22 Acharya 2001a.
23 Acharya 2002: 378.
24 MacFarlane and Khong 2006: 159.
25 Alagappa 1998: 68.
26 It may be interesting to note that the Chinese norm of hierarchy (manifest in its claim to higher culture and universal kingship) was undermined by the Qing dynasty's internal weakness, the rise of Japan as a great power, and the Western powers' rejection of Chinese cultural superiority. Since the end of colonial rule after World War II, Asian states have adopted and defended the Westphalian norm of absolute state sovereignty and resisted any new norms that challenge the traditional statist norm.
27 Alagappa 1998: 68.
28 Ayoob 2004: 106.
29 Berger 1998.
30 Lee 2003.

31 Non-democratic states such as Burma and North Korea, for instance, are opposed to the idea of human security; on the contrary, democratic countries such as Japan, South Korea and Thailand tend to support and promote the idea.
32 On this, I am sympathetic toward Pettman 2005.
33 Tow and Trood 2000: 28.
34 Tow and Trood 2000: 29.
35 Tow and Trood 2000: 14.
36 Sil 2000a, 2000b.
37 Johnson 2002.
38 The literature pays much attention to Japan's policy commitment to non-military security issues. See, for instance, Lam 2006; Kikkawa 2007.
39 A comment he made at the Sentosa Roundtable on Asian Security (17–18 January 2008, organized by the S. Ratjaratnam School of International Studies, Singapore).
40 Tow *et al.* 2000.
41 On Japan's collective capitalism as opposed to the US's managerial capitalism, see Gilpin 2003. On Japan's equitable economic growth, see Kabashima and MacDougal 1999.

1 Critical challenges for globalism in human security studies

1 Keohane and Nye 1977: 229.
2 Buzan, 1991.
3 Kegley 1993.
4 Claude 1966: 110 (italics original).
5 Van Evera 1998: 92.
6 Keohane and Nye 1977: 246.
7 See Peou 2002b, 2008.
8 UNDP 2002: 2.
9 Booth 1991: 313–26; Smith 1991: 325–39.
10 UNDP 1994: 4, 23.
11 Commission on Global Governance 1995: 81.
12 Axworthy 1998: 11.
13 MacFarlane and Khong 2006: ch.6.
14 Walt 1991: 212.
15 Posen 2001.
16 Posen 1993.
17 Canadian Department of Foreign Affairs and International Trade 2000.
18 UNDP 1994; Commission on Human Security 2003.]
19 Commission on Human Security 2003; Ogata and Cels 2003; Thomas 2000.
20 Gasper 2005: 238–39.
21 Booth 1991: 319.
22 UNDP 1994: 23.
23 Kim and Hyun 2000: 39.
24 Commission on Human Security 2003: 4; on 'human dignity' see also Thomas and Wilkin 1999; Tadjbakhsh and Chenoy 2007: chapter 5.
25 Human Security Centre 2005.
26 *Ibid.*: 86, 87.
27 Thomas and Wilkin 1999: 3.
28 Sucharithanarugse 2000: 58.
29 Thomas and Tow 2002b: 181.
30 UNDP 1994: iii.
31 Annan 1999b.
32 MacFarlane and Khong 2006: 243–53.

33 Morgenthau 1993: 10–23.
34 Human Security Centre 2005: viii.
35 See for instance Friedberg 1991: 275–76; Krasner 1983.
36 Sachs 2005: 1.
37 Claude 1966: 6.
38 Kupchan and Kupchan 1991: 119.
39 Kupchan and Kupchan 1998: 399–400.
40 Human Security Centre 2005: viii.
41 ICISS 2001a: 15.
42 Galtung 1975: 282–304.
43 Fore detailed studies on the Law of War, see Detter 2000; Roberts and Guelff 2000; Guttman *et al.* 1999; Bouchet-Saulnier 2002.
44 Nye 2003: 156–57.
45 See Goulding 1993: 451–64; Berdal 1996; Adekanye 1997: 359–66.
46 Human Security Centre 2005: 9, 155.
47 Kumar 1998; Cousens and Kumar 2001.
48 Bassiouni 1996, 1999: 5–810.
49 Pugh 1995: 320–46; Goodhand and Atkinson 2001.
50 Buzan 1991: 57–111.
51 Kupchan and Kupchan 1998.
52 See Miller 2001.
53 *Ibid.*: 250.
54 UNDP, 1994: 39.
55 ICISS 2001a: 13.
56 *Ibid.*: 17.
57 Elaraby 1986: 1–42.
58 Alagappa 1997: 421–41; Knight 1996: 31–52.
59 McKenzie 2001: 151, 153.
60 UNDP 2002: 5.
61 Ottaway and Carothers 2002.
62 Korey 2001.
63 Washburn 1996: 91.
64 International Peace Academy 1992: 4.
65 Holsti 1986: 356.
66 This study draws inspiration from the concept of collaborative/collective human security coined by Sorpong Peou. See Peou 2002a, 2005.
67 See Wolfers 1962: 181–82.
68 Harris 1993: 273.
69 Hampson *et al.* 2002: 38–61.
70 Keohane 1989: 159.
71 *Ibid.*
72 Cited by Richmond 2003: 5.
73 Tadjbakhsh and Chenoy 2007: 240–41.
74 Richmond 2003: 6.
75 *Ibid.*
76 Vincent 1987.
77 Axworthy 1998: 20–21.
78 Walt 2001/02: 76.
79 Annan 1998: 130, 133.
80 Joyner 1999: 333.
81 White 2002: 173; on the General Assembly's role in elections and democratization, see *ibid.*: 180–82.
82 Peou 2002a: 51–68.

83 UN News Service, 28 April 2006.
84 White 2002: 102.
85 McKenzie 2001; MacFarlane and Weiss 1994: 277–95.
86 Alger 2002: 95.
87 Willetts 2000: 191–212.
88 Alger 2002: 101; see also MacFarlane and Weiss 1994: especially 289–90.
89 Smith 2002: 175.
90 Thakur 2006: 111.
91 *Ibid.*: 6.
92 *Ibid.*
93 Ottaway 2001: 266.
94 White 2002: 286, 288.
95 Bergeson and Lunde 1999: 146.
96 Welsh 2002: 503–21.
97 Thakur 2006: 252.
98 Knudsen 1996: 146–65.
99 Wheeler and Morris 1996: 160.
100 *Globe and Mail*, 28 December 2004: A13.
101 Kurth 2005: 88.
102 *Ibid.*: 93–94.
103 Ruggie 2003: 302–3.
104 *Ibid.*: 307.
105 Thakur 2006: 368, 369.
106 *Ibid.*: 369.
107 See for instance Newman 1999–2000: 213–41.
108 Richmond 2003: 2.
109 Ottaway 2001: 265–92.
110 Corpwatch 2000.
111 Kurth 2005: 101.
112 Barnett *et al.* 2007: 36.
113 Richmond 2003: 1.
114 Hampson *et al.* 2002: Ch. 9.
115 Paris 2001b: 90.
116 Barnett *et al.* 2007: 44.
117 Keating and Knight 2006: xiii.
118 Samuels 2007: 107.
119 Cited by *ibid.*: 92.
120 Schweller 2000: 61.
121 Finnemore 1996: 30.
122 Thakur 2006: 84.
123 *Ibid.*: 367–68.
124 Paris 2001a: 100.

2 The western roots of human security

1 UNDP 1994: 24.
2 Tadjbaksh 2005: 10.
3 ICISS 2001a, 2001b; United Nations 2004
4 MacFarlane and Khong 2006: 10.
5 See, among many, Alkire 2003; Rothschild 1995.
6 For a particularly insightful contribution that raises many such questions, see Tadjbaksh 2005.
7 For more on this see Richmond 2005.

8 Ponzio, 2005: 69.
9 Tadjbaksh 2005: 39.
10 MacFarlane and Khong 2006: 30–33.
11 *Ibid.*: 33.
12 *Ibid.*
13 Hobbes 1998 [1651].
14 Locke 1980 [1689].
15 MacFarlane and Khong 2006: 40.
16 Chesterman 2003: 241–42.
17 Rousseau 1998 [1762].
18 MacFarlane and Khong 2006: 23–29.
19 Brown 2002: 42.
20 *Ibid.*
21 *Ibid.*: 43.
22 Kagan 2003: 58.
23 Doyle 1983a: 205–35; 1983b: 323–53; Mandelbaum 2003.
24 Brown 2002: 30.
25 *Ibid.*: 48.
26 *Ibid.*: 26.
27 *Ibid.*: 38.
28 For more detail on these movements see Young 1987.
29 For a fascinating account of Edmund Morel's campaign against slave labour in the Congo see Hochschild 1999.
30 Rieff 2002: 58.
31 *Ibid.*: 59.
32 Seymour 1928: 51, cited by Fromkin 1989: 253.
33 Link *et al.* 1983: 525.
34 Woodrow Wilson, Address to the Senate, 12 January 1917, in *ibid.*: 536–37.
35 *Ibid.*: 525.
36 Nicolson 1928.
37 Seymour 1928: 323–39.
38 MacFarlane and Khong 2006: 53–57.
39 Williams 1998: 79.
40 For more on this see *ibid.*: 127–33.
41 Rieff 2002: 175.
42 Williams 1998: 178 (citing Hankey).
43 Bell 2003: 161.
44 Barash 2000: 149.
45 Brown 2002: 118.
46 *Ibid.*: 18; see also Ignatieff 2002.
47 Brown 2002: 119.
48 Cited by *ibid.*: 122.
49 *Ibid.*: 123.
50 *Ibid.*: 13; Onara O'Neill is associated with this notion of duties.
51 Rieff 2002: 79.
52 *Ibid.*: 80.
53 *Ibid.*: 81.
54 Wheeler 2000.
55 Brown 2002: 145.
56 *Ibid.*
57 Terry 2002: 218–19.
58 See, among others, UNDP 1994: Paris 2001b; Khong 2001.
59 Miall *et al.* 1999: 22.

60 Duffield 1997.
61 Boutros-Ghali 1992: para. 55.
62 Duffield 1997.
63 Rieff 2002: 67.
64 Josselin and Wallace 2001: 11–13.
65 *Ibid.*: 16.
66 Anderson 1999.
67 Josselin and Wallace 2001: 253.
68 *General Assembly Resolution 43/131*, 8 December 1988; *General Assembly Resolution 45/100*, 14 December 1990; *General Assembly Resolution 46/182*, 19 December 1991.
69 Ramsbotham and Woodhouse 1996: 84.
70 Willetts 2000: 206.
71 See Khong 2001.
72 Scholte 2000: 6.
73 Williamson 1999.
74 Soros 1998.
75 Paris 2001b; Khong 2001.
76 Ponzio 2005: 69.
77 Thomas and Wilkin 1999: 3.
78 See for example Bellamy and MacDonald 2002.

3 East versus West? Debate and convergence on human security

1 This chapter is based on a paper that the author prepared for the Global Strategic Review 2007, organized by the International Institute for Strategic Studies, 7–9 September 2007, Geneva.
2 Sato 1999: 7–8.
3 Commission on Human Security 2003: 5; Stares 1998: 11–16.
4 Caballero-Anthony and Emmers 2006: 1–112. Also see Obama 2007: 2–16.
5 Friedman 2006.
6 *Ibid.*: 463.
7 Commission on Human Security 2003.
8 Refer to Human Security Centre 2005, Section IV: Freedom to Live in Dignity: 127–52.
9 Human Security Centre 2005: viii.
10 United Nations General Assembly 2005 A/ReS/60/1: para. 143. http://unpan1.un.org/intradoc/groups/public/documents/UN/UNPAN021752.pdf
11 Shinoda and Uesugi 2005: 291.
12 Government of Japan 2003.
13 Obama 2007: 2–16.
14 Missiroli 2006: 5.
15 Ferrero-Waldner 2005: 6.
16 Based on the author's interview with Mr Tadashi Yamamoto, President of Japan Center for International Exchange, on 20 May 2007.
17 Obuchi 1998a.
18 Obuchi 1998b.
19 Caballero-Anthony and Emmers 2006: 1.
20 Wang 2006: 58–81.
21 Acharya 2006: 239.
22 Kotsopoulos 2006: 11.
23 Based on the author's interview with Canadian officials in July 2007.
24 Commission on Human Security 2003.
25 Council for the Promotion of Cultural Diplomacy 2004: 3.

26 Ministry of Foreign Affairs of Japan 2007.
27 ASEAN Eminent Persons Group 2000.
28 ASEAN 2001.
29 ASEAN 2004a.
30 East Asia Vision Group 2001.
31 ASEAN+3 Summit 2002.
32 ASEAN 2004b.
33 ASEAN Regional Forum 2005.
34 APEC 2003.
35 ASEAN 2003.

4 Southeast Asia's points of convergence on international intervention

1 MacFarlane 2002: 15.
2 See for example Buchanan 2003; Finnemore 2003.
3 Annan 2000.
4 Annan 1999a.
5 Vincent 1974: 13.
6 Jackson 1993: 581.
7 Walzer 1996.
8 Higgins 1984: 34–35.
9 Holzgrefe 2003: 18 (italics added).
10 See discussions by Wheeler and Bellamy 2001: 470–93.
11 Chris Brown, cited by Wheeler and Bellamy 2001: 474.
12 Holzgrefe 2003: 30.
13 Weiss 2004.
14 Finnemore 2003: 56.
15 *Ibid.*: 55.
16 Weiss 2004: 137.
17 See for example Watanabe 2003.
18 For a more detailed discussion on how security concepts and processes have taken place in the region among different state and non-state actors, see Caballero-Anthony 2004b.
19 The appeal is reflected in the way countries such as Japan have used human security as one of the pillars of their foreign policy, and also in the use of this concept in many official statements from the region (e.g. Thailand, Indonesia and the Philippines). See also Caballero-Anthony 2004b.
20 See Canadian Department of Foreign Affairs and International Trade 2000.
21 See UNDP 1994.
22 This has been a subject of much debate since governments in the region did not raise concerns about what was happening in Cambodia prior to the Vietnamese occupation, when arguably it was during the Pol Pot regime when cases of genocide, mass torture and violence occurred in Cambodia. See, among others, Chanda 1986; Peou 1997; Chandler 2000.
23 For a more recent study on the UN Peace Operations in Cambodia, see Peou 2005.
24 For a detailed account of ASEAN's initiatives in getting Cambodia to agree to its terms to restore political stability in the country, see Jarasa 1999: 209–14.
25 For more detailed discussion on the East Timor crisis, see Martin 2001. See also Sebastian and Smith 2000.
26 See Severino 2000.
27 See Acharya 2002.
28 Cited by Byers and Chesterman 2003: 202.
29 The usage of the term track I usually refers to official diplomacy between government officials, while track II refers to non-official activities that usually include epistemic

communities and government officials participating in their personal capacity. For more discussion on the role of track II institutions in East Asia, see Caballero-Anthony 2005: 157–93.

30 See Summary of Discussions of the Seventh Meeting of the CSCAP Working Group on Comprehensive and Cooperative Security in Dickens and Wilson-Roberts 2000.

31 While CSCAP is widely regarded as a non-official, track II organization, its member-state representatives in the 17-member body are also drawn from official circles, albeit participating in CSCAP meetings in their private capacities.

32 The ASEAN People's Assembly (APA) was first convened in 2000 in Batam, Indonesia. Following its success, subsequent meetings were held in Bali in 2002 and Manila in 2003. The fourth (latest) meeting was again held in Manila in May 2005. APA has been considered as the main vehicle for NGOs and other civil society groups in the region to discuss more people-oriented issues and problems in ASEAN, and serves as an important springboard to channel track II policies that could be adopted by governments in the region.

33 See APA 2003a.

34 APA 2001, 2003a.

35 APA 2003b.

36 Morada 2006.

37 For more on the genesis of APA, see Caballero-Anthony 2004a.

38 United Nations 2004.

39 Caballero-Anthony 2005.

40 See for example Banerjee 2005: 15–27.

41 See Caballero-Anthony 2005.

42 *Jakarta Post*, 16 June 2003.

43 See the *Declaration of the ASEAN Concord II (Bali Concord II)*, www.aseansec.org/15160.htm; and *Vientiane Action Programme*, www.aseansec.org./VAP-10thASEANSummit.pdf

44 'Indonesia Proposes Southeast Asian Peacekeeping Force', 21 February 2004, www.aseansec.org/afp/20p.htm

45 *The Straits Times* (Singapore), 8 March 2004.

46 Martin and Mayer-Rieckh 2005: 118.

47 ASEAN 2006: 6.

5 Human Security *in extremis*: East Asian reactions to the responsibility to protect

1 This is an extension of the argument developed in my earlier essay, Evans 2004.

2 Usage of the phrase is increasing in absolute but not relative terms. A Google search assessing the frequency of different adjectives for modifying security (e.g. national security, regime security, comprehensive security, cooperative security, homeland security) in English-language sources in 2002 revealed that less than 0.3 per cent of the references (about 130,000) were to 'human security'. By 2008 that number had increased too about 577,000, but that was still only about 0.5 per cent of total references.

3 A 2007 survey of Canadian academics listed more that 230 at 36 universities who self-identified as having a research or teaching interest in the area of human security. The list and a selection of syllabuses from courses they offer is available online at www.humansecurity.info. Even in Canada, its hold is in question, at least at the political level. A new Conservative government has disavowed the phrase "human security" and unravelled some of the international agenda that was build around it under the previous Liberal government.

4 Christensen 1996: 37.

5 Buzan 2001; Ignatieff 1998; Bain 1999; Luttwak 1999; Paris 2001b: 102.

6 Capie and Evans 2007: 135–44.
7 It also appears to be something of a syndrome or value signifier. A person interested in human security is also probably ambivalent about globalization, liberalization and unfettered markets; committed to international development and more equal distribution of resources; uses terms such as 'social justice' and 'root causes'; supports multilateral institutions including the United Nations, International Criminal Court and the new diplomacy of 'coalitions of the willing' (in the sense used in the antipersonnel landmines campaign, not the war in Iraq); and apoplectic about American unilateralism and exceptionalism.
8 ICISS 2001b.
9 *Ibid.*: 15.
10 *Ibid.*
11 *Ibid.*
12 Mack 2003: 5.
13 Commission on Human Security 2003: 4.
14 Acharya 2001a: 459.
15 Song 2002.
16 Ayoob 2004: 110–14.
17 Chen 1995; JCIE 1999a, 1999b, 2002.
18 It is instructive that of the roughly 60 papers completed between 1999 and 2002 by authors in Northeast Asia, Southeast Asia and South Asia in the first phase of a Ford Foundation research and conference project on non-traditional and human security, only seven dealt directly with issues of violence and intervention. And only ten paid attention to non-state actors as policy players and not just the targets of policy. See Khan 2001; Chari 2001; Zhang 2001; Tan and Boutin 2001; Capie and Evans 2007: 173–78.
19 Acharya 2001a: 444–51.
20 Thiparat 2001: 62.
21 Caballero-Anthony 2002.
22 Thiparat 2001.
23 Lee 2003.
24 Lizée 2002: 509.
25 *Ibid.*: 513.
26 JCIE undated.
27 McRae and Hubert 2001.
28 United Nations 2004.
29 2005 World Summit Outcome (A/RES/60/1), (New York: UN.A/60L.1, September 2005), especially paragraphs 138 and 139. http://unpan1.un.org/intradoc/groups/public/documents/UN/UNPAN021752.pdf
30 UN Security Council, S/RES/1674, 28 April 2006. www.un.org/Docs/sc/unsc_resolutions06.htm
31 *New York Times*, 20 January 2008: 11.
32 Mohanty 2002.
33 Thakur 2003.
34 Acharya 2002: 379; McDougall 2001: 169.
35 Ministry of Foreign Affairs, Government of China 2002.
36 Cited by Thakur 2006: 268.
37 Chu 2000.
38 Cai 2008.
39 ICISS 2001a; Mao 2002.
40 Cited by Ayoob 2004: 108.
41 Chu 2002: 25.
42 Carlson 2002: 32, 29.
43 *International Herald Tribune*, 24 August 2006: 6.

44 Thakur 2006: 286; Position Paper of the People's Republic of China on the United Nations Reforms (Beijing, 7 June 2005), Part III.1, 'Responsibility to Protect'. http://au.china-embassy.org/eng/xw/t199208.htm
45 Speech delivered by Assistant Foreign Minister Cui Tiankai at the Opening Ceremony of China–Norway Peacekeeping Workshop, 26 March 2007.
46 Associated Press, 22 June 2007.

6 East Asian states' collaborative action in UN peace operations for East Timor

1 Chalk 2001; Ishizuka 2004: 271–85; Wheeler and Dunne 2001: 805–27; Cotton 1999: 237–46; Cotton 2004; Dickens 2002; Bell 2000; Maley 2000; Salla 1995.
2 Sado 2005; Gorjão 2002; Nevins 2002.
3 The only exceptions are Dupont 2000; Sado 2005.
4 *New York Times*, 2 August 1974: 1, 26; *New York Times*, 19 October 1974: 2.
5 *Agence France Presse*, 21 January 2002; de Magalhaes 1990: 56.
6 de Magalhaes 1990: 35–38.
7 Kammen 1999: 64.
8 de Magalhaes 1990: 50.
9 Senate Standing Committee on Foreign Affairs and Defense of Australia 1983.
10 Hainsworth 2000: 5.
11 Tiffen 2001: 55.
12 Gunn 1999.
13 *Ibid.*; van Klinken 1998; Tiffen 2001: 55.
14 Greenlees and Garran 2003: ch. 7; Bartu 2000: 81–98.
15 About the increased killing before the ballot, see Greenlees and Garran 2003: ch. 3.
16 *Antara*, 12 June 1999; Fischer 2000: 25; Samuel 2003: 197–230; Martin and Mayer-Rieckh 2005: 125–45 Martin 2001: 70–73.
17 Cotton 2004: 86–87.
18 *The Evening Post*, 8 September 1999: 1.
19 *The Statesman*, 6 September 1999; *United Press International*, 6 September 1999.
20 D. Nason, *The Australian*, 25 February 2005; H. Paterson, *Associated Press Online*, 23 February 2000; United Nations Department of Public Information 2002.
21 *The Australian*, 30 March 2007; Shuto 2004: 39.
22 *Wall Street Journal*, 10 September 1999.
23 Tiffen 2001: 68; S. Pristel, *The Australian*, 28 October 1999: 9.
24 *Agence France Presse*, 18 October 1999; *The Independent*, 23 September 1999.
25 *Japan Economic Newswire*, 16 October 1999.
26 *Associated Press*, 23 February 2000.
27 Smith and Dee 2003: 187–93; *Agence France Presse*, 13 November 2000; D. Nason, *The Australian*, 25 February 2005.
28 *The Irish Times*, 7 April 2007; *The Guardian*, 14 August 2007.
29 UN Documents A/RES/3485, 12 December 1975; A/RES/31/53, 1 December 1976; A/RES/32/34, 28 November 1977; A/RES/33/39, 13 December 1978; A/RES/34/40, 21 November 1979; A/RES/35/27, 11 November 1980; A/RES/36/50, 24 November 1981; A/RES/37/30, 23 November 1982.
30 'Voting Behaviour in the United Nations Concerning the General Assembly Resolutions on the Situation in East Timor between 1975 and 1982', in Krieger 1997: 129–33.
31 UN Documents A/RES/3485 (12 December 1975) and S/RES/384 (22 December 1975).
32 *The Straits Times*, 28 October 1992; 30 October 1992; 10 November 1992; 11 November 1992; 25 December 1992.
33 *Jakarta Post*, 26 December 1996; *Deutsche Presse-Agentur*, 30 November 1996.
34 *The Economist*, November 1996.

35 Ministry of Foreign Affairs of Japan 1999a; Martin 2001: 109; *Japan Economic Newswire*, 6 July 1999; *The Jakarta Post*, 30 July 1999; *Japan Economic Newswire*, 27 August 1999.
36 Martin 2001: 111–12.
37 *Asia Plus*, 9 September 1999.
38 Walton 2004: 240.
39 Ministry of Foreign Affairs of Japan 1999b.
40 *The Straits Times*, 18 October 1999; *Wall Street Journal*, 1 October 1999.
41 *The Daily Telegraph*, 15 September 1999: 28.
42 Sado 2005: 10.
43 *Financial Times*, 14 September 1999.
44 *Korea Times*, 21 September 1999; Cotton 2004: 72–73.
45 Gorjão 2002: 761.
46 Ministry of Foreign Affairs of Japan 1999c.
47 Sado 2005: 7.
48 Cotton 2004: 83.
49 *Japan Economic Newswire*, 14 September 1999.
50 Mak 1999: 102, 108; Cotton 2004: 72.
51 *Jiji Press Ticker Service*, 15 January 2000.
52 *Deutsche Press – Agentur*, 28 October 1999.
53 *Agence France Presse*, 26 October 1999; *Xinhua News Agency*, 21 October 1999.
54 *BBC Monitoring Asia–Pacific*, 11 January 1999; *Japan Economic Newswire*, 4 November 1999.
55 *Malaysia General News*, 30 December 1999.
56 K. Chongkittavorn, *The Nation*, 11 October 1999.
57 *Deutsche Press–Agentur*, 28 October 1999.
58 *BBC Monitoring Asia Pacific*, 1 May 2000.
59 *Japan Economic Newswire*, 4 February 2002.
60 Hijikata *Sekai Shuho*, 28 October 1975: 44–46; Omura 1986: 10–11.
61 Krieger 1997: 129.
62 JETRO 1999; Newman and Kopras 1999.
63 Jardine 1992.
64 *Korea Times*, 21 September 1999; Cotton 2004: 72–73.
65 *International Herald Tribune*, 21 August 1998: 8.
66 Watanabe 1999.
67 Dupont 2000: 165.
68 *The Straits Times*, 26 May 1994.
69 UN Document S/PV/4043, 11 September 1999. About China's policy on intervention, see Gill and Reilly 2000: 41–60; Carlson 2004: 9–27; Jin 2000: 55–58.
70 Simpson 2005: 281–315; Moynihan 1978: 247; Budiardjo and Soei 1984: 8–10; Tayler 1991: 84, 134; Nairn 2000: 43–48.
71 This resolution was passed every year between 1975 and 1982. The USA abstained in 1975 and voted for the support of Indonesia every year from 1976: Hartung and Washburn 1997; Krieger 1997: 133; Scheiner 2000: 119.
72 Monk 2000; *The Sydney Morning Herald*, 12 September 2000, 14 September 2000; *The Age*, 14 September 2000, 20 December 2000; Ishizuka 2004: 275; Simpson 2005: 281–315; Krieger 1997: 333.
73 Jardine 1992; it was incorporated in the HR5368 Foreign Operations, Export Financing, and Related Programs Appropriations Act, 1993.
74 It was incorporated in the HR2295 Foreign Operations, Export Financing, and Related Programs Appropriations Act, 1994.
75 Scheiner 2000: 122–24.
76 HR4328 The Omnibus Consolidated and Emergency Appropriations Act, 1998.

77 Chalk 2001: 40–41; Tiffen 2001: 56.
78 Tiffen 2001: 56; Fischer 2000: 9–18.
79 *BBC Summary of World Broadcasts*, 7 April 1999.
80 Martin 2001: 32.
81 Samuel 2003; Martin and Mayer-Rieckh 2005.
82 *Financial Times*, 13 September 1999: 8.
83 *IPS – Inter Press Service*, 7 September 1999.
84 These actions were controversial, and Australia, along with East Asian countries, opposed such actions: at the time of Indonesian recovery from the Asian Financial Crisis, the suspension of International Monetary Fund and World Bank loans could have destabilized not only the Indonesian economy, but also the entire East Asian regional economy. *Financial Times*, 13 September 1999: 8.
85 Office of the Press Secretary, The White House 1999.
86 Cotton 2004: 82–83.
87 *Ibid.*: 83; *The Hindu*, 10 September 1999.
88 *International Herald Tribune*, 27 September 1999; *Australian Financial Review*, 2 October 1999; Snyder 2006: 327; Jain 2007: 26–41; *Courier Mail*, 18 September 1999.
89 *International Herald Tribune*, 27 September 1999.
90 Caballero-Anthony 1998; Thambipillai 1985; Acharya 2001b: 28. On criticisms of the ASEAN Way see Narine 1997; Moller 1998; Henderson 1999.

7 The limits of collaborative action on criminal justice in East Asia

1 See Kerr 2001.
2 Dickinson 2003: 295–310.
3 Smith 2002: 184.
4 *Ibid.*: 185.
5 *Ibid.*: 184.
6 Hampson *et al.* 2002: 65.
7 *Ibid.*: 66.
8 Kerr 2001: 126.
9 Bassiouni 1999: 796.
10 Feher 2000: 85.
11 Akhavan 1999a.
12 *Ibid.*: 9.
13 Kerr 2001: 129.
14 Bassiouni 1999: 808.
15 Akhavan 1999a; Yacoubian 1999.
16 Kerr 2001: 129.
17 Akhavan 1999a: 7.
18 Watt 1998: 2.
19 Wippman 1999–2000: 474.
20 Thakur 2006: 132.
21 Railsback 1989–90: 457–81.
22 Roht-Arriaza 1999: 484.
23 Goldstone 1995: 607–21.
24 Akhavan 1999b.
25 Akhavan 1999a: 12.
26 *Ibid.*: 13.
27 Roberts 1998: 272.
28 Kerr 2001: 121.
29 Roht-Arriaza 1999: 474–75.
30 Economides 2003: 38.

31 Human Rights Watch 1999b: 5.
32 Economides 2003: 41.
33 Roht-Arriaza 1999: 491.
34 Roberts 1998: 273, 274.
35 UN Integrated Mission in Timor-Leste, 'Report on human rights development in Timor-Leste: August 2006–August 2007': 27.
36 CIJ and OSJI 2004: 1.
37 Human Rights Watch 2003: 1.
38 Open Society Institute 2007: 7.
39 Dickinson 2003: 310.
40 Human Rights Watch 2002a.
41 In October 2001, three international judges for the Special Panels and two for the Court of Appeal were present, but the situation deteriorated in September 2002, when one international judge and both Appeal Court judges left. The problem is, 'Neither the Special Panels ... nor the *ad hoc* tribunal in Jakarta are providing any answer to the problems of bringing the perpetrators of crimes committed in 1999 to justice' and the 'UN has shown little commitment to ensuring that the Special Panels in Dili are adequately resourced' (de Bertodano 2003: 236).
42 Zwanenburg 1999: 124–43.
43 Watt 1998: 6.
44 Kiernan 1993; Railsback 1989–90; Hawk 1988; Heder 2002.
45 JSMP 2004.
46 *Ibid.*: 11.
47 See Amnesty International and JSMP 2004.
48 Call by Cambodian NGOs for Trials of Khmer Rouge (13 November 1998), cited in United Nations 1999: 29.
49 Hammarberg undated: 7.
50 Chang 2002: 2.
51 J. Jeldres, *The Bangkok Post*, 26 February 2002.
52 *The Cambodia Daily*, 5 November 2002: 1, 18.
53 *The Cambodia Daily*, 4 November 2002: 29.
54 *Ibid.*: 52.
55 President Gloria Macapagal Arroyo, for instance, commented as follows: 'As a leader of a democratic country, I feel that all countries are ready for democracy. But whether I would interfere and impose my values on another country outside the UN system is another thing. ASEAN has different cultures, different political systems, different histories, different religions, different social organizations. And one country cannot impose its system on another.' *The Cambodia Daily*, 4 November 2002: 26.
56 Human Rights Watch 2002b: 4.
57 Human Rights Watch 1999c.
58 Ziauddin 2001.
59 Toon 2004: 226; see Coalition for the International Criminal Court, www.iccnow.org.
60 Popovski 2000: 415.
61 Human Rights Watch press release, 'Human Rights Watch Welcomes New Japanese Position on International Court', 28 June 1998, http://hrw.org/press98/june/japn0626.htm
62 Adams, *The Japan Times*, 16 January 2002.
63 Global Policy Forum, 17 May 2004; East Timor's Foreign Minister Jose Ramos Horta made it clear that his government would 'explore some ideas based on [our] interest and concern including the issue of justice, without losing focus ... of the strong bilateral ties between Timor-Leste and Indonesia'. Judicial System Monitoring Programme: 'Timor-Leste Wants Solution to Crimes Against Humanity "acceptable to all": foreign minister', (Dili: 16 May 2004); 'Timor-Leste Can't Annul Arrest Warrant for Indonesian General', (Dili: 16 May 2004).

64 Annan 2002.
65 CIJ and OSJI 2004: 1–2.
66 UN Integrated Mission in Timor-Leste, 'Report on human rights development in Timor-Leste: August 2006-August 2007': 27.
67 CIJ and OSJI 2004: 1.
68 *Jakarta Post*, 31 July 2007: 12.
69 Human Rights Watch 2002a.
70 UN News Centre, 10 May 2004.
71 See 'Special report of the Secretary-General on the United Nations Mission of Support in Timor-Leste', UN Doc. S/2004/117, 13 February 2004: 7; S/2002/333, 29 April 2004: 7.
72 Human Rights Watch 2002b: 5.
73 Ministry of Foreign Affairs, Government of China 2003.
74 Hammarberg undated: 3.
75 Marks 1999: 713.
76 Hammarberg undated: 1.
77 *Reasmei Kampuchea Daily*, 20 February 2002 (translated by Bunsou Sour).
78 *International Herald Tribune* & *Asahi Shimbun*, 23 November 2007.
79 Economides 2003: 46.
80 Cited by Bell 1996: 659.
81 Noguchi 2006: 587–92.
82 Hampson *et al.* 2002: 77.
83 Department of Foreign Affairs, Philippines, 29 December 2000, Press Release No. 171-00.
84 Xinhua General News Service, 6 June 2002.
85 Hampson *et al.* 2002: 77.
86 Nguyen Thi Thanh Ha, 'On Agenda Item 76: Report of the International Criminal Court', New York: 1 November 2007.
87 Christie 1995: 204–18; Toon 2004: 219, 230.
88 Christie 1995: 204.
89 *Cambodia Daily*, 15–16 September 2001.
90 United Nations 1999: 29.
91 *Khmer Intelligence* (sent to undisclosed list of recipients, 19 October 2002).
92 *Bangkok Post*, 23 November 2006.
93 *Agence France-Presse*, 6 September 2002.
94 Bell 1996: 644.
95 Judicial System Monitoring Program Press Release, 22 June 2004.
96 Cited by D. Greenlees, *Weekend Australian*, 4–5 May 2002, cited by Thakur 2006: 128.
97 Thakur 2006: 120; see also Hayden 2003: 259–85.
98 Thakur 2006: 132.

8 The neoliberalization of security and violence in Cambodia's transition

1 On the importance of a Marxian political economy approach in understanding contemporary encounters with violence, inequality and poverty, each of which is an important obstacle to human security, see Springer 2008.
2 Peck and Tickell 2002.
3 On 'actually existing neoliberalism' see Brenner and Theodore 2002; for its application in Cambodia see Springer 2009.
4 UNDP 1994.
5 Commission on Human Security 2003.
6 Bain 2001: 283.
7 King *et al.* 2002.
8 *Ibid.*: 264.

9 Despite variance in doses among regions, states and cities, the basic neoliberal policy treatment is underpinned by a vision of naturalized market relations seeking to
   eradicate obstacles to the operation of markets; stifle collective initiative and public
   expenditure, primarily via privatization of common assets and imposition of user fees;
   advocate individualism, competitiveness and economic self-sufficiency as fundamental virtues; attenuate or nullify social protections and transfer programs; and actively
   'recruit' the poor and marginalized into a flexible labor regime of precarious work and
   low-wage employment (Peck and Tickell 2002).
10 UNDP 1999: 3.
11 Harvey 2005.
12 *Ibid.*: 41.
13 Bain 2001.
14 Michel 2005.
15 Commission on Human Security 2003: 75.
16 Lizée 2002.
17 Bain 2001: 285.
18 Hay 2003: 165–206.
19 Harvey 2005.
20 Foucault 1991: 53–72.
21 Gordon 1991: 1–52.
22 Harvey 2005.
23 Commission on Human Security 2003.
24 Alagappa 1997.
25 Evans 2004.
26 Lizée 2002.
27 Mish 2003: 243.
28 Lummis 1996; Mouffe 1992.
29 Jain 2002.
30 Irvin 1993; St John 1997.
31 Evans 2004.
32 Alagappa 1997: 423.
33 Um 1990.
34 Ojendal 1996.
35 Roberts 2001.
36 The abandonment is attributable to America's embarrassment with its war effort in
   Vietnam, as it was Vietnamese troops who had brought down the Khmer Rouge and
   continued to rule Cambodia as a client state throughout the 1980s. Using Cambodia as
   the instrument of Vietnam's punishment, Washington compelled the UN to withhold
   development aid and bar Cambodia from all international agreements on trade and
   communications (Roberts 2001).
37 Brown and Timberman 1998.
38 Doyle 1995.
39 Ear 1997: 73.
40 Jones and PoKempner 1993: 43–68.
41 'Shadow state politics' refers to the system through which leaders draw authority from
   their abilities informally to control markets and material rewards. Rather than oppose
   the dominant paradigm of neoliberal reform, third world governments often assimilate
   the interests of international financial institutions, reshaping them into instruments of
   power. The emergence of the shadow state is indicative of the contradictions between
   neoliberal theory and its actual practice, because it allows elites to amass astonishing
   wealth obtained through unofficial channels that are pocketed rather than put back
   into developing the country, thereby reinforcing systems of clientelism and patronage.
   Thus the neoliberal axiom asserting that if individuals are left to pursue their narrow

self-interest, then society as a whole will benefit, is clearly erroneous. Rather, only an elite few along with their circle of patrons benefit, while the much-touted neoliberal assumption of the 'trickle-down' effect fails to materialize as the forthcoming developmental rewards promised to those on 'the bottom' are swallowed in the vagaries of the shadow state. On shadow state politics see Reno 1995. For its application in the Cambodian context see Le Billon and Springer 2007. On the contradictions of neoliberalism and its practice see Harvey 2005.

42 Hughes 2003.
43 Jones and PoKempner 1993.
44 Peou 2000.
45 *Ibid.*
46 Hughes 2003.
47 *Ibid.*: 19.
48 For example, Minister of Economy and Finance Keat Chhon was educated at the National Institute of Nuclear Science and Technology in Saclay, France; Minister of International Cooperation and Foreign Affairs Hor Namhong studied at the University of Paris: Ministry of Economy and Finance, Kingdom of Cambodia 2006; Ministry of Foreign Affairs and International Cooperation, Kingdom of Cambodia 2006.
49 Hendrickson 2002.
50 LICADHO 2006.
51 Le Billon and Springer 2007.
52 Global Witness 2007.
53 Le Billon and Springer 2007.
54 Global Witness 2007.
55 Heder 1996: 73–113.
56 *Ibid.*
57 Findlay 1995.
58 Vickery 2007; Roberts 2001.
59 Brown and Zasloff 1998; Hughes 2003; Peou 2000.
60 Shawcross 2002.
61 Doyle 1995.
62 Harvey 2005.
63 Heder 1996; Shawcross 2002.
64 Brown and Zasloff 1998.
65 Gallup 2002: 165–85.
66 Shawcross 2002; Um 1994.
67 Boutros-Ghali 1995; Doyle 1995.
68 Shawcross 2002.
69 Peou 2000: 255.
70 Lizée 1993.
71 Ear 1997.
72 Chandler 2000; McCargo 2005.
73 For discussions of the 1997 coup see Human Rights Watch 1997; Peou 1998c; Springer 2009.
74 St John 1995.
75 Jennar 1995: 17.
76 Findlay 1995.
77 Brown and Zasloff 1998; Jeldres 1996; Lizée 1996.
78 Hendrickson 2002.
79 Um 1994.
80 Hendrickson 2002; Lizée 1996.
81 Godfrey *et al.* 2002.
82 Kirby 1995: 31.

83 The Gini coefficient is a number between 0 and 100, where 0 corresponds with perfect equality (where everyone has the same income) and 100 corresponds with perfect inequality (where one person has all the income, and everyone else has zero income). Prior to UNTAC in 1990, Cambodia's Gini coefficient was 41.6. In 2004 it represented the highest recorded value to date at 46.3 (World Bank 2004).
84 St John 1997.
85 Hendrickson 2002: 99.
86 Irvin 1993.
87 Hendrickson 2002.
88 van der Kroef 1991.
89 Hendrickson 2002.
90 Human Rights Watch 1999a.
91 US Ambassador Joseph A. Mussomeli suggested that the 'culture of impunity that we see throughout Cambodia today is rooted in the irrefutable belief among its people that no crime is so great that it must be punished' (Mussomeli 2006).
92 Peou 2000.
93 Lizée 1996.
94 Jeldres 1996.
95 Lizée 1996.
96 Heder 1995: 425.
97 *Ibid.*: 428.
98 Canterbury 2005; Springer 2009.
99 Harvey 2005.
100 Tan 2002.
101 Jain 2002.
102 Lizée 1993.

Conclusion

1 Peou 2008.
2 Abad 2000.
3 Tow 2000: 3.
4 Burke 2001.
5 Thomas and Tow 2002b: 381.
6 Tow 2000: 5.
7 Tadjbakhsh and Chenoy 2007: 153.
8 Peou, 2008a, 2008b.
9 Kiernan 1996.
10 Kolko 1997: 6.
11 *Ibid.*: 13.
12 *Ibid.*: 12.
13 See for instance Schwartz 1996.
14 Thakur 2006: 190.
15 Sen 1999: 92.
16 Akiko Fukushima, the author of Chapter 3, brought out this point.
17 Sanders 2002: 62.
18 See for instance Atack 2002.
19 Thakur 1994; Makinda 1993.
20 Burke 2001: 224.
21 Dosch 2006: 92, 94, 104, 105–6, 107.
22 Welsh 2002.
23 Hampson *et al.* 2002: 146–47.
24 Gallis 2008: 2, 18.

25 Reuters, 23 January 2008.
26 *CNN News* (Jonathan Mann), 19 March 2008.
27 Urquhart 1983: 165.
28 Thakur 2006: 46.
29 *Ibid.*: 47.
30 *Ibid.*
31 *Ibid.*: ch. 6; Chesterman and Pouligny 2003; Brzoska 2003; Tostensen and Bull 2002; Mack and Khan 2000; Weiss *et al.* 1997.
32 Mack and Khan 2000: 279.
33 Thakur 2006: 145–51; Mack and Khan 2000: 284; Brzoska 2003: 520.
34 Tostensen and Bull 2002: 397.
35 See Nossal 1999: 127–49, cited by Mack and Khan 2000: 282.
36 Chesterman and Pouligny 2003: 511.
37 Tostensen and Bull 2002: 403.
38 Mack and Khan 2000: 282.
39 Tostensen and Bull 2002: 397.
40 Thakur 2006: 141.
41 Mack and Khan 2000: 279; Chesterman and Pouligny 2003: 507, 513–15; Brzoska 2003: 523, 526, 529, 534; Thakur 2006: 135, 138, 140, 142.
42 Kerr 2001: 128.
43 Fatic 1996; Wedgwood 1999; Bolton 1999; Charney 1999.
44 Rieff 1995, 2000.
45 Reisman 1998.
46 Guéhenno 2002: 71.
47 Carr 1946: ch. 4.
48 Bolton 1999.
49 Tucker 2001: 80.
50 Snyder and Vinjamuri 2003/04: 43.
51 *Ibid.*: 6.
52 Newman and Richmond 2006: 11.
53 *Ibid.*: 9, 12.
54 *Ibid.*: 12.
55 *Ibid.*: 10.
56 *Ibid.*: 11.
57 Berger 1998.
58 Burke 2001.
59 Dosch 2006: 96, 97, 98, 99, 106, 208–9.
60 Peou 2007.

Bibliography

Abad Jr, M. C. (2000) 'The Challenge of Balancing State Security with Human Security', *Indonesian Quarterly*, 28(4): 403–10.

Acharya, A. (2001a) 'Human Security: East versus West', *International Journal*, 61(3): 442–60.

—— (2001b) *Constructing a Security Community in Southeast Asia: ASEAN and the Problem of Regional Order*, London and New York: Routledge.

—— (2002) 'Redefining the Dilemmas of Humanitarian Intervention', *Australian Journal of International Affairs*, 56(3): 373–82.

—— (2006) 'Securitization in Asia: Functional and Normative Implications', in M. Caballero-Anthony *et al.* (eds) *Non-traditional Security in Asia: Dilemmas in Securitization*, Hampshire: Ashgate.

Adekanye, J. B. (1997) 'Review Essay: Arms and Reconstruction in Post-Conflict Societies', *Journal of Peace Research*, 34(3): 359–66.

Alagappa, M. (1997) 'Regional Institutions, the UN and International Security: A Framework for Analysis', *Third World Quarterly*, 18(3): 421–41.

—— (1998) 'International Politics in Asia: The Historical Context', in M. Alagappa (ed.) *Asian Security Practice*, Stanford, CA: Stanford University Press.

Alger, C. F. (2002) 'The Emerging Roles of NGOs in the UN System: From Article 71 to a People's Millennium Assembly', *Global Governance* 8(1): 93–117.

Alkire, S. (2003) *A Conceptual Framework for Human Security*, CRISE Working Paper 2, Oxford: Centre for Research on Inequality, Human Security and Ethnicity, Queen Elizabeth House, University of Oxford.

Akhavan, P. (1999a) 'Beyond Impunity: Can International Criminal Justice Prevent Future Atrocities?', *American Journal of International Law*, 95(1): 7–31.

—— (1999b) 'Justice in The Hague: Peace in the former Yugoslavia?' *Human Rights Quarterly*, 20(4): 737–816.

Amnesty International and JSMP (2004) *Justice for Timor-Leste: The Way Forward*, Dili, East Timor: Justice System Monitoring Programme, www.jsmp.minihub.org

Anderson, M. B. (1999) *Do No Harm: How Aid Can Support Peace – or War*, London: Lynne Rienner.

Annan, K. (1998) 'The Quiet Revolution', *Global Governance*, 4(2): 123–38.

—— (1999a) 'The Question of Intervention: Statements by the Secretary General', New York: United Nations Department of Public Information.

—— (1999b) 'Speech of the UN Secretary-General to the General Assembly', New York: United Nations.

—— (2000) 'Opening Remarks at the Symposium on Humanitarian Action', New York: International Peace Academy.

—— (2002) 'Dili, East Timor – Press Encounter upon Arrival (unofficial transcript)', 19 May, UN Secretary General, 'Off the Cuff'. www.un.org/apps/sg/offthecuff. asp?nid=61

APA (2001) *An ASEAN of the People, by the People, for the People: Report of the First ASEAN People's Assembly*, Batam, Jakarta: Centre for Strategic and International Studies.

—— (2003a) *APA 2002 Report: Challenges Facing the ASEAN People*, Jakarta: Centre for Strategic and International Studies.

—— (2003b) *Towards an ASEAN Community of Caring Societies*, Manila: Institute for Strategic and Development Studies.

APEC (2003) *Leaders' Declaration: Bangkok Declaration on Partnership for the Future*, Bangkok: Asia-Pacific Economic Cooperation. www.apec.org/apec/leaders_declarations/2003.html

ASEAN (2001) *7th ASEAN Summit Declaration on HIV/AIDS*, Jakarta: Association of Southeast Asian Nations. www.aseansec.org/8582.htm

—— (2003) *The ASEAN People's Declaration 2003: Towards a Community of Caring Societies*, Jakarta: Association of Southeast Asian Nations. www.asean-isis-aseanpeoplesassembly.net/declarations.htm

—— (2004a) *The ASEAN Socio-Cultural Community (ASCC) Plan of Action*, Jakarta: Association of Southeast Asian Nations. www.aseansec.org/16832.htm

—— (2004b) *Co-chairs' Summary Report of the Meeting of the ASEAN Regional Forum Inter-sessional Support Group on Confidence Building Measures*, Jakarta: Association of Southeast Asian Nations. www.aseansec.org/16096.htm

—— (2006) *Report of the Eminent Persons Group on the ASEAN Charter*, Jakarta: Association of Southeast Asian Nations. www.aseansec.org/19247.pdf

ASEAN+3 Summit (2002) *Final Report of the East Asia Study Group*, Jakarta: Association of Southeast Asian Nations. www.aseansec.org/pdf/easg.pdf

ASEAN Eminent Persons Group (2000) *Vision 2020*, Jakarta: Association of Southeast Asian Nations. www.aseansec.org/5304.htm

ASEAN Regional Forum (2005) *Co-chair's Summary Report of the ARF Workshop on 'Evolving Changes in the Security Perceptions of the ARF Countries'*, Jakarta: Association of Southeast Asian Nations.

Atack, I. (2002) 'Ethical Objections to Humanitarian Intervention', *Security Dialogue*, 33(3): 279–92.

Axworthy, L. (1998) 'The New Diplomacy: The UN, The International Criminal Court and the Human Security Agenda', paper presented at Conference on UN Reform, Kennedy School, Harvard University, Cambridge, MA, USA, 25 April 1998.

Ayoob, M. (2004) 'Third World Perspectives on Humanitarian Intervention and International Administration', *Global Governance*, 10(1): 99–118.

Bain, W. (1999) 'Against Crusading: The Ethic of Human Security and Canadian Foreign Policy', *Canadian Foreign Policy*, 6(3): 85–98.

—— (2001) 'The Tyranny of Benevolence: National Security, Human Security, and the Practice of Statecraft', *Global Society: Journal of Interdisciplinary International Relations*, 15: 277–94.

Banerjee, D. (2005) 'Current Trends in UN Peacekeeping: A Perspective from Asia', in M. Caballero-Anthony and Amitav Acharya (eds), *UN Peace Operations and Asian Security*, London/New York: Routledge.

Barash, D. (1999) 'Human Rights', in D. Barash (ed.) *Approaches to Peace*, New York: Oxford University Press.

—— (2000) *Approach to Peace*, New York: Oxford University Press.

Barnett, M., Kim, H., O'Donnell, M. and Sitea, L. (2007) 'Peacebuilding: What is in a Name?', *Global Governance*, 13(1): 35–58.

Bartu, P. (2000) 'The Militia, the Military, and the People of Bobonaro District', in D. Kingsbury (ed.) *Guns and Ballot Boxes: East Timor's Vote for Independence*, Victoria, Australia: Monash Asia Institute.

Bassiouni, M. C. (1996) 'Searching for Peace and Achieving Justice: The Need for Accountability', *Law and Contemporary Problems*, 59(4): 9–28.

—— (1999) 'Policy Perspectives Favoring the Establishment of the International Criminal Court', *Journal of International Affairs*, 52(2): 795–810.

Bauer, O. R. and Bell, D. A. (eds) (1999) *The East Asian Challenge for Human Rights*, Cambridge and New York: Cambridge University Press.

Bell, C. (2000) 'East Timor, Canberra and Washington: A Case Study in Crisis Management', *Australian Journal of International Affairs*, 54(2): 171–76.

—— (2003) 'Human Rights and Minority Protection', in J. Darby and R. MacGinty (eds) *Contemporary Peacemaking: Conflict, Violence and Peace Processes*, London: Palgrave.

Bell, D. A. (1996) 'The East Asian Challenge to Human Rights: Reflections on an East West Dialogue', *Human Rights Quarterly*, 18(3): 641–67.

Bellamy, A. and MacDonald, M. (2002) 'The Utility of Human Security: Which Humans, What Security? A Reply to Thomas and Tow', *Security Dialogue*, 33(3): 373–77.

Berdal, M. (1996) *Disarmament and Demobilization after Civil Wars: Arms, Soldiers and the Termination of Armed Conflict*, Adelphi Paper 303, Oxford: Oxford University Press.

Berger, T. U. (1998) *Cultures of Antimilitarism: National Security in Germany and Japan*, Baltimore, MD: Johns Hopkins University Press.

Bergeson, H. O. and Lunde, L. (1999) *Dinosaurs or Dynamos? The United Nations and the World Bank at the Turn of the Century*, London: Earthscan.

de Bertodano, S. (2003) 'Current Developments in International Courts', *Journal of International Criminal Justice*, 1: 226–44.

Betts, R. K. (1994) 'The Delusion of Impartial Intervention', *Foreign Affairs*, 73(6): 20- 33.

Bolton, J. (1999) 'The Global Prosecutors: Hunting Criminals in the Name of Utopia', *Foreign Affairs*, 78(1): 157–64.

Booth, K. (1991) Security and Emancipation', *Review of International Studies*, 17(4): 313–26.

Bouchet-Saulnier, F. (2002) *The Practical Guide to International Law*, Lanham, MD: Rowman & Littlefield.

Boutros-Ghali, B. (1992) *An Agenda for Peace*, New York: United Nations.

—— (1995) *The United Nations and Cambodia 1991–1995*, New York: United Nations Department of Public Information.

Brenner, N. and Theodore, N. (2002) 'Cities and the Geographies of 'Actually Existing Neoliberalism', *Antipode*, 34: 349–79.

Brown, C. (2002) *Sovereignty, Rights and Justice: International Political Theory Today*, Cambridge: Polity Press.

Brown, F. and Timberman, D. G. (1998) 'Peace, Development, and Democracy in Cambodia: Shattered Hopes', in F. Z. Brown and D. G. Timberman (eds) *Cambodia and the International Community: The Quest for Peace, Development, and Democracy*, New York: Asia Society.

Brown, M. and Zasloff, J. J. (1998) *Cambodia Confounds the Peacemakers 1979–1998*, Ithaca: Cornell University Press.

Brzoska, M. (2003) 'From Dumb to Smart? Recent Reforms of UN Sanctions', *Global Governance*, 9(4): 519–35.

Buchanan, A. (2003) 'Reforming the Law of Humanitarian Intervention', in J. L. Holzgrefe and R. O. Keohane (eds) *Humanitarian Intervention: Ethical, Legal and Political Dilemmas*, Cambridge: Cambridge University Press.

Budiardjo, C. and Soei, L. L. (1984) *The War against East Timor*, London: Zed Books.

Burke, A. (2001) 'Caught between National and Human Security: Knowledge and Power in Post-crisis Asia', *Pacific Review*, 13(3): 215–39.

Buzan, B. (1991) *People, States and Fear: An Agenda for International Security Studies in the Post-Cold War Era*, 2nd edn, Boulder, CO: Lynne Rienner.

—— (2001) 'Human Security in International Perspective', in M. Anthony- Caballero and M. J. Hassan (eds) *The Asia Pacific in the New Millennium*, Kuala Lumpur: ISIS Malaysia.

Byers, M. and Chesterman, S. (2003) 'Changing the Rules about Rules?', in J. L. Holzgrefe and R. Keohane (eds) *Humanitarian Intervention: Ethical, Legal and Political Dilemmas*, Cambridge: Cambridge University Press.

Caballero-Anthony, A. (2002) 'Human Security in the Asia-Pacific: Current Trends and Prospects', in D. Dickens (ed.) *The Human Face of Security: Asia-Pacific Perspectives*, Canberra: Strategic and Defence Studies Centre.

Caballero-Anthony, M. (1998) 'Mechanisms of Dispute Settlement: The ASEAN Experience', *Contemporary Southeast Asia*, 20(1): 38–66.

—— (2004a) 'Non-State Regional Governance Mechanism for Economic Security: The Case of the ASEAN Peoples' Assembly', *Pacific Review*, 17(4): 567–85.

—— (2004b) 'Revisioning Human Security in Southeast Asia', *Asian Perspectives*, 28(3): 155–89.

—— (2005) *Regional Security in Southeast Asia: Beyond the ASEAN Way*, Singapore: Institute of Southeast Asian Studies.

Caballero-Anthony, M. and Emmers, R. (2006) 'Understanding the Dynamics of Securitizing Non-Traditional Security', in M. Caballero-Anthony, R. Emmers and A. Acharya (eds) *Non-traditional Security in Asia: Dilemmas in Securitization*, Hampshire: Ashgate.

Cai, P. (2008) 'China and ASEAN in Non-Traditional Security Cooperation', in A. S. P. Baviera (ed.) *Regional Security in East Asia: Challenges to Cooperation and Community Building*, Diliman, Quezon City: Asian Center, University of the Philippines.

Canadian Department of Foreign Affairs and International Trade (2000) *Freedom from Fear: Canada's Foreign Policy for Human Security*, Ottawa: Department of Foreign Affairs and International Trade.

Canterbury, D. C. (2005) *Neoliberal Democratization and New Authoritarianism*, Burlington, VT: Ashgate.

Capie, D. and Evans, P. (2007) *The Asia-Pacific Security Lexicon*, Singapore: Institute of Southeast Asian Studies.

Carey, H. F. and Richmond, O. P. (2003a) 'Mitigating Conflict: The Role of NGOs', *International Peacekeeping*, Special Issue, 10(1): 1–8.

—— (eds) (2003b) *Mitigating Conflict: The Role of NGOs*, London: Frank Cass.

Carlson, A. (2002) *Protecting Sovereignty, Accepting Intervention: The Dilemma of Chinese Foreign Relations in the 1990s*, China Policy Series No. 18, New York: National Committee on United States–Japan Relations.

—— (2004) 'Helping to Keep the Peace (Albeit Reluctantly): China's Recent Stance on Sovereignty and Multilateral Intervention', *Pacific Affairs*, 77(1): 9–27.

Carr, E. H. (1946) *The Twenty Years' Crisis, 1919–1939*, London: Macmillan.

Chanda, N. (1986) *Brother Enemy*, New York: Harcourt Brace Jovanovich.

Chandler, D. (2000) *The Tragedy of Cambodian History*, Boulder, CO: Westview Press.

Chalk, P. (2001) *Australian Foreign and Defense Policy in the Wake of the 1999/2000 East Timor Intervention*, Santa Monica, CA: Rand.

Chang, Y. (2002) 'The Right to Life', paper presented at Conference on '*The Experiences of Local Actors in Peace-building Reconstruction and the Establishment of Rule of Law*', 23–25 March, Singapore (unpublished).

Chari, P. R. (ed.) (2001) *Security and Governance in South Asia*, Colombo: Regional Centre for Strategic Studies.

Chen, L. (1995) 'Human Security: Concepts and Approaches', in T. Matsumae and L. Chen (eds) *Common Security in Asia: New Concepts of Human Security*, Tokyo: Tokai Press.

Chesterman, S. (2003) *Just War or Just Peace? Humanitarian Intervention and International Law*, Oxford: Oxford University Press.

Chesterman, S. and Pouligny, B. (2003) 'Are Sanctions Meant to Work? The Politics of Creating and Implementing Sanctions through the United Nations', *Global Governance*, 9(4): 503–18.

Christensen, T. (1996) 'Chinese Realpolitik', *Foreign Affairs*, 75(5): 37–52

Christie, K. (1995) 'Regime Security and Human Rights in Southeast Asia', *Political Studies*, XLIII (Special Issue): 204–18.

Chu, S. (2000) *China, Asia, and Issues of Sovereignty and Intervention*, Beijing: China Institute of International Relations.

—— (2002) *China and Human Security*, North Pacific Policy Paper 8. Vancouver: Program on Canada–Asia Policy Studies, Institute of Asian Research, University of British Columbia.

CIJ and OSJI (2004) *Unfulfilled Promises: Achieving Justice for Crimes Against Humanity in East Timor*, New York: Coalition for International Justice and Open Society Justice Initiative.

Claude, I. L. (1966) *Power and International Relations*, New York: Random House.

Commission on Global Governance (1995) *Our Global Neighborhood*, New York: Oxford University Press.

Commission on Human Security (2003) *Human Security Now: Protecting and Empowering People*, New York: United Nations Publications.

Corpwatch (2000) *Tangled up in Blue: Corporate Partnership at the United Nations*, San Francisco, CA: Transnational Resource and Action Center.

Cotton, J. (1999) ' "Peacekeeping" in East Timor: An Australian Policy Departure', *Australian Journal of International Affairs* 53(3): 237–46.

—— (2004) *East Timor, Australia and Regional Order: Intervention and its Aftermath in Southeast Asia*, London and New York: Routledge Curzon.

Council for the Promotion of Cultural Diplomacy (2004) *Establishing Japan as a 'Peaceful Nation of Cultural Exchange'*, Cabinet Secretariat. www.kantei.go.jp/foreign/policy/bunka/050711bunka_e.html

Cousens, E. and Kumar C. (eds) (2001) *Peacebuilding as Politics: Cultivating Peace in Fragile Societies*, Boulder, CO: Lynne Rienner.

Detter, I. (2000) *The Law of War*, 2nd edn, Cambridge: Cambridge University Press.

Dickens, D. (2002) 'Can East Timor be a Blueprint for Burden Sharing?', *Washington Quarterly*, 25(3): 29–40.

Dickens, D. and Wilson-Roberts, G. (eds) (2000) *Non-Intervention and State Sovereignty in the Asia-Pacific*, Wellington: Centre for Strategic Studies.

Dickinson, L. A. (2003) 'Notes and Comments: the Promise of Hybrid Courts', *American Journal of International Law*, 97(2): 295–310.

Dosch, J. (2006) *The Changing Dynamics of Southeast Asian Politics*, Boulder, CO: Lynne Rienner.

Doyle, M. (1983a) 'Kant, Liberal Legacies, and Foreign Affairs', *Philosophy and Public Affairs*, 12(3): 205–35.

—— (1983b) 'Kant, Liberal Legacies, and Foreign Affairs, Part 2', *Philosophy and Public Affairs*, 12(4): 323–53.

—— (1995) *UN Peacekeeping in Cambodia: UNTAC's Civil Mandate*, Boulder, CO: Lynne Rienner.

Duffield, M. (1997) 'NGO Relief in War Zones', *Third World Quarterly*, 18(3): 527–42.

Dupont, A. (2000) 'ASEAN's Response to the East Timor Crisis', *Australian Journal of International Affairs*, 54(2): 163–70.

Ear, S. (1997) 'Cambodia and the 'Washington consensus', *Crossroads: An Interdisciplinary Journal of Southeast Asian Studies*, 11: 73–97.

East Asia Vision Group (2001) *Towards an East Asia Community: Region of Peace, Prosperity and Progress*. www.mofa.go.jp/region/asia-paci/report2001.pdf

Economides, S. (2003) 'The International Criminal Court: Reforming the Politics of International Justice', *Government and Opposition*, 38(1): 29–51.

Edström, B. (2003) 'Japan's Foreign Policy and Human Security', *Japan Forum*, 15(2): 209–25

Elaraby, N. (1986) 'The Office of the Secretary-General and the Maintenance of International Peace and Security', *Revue Egyptienne du Droit International*, 42: 1–42.

Evans, P. (2004) 'Human Security and East Asia: In the Beginning', *Journal of East Asian Studies*, 4: 263–84.

Fatic, A. (1996) 'The Need for Politically Balanced Works of the Hague International War Crimes Tribunals', *Review of International Affairs*, XLVII (2): 8–11.

Feher, M. (2000) *Powerless by Design: The Age of the International Community*, Durham, NC: Duke University Press.

Ferrero-Waldner, B. (2005) 'Human Rights, Security and Development in a Global World', speech to Women Building Peace Conference, Soroptimist International, Vienna, 8 July 2005. European Commission, http://ec.europa.eu/external_relations/news/ferrero/2005/sp05_428.htm

Findlay, T. (1995) *Cambodia: The Legacy and Lessons of UNTAC*, New York: Oxford University Press.

Finnemore, M. (1996) *National Interests in International Society*, Ithaca, NY: Cornell University Press.

—— (2003) *The Purpose of Intervention: Changing Beliefs about the Use of Force*, Ithaca, NY: Cornell University Press.

Fischer, T. (2000) *Seven Days in East Timor*, St Leonards, New South Wales: Allen & Unwin.

Foucault, M. (1991) 'Governmentality', in G. Burchell *et al.* (eds) *The Foucault Effect: Studies in Governmentality, with Two Lectures by and an Interview with Michel Foucault*, Chicago, IL: University of Chicago Press.

Friedberg, A. L. (1991) 'The Changing Relationship between Economics and National Security', *Political Science Quarterly*, 106(2): 265–76.

Friedman, T. L. (2006) *The World is Flat: A Brief History of the 21st Century*, London: Penguin.

Gallis, P. (2008) *NATO in Afghanistan: A Test of the Transatlantic Alliance*, Congressional Research Report for Congress. http://infoalert.usembassy.de/trans/fl1_507.htm

Gallup, J. C. (2002) 'Cambodia: A Shaky Start for Democracy', in J. F. Hsieh and D. Newman (eds) *How Asia Votes*, New York: Chatham House/Seven Bridges Press.

Gasper, D. (2005) 'Securing Humanity: Situating "Human Security" as Concept and Discourse', *Journal of Human Development*, 6(2): 221–45.

Gill, B. and Reilly, J. (2000) 'Sovereignty, Intervention and Peacekeeping: The View From Beijing', *Survival*, 42(3): 41–60.

Gilpin, R. (2003) 'Sources of American–Japanese Economic Conflict', in J. Ikenberry and M. Mastanduno (eds) *International Relations Theory and the Asia-Pacific*, New York: Columbia University Press.

Global Witness (2007) *Cambodia's Family Trees: Illegal Logging and the Stripping of Public Assets* by *Cambodia's Elite*, London: Global Witness. www.globalwitness.org

Godfrey, M., Sophal, C., Kato, T., Piseth, L. V., Dorina, P., Saravy, T., Savora, T. and Sovan-narith, S. (2002) 'Technical Assistance and Capacity Development in an Aid-Dependent Economy: The Experience of Cambodia', *World Development*, 30: 355–73.

Goldstone, R. (1995) 'Exposing Human Rights Abuses: A Help or Hindrance to Reconcili-ation', *Hastings Constitutional Law Quarterly*, 22(3): 607–21.

Goodhand, J. and Atkinson, P. (2001) *Conflict and Aid: Enhancing the Peacebuilding Impact of International Engagement: A Synthesis of Findings from Afghanistan, Liberia and Sri Lanka*, London: International Alert.

Gordon, C. (1991) 'Governmental Rationality: An Introduction', in G. Burchell, C. Gor-don and P. Miller (eds) *The Foucault Effect: Studies in Governmentality, with Two Lectures by and an Interview with Michel Foucault*, Chicago, IL: University of Chicago Press.

Gorjão, P. (2002) 'Japan's Foreign Policy and East Timor, 1975–2002', *Asian Survey*, 42(5): 754–71.

Goulding, M. (1993) 'The Evolution of United Nations Peacekeeping', *International Affairs*, 69: 451–64.

Government of Japan (2003) *Japan's Official Development Assistance Charter*. www.mofa.go.jp/policy/oda/reform/revision0308.pdf

Greenlees, D. and Garran, R. (2003) *Deliverance: The Inside Story of East Timor's Fight for Freedom*, Crows Nest, New South Wales: Allen & Unwin.

Guéhenno, J. M. (2002) 'On the Challenges and Achievements of Reforming UN Peace Operations', in E. Newman and A. Schnabel (eds) *Recovering from Civil Conflict: Rec-onciliation, Peace and Development*, London: Frank Cass.

Galtung, J. (1975) 'Three Approaches to Peace: Peacekeeping, Peacemaking and Peace-building', in J. Galtung (ed.) *Peace, War and Defense – Essays in Peace Research Vol.2*, Copenhagen: Christian Ejlers.

Gunn, G. (1999) 'Lost and Found: How did the World Rediscover the "Lost Cause" of East Timor?', *Inside Indonesia*, 60(Oct/Dec). www.insideindonesia.org/edit60/gunn.htm

Guttman, R. and Rieff, D. (eds) (1999) *Crimes of War: What the Public Should Know*, New York: W.W. Norton.

Hainsworth, P. (2000) *The East Timor Question: The Struggle for Independence from Indo-nesia*, London: I.B. Tauris.

Hammarberg, T. (2000) *Situation of Human Rights in Cambodia*, Report of the Special Representative of the Secretary-General of Human Rights in Cambodia, New York: United Nations Economic and Social Council.

—— (undated) 'How the Khmer Rouge Tribunal was Agreed: Discussions between the Cambodian Government and the UN: Part II, March 1999–January 2001', *Searching for the Truth! A Magazine of the Documentation Center of Cambodia*, 20 (August): 42–46. www.dccam.org/Projects/Magazines/Previous%20Englis/Issue20.pdf

Hampson, F. O., Daudelin, J., Hay, J., Reid, H. and Martin, T. (2002) *Madness in the Mul-titude: Human Security and World Disorder*, Ontario: Oxford University Press.

Harris, S. (1993) 'Economic Cooperation and Institution Building in the Asia-Pacific Region', in R. Higgott, R. Leaver and J. Ravenhill (eds) *Pacific Economic Relations in the 1990s: Cooperation or Conflict?*, Boulder, CO: Lynne Rienner.

Hartung, W. D. and Washburn, J. (1997) *US Arms Transfer to Indonesia 1975–1997: Who's Influencing Whom?* New York: World Policy Institute.

Harvey, D. (2005) *A Brief History of Neoliberalism*, New York: Oxford University Press.

Hawk, D. (1998) 'The Cambodian Genocide', in I. W. Charney (ed.) *Genocide: A Critical Bibliographic Review*, New York: Facts on File Publications.

Hay, J. (2003) 'Unaided Virtues: The (Neo)Liberalization of the Domestic Sphere and the New Architects of Community', in J. Z. Bratich, J. Packer and C. McCarthy (eds) *Foucault, Cultural Studies, and Governmentality*, Albany, NY: State University of New York Press.

Hayden, R. M. (2003) Biased Justice: 'Humanrightism' and the International Criminal Tribunal for the Former Yugoslavia,' in R. G. C. Thomas (ed.) *Yugoslavia Unravelled: Sovereignty, Self-Determination, and Intervention*, Lanham, MD: Lexington Books.

Heder, S. (1995) 'Cambodia's Democratic Transition to Neoauthoritarianism', *Current History*, 94: 425–29.

—— (1996) 'The Resumption of Armed Struggle by the Party of Democratic Kampuchea: Evidence from National Army of Democratic Kampuchea 'Self-Demobilizers', in S. Heder and J. Ledgerwood (eds) *Propaganda, Politics, and Violence in Cambodia: Democratic Transition under United Nations Peace-Keeping*, Armonk, NY: M.E. Sharpe.

—— (2002) 'Dealing with Crimes against Humanity', *Southeast Asian Affairs 2001*, Singapore: Institute of Southeast Asian Affairs, 129–41.

Henderson, J. (1999) *Reassessing ASEAN*, Adelphi Paper 328, Oxford: Oxford University Press.

Hendrickson, D. (2002) 'Globalisation, Insecurity and Post-War Reconstruction: Cambodia's Precarious Transition', *IDS Bulletin*, 32: 98–105.

Higgins, R. (1984) 'Intervention and International Law', in H. Bull (ed.) *Intervention in World Politics*, Oxford: Oxford University Press.

Hobbes, T. (1998 [1651]) *Leviathan*, Oxford: Oxford University Press.

Hochschild, A. (1999) *King Leopold's Ghost*, London: Macmillan.

Holsti, K. J. (1986) 'The Horseman of the Apocalypse: At the Gate, Detoured, or Retreating', *International Studies Quarterly*, 30: 355–72.

Holzgrefe, J. L. (2003) 'The Humanitarian Intervention Debate', in J. L. Holzgrefe and R. Keohane (eds) *Humanitarian Intervention: Ethical, Legal and Political Dilemmas*, Cambridge: Cambridge University Press.

Hughes, C. (2002) 'International Intervention and the People's Will: The Demoralization of Democracy in Cambodia', *Critical Asian Studies*, 34: 539–62.

—— (2003) *The Political Economy of Cambodia's Transition, 1991–2001*, New York: Routledge Curzon.

Human Rights Watch (1997) 'Aftermath of the Coup'. www.hrw.org/reports/1997/cambodia

—— (1998) 'Human Rights Watch Welcomes New Japanese Position on International Court', Rome: 28 June. http://hrw.org/press98/june/japn0626.htm

—— (1999a) 'Impunity in Cambodia: How Human Rights Offenders Escape Justice'. www.hrw.org/reports/1999/cambo2/

—— (1999b) World Report 1999: Special Issues and Campaigns – International Criminal Court. www.hrw.org/worldreport99/special/icc.html

—— (1999c) 'International Criminal Court', Issue 10. www.hrw.org/wr2k/Issues-09.htm

—— (2002a) 'Justice Denied for Timor-Leste'. Human Rights Watch: *Backgrounders*. www.hrw.org/backgrounder/asia/timor/etimor1202bg.htm

—— (2002b), World Report: 'International Justice', www.hrw.org/wr2k2/internationaljustice. html

—— (2003) *Serious Flaws: Why the UN General Assembly Should Require Changes to the Draft Khmer Rouge Tribunal Agreement.* www.hrw.org/backgrounder/asia/ cambodia040303-bck.htm

—— (undated) 'International Justice'. www.hrw.org/wr2k2/international justice.html

Human Security Centre (2004) *Human Security Report 2004*, Vancouver: University of British Columbia.

—— (2005) *Human Security Report 2005: War and Peace in the 21st Century*, New York/ Oxford: Oxford University Press.

ICISS (2001a) 'Beijing: Roundtable Consultation with Nongovernmental and other Interested Organizations, June 14 2001', in *Regional Roundtables and National Consultations*, International Commission on Intervention and State Sovereignty, pp. 391–94, www.iciss.ca

—— (2001b) *The Responsibility to Protect*, International Commission on Intervention and State Sovereignty, www.iciss.ca

Ignatieff, M. (1998) *The Warrior's Honour: Ethnic War and the Modern Conscience*, New York: Viking Press.

—— (2002) *Virtual War*, London: Vintage.

International Peace Academy (1992) *Options for Promoting Corporate Responsibility in Conflict Zones: Perspectives from the Private Sector*, New York: International Peace Academy.

Irvin, G. (1993) 'Cambodia: Why recovery is unlikely in the short term', *European Journal of Development Research*, 5: 123–41.

Ishizuka, K. (2004) 'Australia's Policy towards East Timor', *Round Table*, 93(374): 271–85.

Jackson, R. H. (1993) 'Armed Humanitarianism', *International Journal*, 48(4): 579–606.

Jain, P. (2007) 'Australia's Attitude toward Asian Values and Regional Community Building', *Politics & Policy*, 35(1): 26–41.

Jain, R. (2002) 'Globalisation, Liberalisation and Human Security in India: Challenges for Governance', *Journal of Developing Societies*, 17: 111–29.

JCIE (1999a) *The Asian Crisis and Human Security: An Intellectual Dialogue on Building Asia's Tomorrow*, Tokyo: Japan Center for International Exchange.

—— (1999b) *Sustainable Development and Human Security: Second Intellectual Dialogue on Building Asia's Tomorrow*, Tokyo/Singapore: Japan Center for International Exchange/Institute of Southeast Asian Studies.

—— (2002) *Health and Human Security: Moving from Concept to Action*, Tokyo: Japan Center for International Exchange. www.jcie.or.jp/thinknet/tomorrow/4.html

—— (undated) *Dialogue and Research Monitor: Inventory of Multilateral Meetings on Asia Pacific Security and Community Building, 1994–2002*, Tokyo: Japan Center for International Exchange. www.jcie.or.jp/drm

Jarasa, J. (1999) 'The ASEAN Troika on Cambodia: A Philippine Perspective', in D. Ball and A. Acharya (eds) *The Next Stage: Preventive Diplomacy and Security Cooperation in the Asia-Pacific*, Canberra: Strategic and Defence Studies Centre.

Jardine, M. (1992) 'Forgotten Genocide', *Progressive* 56(12): 19–21.

Jeldres, J. A. (1996) 'Cambodia's fading hopes', *Journal of Democracy*, 7: 148–57.

Jennar, R. M. (ed.) (1995) *The Cambodian Constitutions (1953–1993)*, Bangkok: White Lotus.

182   *Bibliography*

JETRO (1999) *Nihon no Boeki Aitekoku Top 50: 1999* [Japan's Trade Partners Top 50: 1999], Tokyo: Japan External Trade Organization. www.jetro.go.jp/jpn/stats/trade/excel/rank1999.xls

Jin, L. (2000) 'The Principle of Non-intervention in the Asia Pacific Region: A Chinese Perspective', in D. Dickens and G. Wilson-Roberts (eds) *Non-Intervention and State Sovereignty in the Asia-Pacific*, Wellington: Center for Strategic Studies.

Johnson, J. (2002) 'How Conceptual Problems Migrate: Rational Choice, Interpretation, and the Hazards of Pluralism', *Annual Review of Political Science*, 5: 223–48.

Jones, S. and PoKempner, D. (1993) 'Human Rights in Cambodia: Past, Present, and Future' in F. Z. Brown (ed.) *Rebuilding Cambodia: Human Resources, Human Rights and Law*, Arlington, VA: Johns Hopkins Foreign Policy.

Josselin, D. and Wallace, W. (eds) (2001) *Non-State Actors in World Politics*, London: Palgrave.

Joyner, C. (1999) 'The United Nations and Democracy', *Global Governance*, 5: 333–57.

JSMP (2004) *The Future of the Serious Crimes Unit*, Dili, East Timor: Judicial System Monitoring Programme, www.jsmp.minihub.org/Reports

Kabashima, I. and MacDougal, T. (1999) 'Japan: Democracy with Growth and Equity', in J. W. Morley (ed.) *Driven by Growth: Political Change in the Asia-Pacific Region*, Armonk, NY and London: M.E. Sharpe.

Kagan, R. (2003) *Paradise and Power*, London: Atlantic Books.

Kammen, D. (1999) 'Notes on the Transformation of the East Timor Military Command and its Implications for Indonesia', *Indonesia*, 67: 61–76.

Kaufmann, C. (1996) 'Possible and Impossible Solutions to Ethnic Civil Wars', *International Security*, 20(4): 136–75.

Keating, T. and Knight, A. (eds) (2006) *Building Sustainable Peace*, New Delhi: Academic Foundation.

Kegley, C. (1993) 'The Neoidealist Moment in International Studies? Realist Myths and the New Internationalist Realities', *International Studies Quarterly*, 37: 131–46.

Keohane, R. (1989) *International Institutions and State Power*, Boulder, CO, San Francisco, CA and London: Westview Press.

Keohane, R. and Nye, J. (1977) *Power and Interdependence: World Politics in Transition*, Boston, HA: Little, Brown.

Kerr, R. (2001) 'International Peace and Security and International Criminal Justice', in E. Newman and O. Richmond (eds) *The United Nations and Human Security*, London: Palgrave Macmillan.

Khan, A. R. (ed.) (2001) *Globalization and Non-Traditional Security in South Asia*, Colombo: Regional Centre for Strategic Studies.

Khong, Y. F. (2001) 'Human Security: A Shotgun Approach to Alleviating Human Misery?', *Global Governance*, 7(3): 231–36.

Kiernan, B. (ed.) (1993) *Genocide and Democracy in Cambodia: The Khmer Rouge, the United Nations and the International Community*, New Haven, CT: Yale University Southeast Asian Studies.

—— (1996) *The Pol Pot Regime: Race, Power and Genocide in Cambodia under the Khmer Rouge*, New Haven, CT: Yale University Press.

Kikkawa, F. (2007) 'Japan and East Timor: Change and Development of Japan's Security Policy and the Road to East Timor', *Japanese Studies*, 27(3): 247–61.

Kim, Woosang and Hyun, In-Taek (2000) 'Toward a New Concept of Security: Human Security in World Politics', in W. T. Tow, R. Thakur and I. Hyun (eds) *Asia's Emerging Regional Order: Reconciling Traditional and Human Security*, Tokyo: United Nations Press.

King, G., Murray, C. and Christopher, J. L. (2002) 'Rethinking Human Security', *Political Science Quarterly*, 116(4): 585–610.

Kirby, M. (1995) 'Human rights, the United Nations and Cambodia', *Australia Quarterly*, 67: 26–39.

van Klinken, G. (1998) 'No Autonomy for East Timor without Democracy in Indonesia', *Inside Indonesia Digest* 72: 4 December, http://insideindonesia.org/digest/dig72.htm

Knight, A. (1996) 'Toward a Subsidiarity Model for Peacemaking and Preventive Diplomacy', *Third World Quarterly*, 17(1): 31–52.

Kolko, G. (1997) *Vietnam: Anatomy of a Peace*, London and New York: Routledge.

Kondoch, B. (2001) 'The United Nations Administration of East Timor', *Journal of Conflict and Security Law*, 6(2): 245–65.

Kotsopoulos, J. (2006) *A Human Security Agenda for the EU?* EPC Issue Paper 48, European Policy Centre. www.epc.eu/TEWN/pdf/245249_Human%20Security%20IP.pdf

Knudsen, T. B. (1996) 'Humanitarian Intervention Revisited: Post-Cold War Responses to Classical Problems', *International Peacekeeping*, 3(4): 146–65.

Korey, W. (2001) *NGOs and the Universal Declaration of Human Rights*, New York: Palgrave.

Krasner, S. D. (1983) 'National Security and Economics', in T. Trout and J. G. Harf (eds) *National Security Affairs*, New Brunswick, NJ: Transaction Books.

Krieger, H. (ed.) (1997) *East Timor and the International Community: Basic Documents*, Cambridge: Cambridge University Press.

van der Kroef, J. M. (1991) 'Cambodia in 1990: The Elusive Peace', *Asian Survey*, 31(1): 94–102.

Kumar, K. (ed.) (1998) *Post-Conflict Elections, Democratization and International Assistance*, Boulder, CO: Lynne Rienner Publishers.

Kupchan C. A. and Kupchan, C. A. (1991) 'Concerts, Collective Security, and the Future of Europe', *International Security*, 16(1): 114–61.

—— (1998) 'The Promise of Collective Security', in M. E. Brown, O. R. Coté Jr, S. M. Lynn-Jones and S. E. Miller (eds) *Theories of War and Peace: An International Security Reader*, Cambridge, MA and London: MIT Press.

Kurth, J. (2005) 'Humanitarian Intervention after Iraq: Legal Ideals vs. Military Realities', *Orbis*, 50(1): 87–101.

Lam, P. E. (2006) 'Japan's Human Security Role in Southeast Asia', *Contemporary Southeast Asia*, 28(1): 141–59

Lawless, R. (1976) 'The Indonesian Takeover of East Timor', *Asian Survey* 16(10): 948–64.

Leaver, R. (2001) 'Introduction: Australia, East Timor and Indonesia', *Pacific Review* 14(1): 1–14.

Le Billon, P. (2000) 'The Political Ecology of Transition in Cambodia, 1989–99: War, Peace and Forest Exploitation', *Development and Change*, 31: 785–805.

Le Billon, P. and Springer, S. (2007) 'Between War and Peace: Violence and Accommodation in the Cambodian Logging Sector', in W. de Jong, D. Donovan and K. Abe (eds) *Extreme Conflict and Tropical Forests*, New York: Springer.

Lee, C. (2003) *Human Security: Implications for Taiwan's International Roles*. Canadian Consortium on Human Security. www.humansecurity.info

LICADHO (2006) *Human Rights in Cambodia: The Façade of Stability*, Phnom Penh: Cambodian League for the Promotion and Defense of Human Rights. www.licadho.org

Link, A. S., Hirst, D. W., Little, J. E. and Aandahl, F. (eds) (1983) *The Papers of Woodrow Wilson*, 41, January 24–April 6, 1917, Princeton, NJ: Princeton University Press.

Lizée, P. (1993) 'The challenge of conflict resolution in Cambodia', *Canadian Defence Quarterly*, 23: 35–44.

—— (1996) 'Cambodia in 1995: From hope to despair', *Asian Survey*, 36: 83–88.

—— (2002) 'Human security in Vietnam, Laos, and Cambodia', *Contemporary Southeast Asia: A Journal of International & Strategic Affairs*, 24: 509–28.

Locke, J. (1980 [1689]) *Second Treatise on Government*, London: Hackett Publishing Co.

Lummis, C. D. (1996) *Radical Democracy*, Ithaca, NY: Cornell University Press.

Luttwak, E. (1999) 'Give War a Chance', *Foreign Affairs*, 78(4): 36–44.

MacFarlane, S. N. (2002) *Intervention in Contemporary World Politics*, Adelphi Paper 350, London: International Institute for Strategic Studies.

MacFarlane, S. N. and Khong, Y. F. (2006) *The UN and Human Security: A Critical History*, Bloomington and Indianapolis, IN: Indiana University Press.

MacFarlane, S. N. and Weiss, T. G. (1994) 'The United Nations, Regional Organizations and Human Security: Building Theory in Central America', *Third World Quarterly*, 15(2): 277–95.

Mack, A. (2003) 'The Human Security Report Project', unpublished, Vancouver: Human Security Centre.

Mack, A. and Khan, A. (2000) 'The Efficacy of UN Sanctions', *Security Dialogue*, 31(3): 279–92.

de Magalhaes, A. B. (ed.) (1990) *East Timor: Land of Hope*, Apartado: Oporto University.

Mak, J. N. (1999) 'The Security Environment in Southeast Asia', in D. Ball (ed.) *Maintaining the Strategic Edge: The Defence of Australia in 2015*, Canberra: Strategic and Defense Studies Centre.

Makinda, S. M. (1993) *Seeking Peace from Chaos: Humanitarian Intervention in Somalia*, Boulder, CO: Lynne Rienner.

Maley, W. (2000) 'Australia and the East Timor Crisis: Some Critical Comments', *Australian Journal of International Affairs*, 54(2): 151–61.

Mandelbaum, M. (2003) *The Ideas that Conquered the World: Peace, Democracy, and Free Markets in the Twenty-first Century*, Oxford: Public Affairs.

Marks, S. P. (1999) 'Elusive Justice for the Victims of the Khmer Rouge', *Journal of International Affairs*, 52(2): 691–718.

Martin, I. (2001) *Self-Determination in East Timor: The United Nations, the Ballot, and International Intervention*, Boulder, CO and London: Lynne Rienner.

Martin, I. and Mayer-Rieckh, M. (2005) 'The United Nations and East Timor: From Self-Determination to State-Building', *International Peacekeeping*, 12(1): 125–45, reprinted in M. Caballero-Anthony and A. Acharya (eds) (2005) *UN Peace Operations and Asian Security*, London: Routledge.

McCargo, D. (2005) 'Cambodia: Getting Away with Authoritarianism', *Journal of Democracy*, 16: 98–112.

McDougall, D. (2001) 'Regional Institutions and Security: Implications of the 1999 East Timor Crisis', in A. Tan and K. Boutin (eds) *Non-Traditional Security Issues in Southeast Asia*, Singapore: Select Publishing.

McKenzie, M. M. (2001) 'The UN and Regional Organizations', in E. Newman and O. Richmond (eds) *The United Nations and Human Security*, London: Palgrave/Macmillan.

McRae, R. and Hubert, D. (eds) (2001) *Human Security and the New Diplomacy: Protecting People, Promoting Peace*, Montreal and Kingston: McGill–Queen's University Press.

Mearsheimer, J. J. (1998a) 'The False Promise of International Institutions', in M. E. Brown, O. R. Coté Jr, S. M. Lynn-Jones and S. E. Miller (eds) *Theories of War and Peace: An International Security Reader*, Cambridge, MA: MIT Press.

—— (1998b) 'Back to the Future: Instability in Europe after the Cold War', in M. E. Brown, O. R. Coté Jr, S. M. Lynn-Jones and S. E. Miller (eds) *Theories of War and Peace: An International Security Reader*, Cambridge, MA: MIT Press.

—— (2001) *The Tragedy of Great Power Politics*, New York/London: W.W. Norton.

Mearsheimer, J. J. and Pape, R. (1993) 'The Answer: A Partisan Plan for Bosnia', *New Republic*, (14 June): 22–28.

Mearsheimer, J. J. and Van Evera, S. (1995) 'When Peace Means War', *New Republic*, (18 December): 16–21.

Miall, H., Ramsbotham, O. and Woodhouse, T. (1999) *Contemporary Conflict Resolution*, Oxford: Polity Press.

Michel, J. (2005) 'Human Security and Social Development: Comparative Research in Four Asian Countries', working paper for World Bank Conference 'New Frontiers of Social Policy: Development in a Globalizing World', 12–15 December, Arusha, Tanzania. http://siteresources. worldbank.org/INTRANETSOCIALDEVELOPMENT/Resources/Michel.rev.pdf

Miller, L. H. (2001) 'The Idea and the Reality of Collective Security', in P. F. Diehl (ed.) *The Politics of Global Governance: International Organizations in an Interdependent World*, Boulder, CO: Lynne Rienner.

Ministry of Economy and Finance, Kingdom of Cambodia (2006) 'A Lifelong Record of Outstanding and Visionary Leadership'. www.mef.gov.kh/Department/department.html

Ministry of Foreign Affairs, Government of China (2002) 'China's Position Paper on Cooperation in the Field of Non-Traditional Security Issues'. www.fmprc.gov.cn

—— (2003) 'China and the International Criminal Court'. www.fmprc.gov.cn/eng/wjb/ zzjg/tyfls/tyfl/2626/2627/t15473.htm

Ministry of Foreign Affairs and International Cooperation, Kingdom of Cambodia (2006) 'Hor Namhong Curriculum Vitae'. www.mfaic.gov.kh/mhor.php

Ministry of Foreign Affairs of Japan (1999a) 'Dispatch of Civilian Police Officers to the United Nations Mission in East Timor (UNAMET)'. www.mofa.go.jp/announce/ announce/1999/6/629.html

—— (1999b) 'Japan's Position in Regard to the East Timor Issue and the Possibility of Japan Participating in United Nations Peacekeeping Forces', Press Conference by the Press Secretary. www.mofa.go.jp/announce/press/1999/9/910.html#3

—— (1999c) *'Higashi Chimoru ni Tenkai suru Takokusekigun no tameno Shikin Kyoshutsu ni tsuite* [On Financial Support for the Multilateral Force Operating in East Timor]'. www.mofa.go.jp/mofaj/area/easttimor/kyoshutu.html

Mish, F. C. (ed.) (2003) *Merriam-Webster's Collegiate Dictionary*, 11th edn, Springfield, MA: Merriam-Webster.

Missiroli, A. (2006) 'Foreword' in J. Kotsopoulos, *A Human Security Agenda for the EU?* EPC Issue Paper 48, Brussels: European Policy Centre.

Mohanty, M. (2002) 'Humanitarian Intervention in an Unequal World – A View from Below', paper presented at the International Seminar on Humanitarian Intervention, Beijing, 27–28 August (unpublished).

Moller, K. (1998) 'Cambodia and Burma: The ASEAN Way Ends Here', *Asian Survey*, 38(12): 1087–104.

Monk, P. M. (2000) *A Slippery Slope to Complicity: Australian Policy on Portuguese Timor 1963–76 as Revealed by the National Archives*, Melbourne: Australian Thinking Skills Institute. www.austhink.org/monk/SLIPPERY.pdf

Morada, N. (2006) 'R2P Roadmap in Southeast Asia: Challenges and Prospects', *UNISCI Discussion Papers*, (11): 59–70. www.responsibilitytoprotect.org/index.php?module=u ploads&func=download&fileId=229

Morgenthau, H. (1993) *Politics Among Nations: The Struggle for Power and Peace*, New York: McGraw Hill.

Mouffe, C. (1992) *Dimensions of Radical Democracy: Pluralism, Citizenship, Community*, New York: Verso.

Moynihan, D. P. (1978) *A Dangerous Place*, Boston: Little, Brown.

Mussomeli, J. A. (2006) 'The Khmer Rouge Genocide and the Need for Justice'. http://cambodia.usembassy.gov/sp_032806.html

Nairn, A. (2000) 'US Support for the Indonesia Military: Congressional Testimony', *Bulletin of Concerned Asian Scholars*, 32(1/2): 43–48.

Narine, S. (1997) 'ASEAN and the ARF: The Limits of the "ASEAN Way" ', *Asian Survey*, 37(10): 961–78.

Nevins, J. (2002) 'The Making of "Ground Zero" in East Timor in 1999: an Analysis of International Complicity in Indonesia's Crimes', *Asian Survey*, 42(4): 623–41.

Newman, D. (1999–2000) 'A Human Security Council? Applying a "Human Security" Agenda to Security Council Reform', *Ottawa Law Review*, 31(2): 213–41.

Newman, E. and Richmond, O. (eds) (2006) *Challenges to Peacebuilding: Managing Spoilers during Conflict Resolution*, New York: United Nations University.

Newman, G. and Kopras, A. (1999) *Australia's Trade with Indonesia*, Parliament of Australia, Research Note 5 1999–2000. www.aph.gov.au/Library/Pubs/RN/1999–2000/2000rn05.htm

Nicolson, H. (1928) *Peacemaking 1919*, London: Constable & Co.

Noguchi, M. (2006) 'Criminal Justice in Asia and Japan and the International Criminal Court', *International Criminal Law Review*, 6: 585–604.

Nossal, K. R. (1999) 'Liberal–Democratic Regimes, International Sanctions and Global Governance', in R. Väyrynen (ed.) *Global Governance and Enforcement: Issues and Strategies*, Lanham, MD: Rowman & Littlefield.

Nye, J. S. (2003) *Understanding International Conflicts: An Introduction to Theory and History*, New York: Longman.

Obama, B. (2007) 'Renewing American Leadership', *Foreign Affairs*, (July/August): 2–16.

Obuchi, K. (1998a) 'Opening Remarks at a Meeting on "Intellectual Dialogue on Building Asia's Tomorrow", Tokyo, 2 December 1998', in *The Asian Crisis and Human Security* (1999), Tokyo: Japan Center for International Exchange.

—— (1998b) 'Toward the Creation of a Bright Future for Asia', speech at the Lecture Program hosted by the Institute for International Relations, Hanoi, Vietnam, 16 December. Tokyo: Ministry of Foreign Affairs of Japan, www.mofa.go.jp/region/asia-paci/asean/pmv9812/policyspeech.html

Ogata, S. and Cels, J. (2003) 'Human Security – Protecting and Empowering the People', *Global Governance*, 9(3): 273–82.

Ojendal, J. (1996) 'Democracy Lost? The Fate of the UN-implanted Democracy in Cambodia', *Contemporary Southeast Asia*, 18: 193–218.

Omura, K. (1986) *Indoneshia Seiji Doyo no Kozu* [The Structure of Political Instability of Indonesia], Tokyo: Yuhikaku.

Open Society Institute (2007) *Recent Developments at the Extraordinary Chambers in the Courts of Cambodia*, August Update, New York: Open Society Institute, www.soros.org/resources/articles_publications/publications/eccc_20070803

Ottaway, M. (2001) 'Corporatism Goes Global: International Organizations, Nongovernmental Organization Networks, and Transnational Business', *Global Governance*, 7: 265–92.

Ottaway, M. and Carothers, T. (2002) *Funding Virtue: Civil Society Aid and Democracy Promotion*, Washington, DC: Carnegie Endowment for International Peace.

Paris, R. (1997) 'Peacebuilding and the Limits of Liberal Internationalism', *International Security*, 22(2): 54–89.

—— (2001a) 'Echoes of the Mission *Civilisatrice*: Peacekeeping in the Post-Cold War Era', in E. Newman and O. Richmond (eds) *The United Nations and Human Security*, New York: St Martin's Press.

—— (2001b) 'Human Security: Paradigm Shift or Hot Air?', *International Security*, 26(2): 87–102.

Peck, J. and Tickell, A. (2002) 'Neoliberalizing space', *Antipode*, 34: 380–404.

Peou, S. (1997) *Conflict Neutralization in the Cambodia War: From Battlefield to Ballot-Box*, Kuala Lumpur, New York and Singapore: Oxford University Press.

—— (1998a) 'Cambodia in 1997: Back to Square One?', *Asian Survey*, 38: 69–74.

—— (1998b) 'Diplomatic Pragmatism: ASEAN's Response to the July 1997 Coup', in D. Hendrickson (ed.) *Safeguarding Peace: Cambodia's Constitutional Challenge, Accord: An International Review of Peace Initiatives*, London: Conciliation Resources.

—— (1998c) 'Hun Sen's Pre-emptive Coup: Causes and Consequences', *Southeast Asian Affairs*, 86–102.

—— (1998d) 'The Subsidiarity Model of Global Governance in the UN–ASEAN Context', *Global Governance*, 4: 439–59.

—— (2000) *Intervention and Change in Cambodia: Towards Democracy?* New York: St Martin's Press.

—— (2002a) 'The UN, Peacekeeping and Collective Human Security: From an Agenda for Peace to the Brahimi Report', in E. Newman and A. Schanabel (eds) *Recovering from Civil Conflict: Reconciliation, Peace and Development*, London: Frank Cass.

—— (2002b) 'Constructivism in Contemporary East-Asian Security Studies: Assessing its Strengths and Weaknesses', *Pacific Focus*, 17(2): 177–211.

—— (2005) 'Collaborative Human Security? The UN and other Actors in Cambodia', *International Peacekeeping*, 12(1): 105–24; reprinted in M. Caballero-Anthony and A. Acharya (eds) *UN Peace Operations and Asian Security*, London and New York: Routledge.

—— (2007) *International Democracy for Peacebuilding: Cambodia and Beyond*, New York: Palgrave Macmillan.

—— (2008a) 'Regional Security Communities: Theory, Practice, and Future Prospects for East Asia,' in A. S. P. Baviera (ed.) *Regional Security in East Asia: Challenges to Cooperation and Community Building*, Quezon City: University of the Philippines Asian Center.

—— (2008b) 'Security Community Building in Pacific Asia: Liberal Democratic Norms, Leadership, and Prospects', in W. Tow (ed.) *Re-envisioning Asia-Pacific Security: A Regional-Global Nexus?*, Cambridge: Cambridge University Press.

Pettman, R. (2005) 'Human Security as a Global Security: Reconceptualizing Strategic Studies', *Cambridge Review of International Affairs*, 18(1): 137–50.

Pinto, C. and Jardine, M. (1997) *East Timor's Unfinished Struggle: Inside the Timorese Resistance*, Boston, MA: South End Press.

Ponzio, R. (2005) 'Why Human Security is a New Concept with Global Origins', *Stair*, 1(2): 66–71.

Popovski, V. (2000) 'A Necessary Step towards Global Justice', *Security Dialogue*, 31(4): 405–19.

Posen, B. R. (1993) 'The Security Dilemma and Ethnic Conflict', *Survival*, 35(1): 27–47.

—— (2001) 'The Struggle Against Terrorism: Grand Strategy, Strategy and Tactics', *International Security*, 26(3): 39–55.

Pugh, M. (1995) 'Peacebuilding as Developmentalism: Concepts from Disaster Research', *Contemporary Security Policy*, 16(3): 320–46.

Railsback, K. (1989–90) 'A Genocide Convention Action against the Khmer Rouge: Preventing a Resurgence of the Killing Fields', *Connecticut Journal of International Law*, 5(457): 457–81.

Ramsbotham, O. and Woodhouse, T. (1996) *Humanitarian Intervention in Contemporary Conflict*, Cambridge: Polity Press.

Reisman, M. (1998) 'Stopping Wars and Making Peace: Reflections on the Ideology and Practice of Conflict Termination in Contemporary World Politics', *Tulane Journal of International and Comparative Law*, 6: 46–49.

Reno, W. (1995) *Corruption and State Politics in Sierra Leone*, New York: Cambridge University Press.

Richmond, O. (2003) 'Introduction: NGOs, Peace and Human Security', in H. F. Carey and O. P. Richmond (eds) *Mitigating Conflict: The Role of NGOs*, London: Frank Cass, p. 6.

—— (2005) *The Transformation of Peace*, London: Palgrave Macmillan.

Rieff, D. (1995) 'The Lessons of Bosnia: Morality and Power', *World Policy Journal*, 12(1): 76–88.

—— (2000) 'International Conference: Are Good Intentions Good Enough? The Limits of the New World of International Justice', *McGill Law Journal*, 46: 173–77.

—— (2002) *A Bed for the Night: Humanitarianism in Crisis*, London: Vintage.

Roberts, A. (1998) 'Implementation of the Laws of War in late 20th Century Conflicts: Part II', *Security Dialogue*, 29(3): 265–89.

Roberts, A. and Guelff, R. (eds) (2000), *Documents on the Law of War*, 3rd edn, Oxford: Oxford University Press.

Roberts, D. (2001) *Political Transition in Cambodia 1991–99: Power, Elitism and Democracy*, Richmond: Curzon Press.

Roht-Arriaza, N. (1999) 'Institutions of Justice', *Journal of International Affairs*, 52(2): 474–84.

Rothschild, E. (1995) 'What is Security?' *Daedalus*, 124(3): 53–98.

Rousseau, J. J. (1998 [1762]) *The Social Contract*, London: Wordsworth.

Rubin, A. R. (1999) 'Challenging the Conventional Wisdom: Another View of the International Criminal Court', *Journal of International Affairs*, 52(2): 783–94.

Ruggie, J. G. (2003) 'The United Nations and Globalization: Patterns and Limits of Institutional Adaptation', *Global Governance*, 9: 301–22.

Sachs, J. (2005) *The End of Poverty: Economic Possibilities for our Time*, New York: Penguin.

Sado, N. (2005) '*Higashi Timoru ni okeru Nichi ASEAN Kyoryoku* [Japan–ASEAN Cooperation in East Timor]', Report of the Japan Institute of International Affairs, 31 March. www2.jiia.or.jp/pdf/resarch/h16_east_timor/east_timor_sado.pdf

Salla, M. E. (1995) 'Australian Foreign Policy and East Timor', *Australian Journal of International Affairs*, 49(2): 207–22.

Samuel, T. (2003) 'East Timor: the path to self-determination', in C. L. Sriram and K. Wermester (eds) *From Promise to Practice: Strengthening UN Capacities for the Prevention of Violent Conflict*, Boulder, CO: Lynne Rienner.

Samuels, R. J. (2007) *Securing Japan: Tokyo's Grand Strategy and the Future of East Asia*, Ithaca/London: Cornell University Press.

Sanders, D. (2002) 'Behaviouralism', in D. Marsh and G. Stoker (eds), *Theory and Methods in Political Science*, New York: Palgrave Macmillan.

Sato, S. (1999) 'Kokubo ga Naze Anzenhosho ni Nattanoka [Why has defence shifted to security?]', *Gaiko Forum*, Special Issue: 5–6.

Scheiner, C. (2000) 'The United States: from complicity to ambiguity', in P. Hainsworth and S. McCloskey (eds) *The East Timor Question: The Struggle for Independence from Indonesia*, London and New York: I.B. Tauris.

Scholte, J. A. (2000) *Globalization*, London: Macmillan.

Schwartz, J. M. (1996) *The Permanence of the Political: A Democratic Critique of the Radical Impulse to Transcend Politics*, Princeton, NJ: Princeton University Press.

Schweller, R. (2000) 'US Democracy Promotion: Realist Reflections', in M. Cox, J. Ikenberry and T. Inoguchi (eds) *American Democracy Promotion: Impulses, Strategies, and Impacts*, New York: Oxford University Press.

Scott, J. C. (1995) *Weapons of the Weak: Everyday Forms of Peasant Resistance*, New Haven, CT: Yale University Press.

Sebastian, L. and Smith, A. L. (2000) *The East Timor Crisis: A Test Case for Humanitarian Intervention*, Southeast Asian Affairs 2000, Singapore: Institute of Southeast Asian Studies.

Sen, A. (1999), 'Human Rights and Economic Achievements', in J. R. Bauer and D. A. Bell (eds) *The East Asian Challenge for Human Rights*, Cambridge and New York: Cambridge University Press.

Senate Standing Committee on Foreign Affairs and Defense of Australia (1983) *The Human Rights and Conditions of the People of East Timor*, Canberra: Australian Government Publishing Service.

Severino, R. (2000) 'Sovereignty, Intervention and the ASEAN Way', address by the Secretary General at the ASEAN Scholars' Roundtable, Singapore, 3 July 2000.

Seymour, C. (1928) *The Intimate Papers of Colonel House*, Vol. 3, Boston: Houghton Mifflin, cited by D. Fromkin (1989) *A Peace to End All Peace*, London: Phoenix Press.

Shawcross, W. (2002) 'Cambodia and the Perils of Humanitarian Intervention' *Dissent*, Spring: 47–53.

Shinoda, H. and Uesugi, Y. (eds) (2005) *Funso to Ningen no Anzenhosho* [Conflict and Human Security], Tokyo: Kokusai Shoin.

Shuto, M. (2004) '*Higashi Timoru no Kokka Keisei to Funso Yobo no Kadai* [The Nation Building in East Timor and the Issues for Conflict Prevention]', in Heisei 15 nendo *Gaimusho Itaku Kenkyu 'Funso Yobo'*. www.jiia.or.jp/pdf/global_issues/h15_funsou-yobou/4_shutou.pdf

Sil, R. (2000a) 'The Foundations of Eclecticism: The Epistemological Status of Agency, Culture, and Structure in Social Theory', *Journal of Theoretical Politics*, 12(3): 353–87.

—— (2000b) 'Against Epistemological Absolutism: Towards a Pragmatic Center", in E. Sil and E. Doherty (eds), *Beyond Boundaries? Disciplines, Paradigms and Theoretical Integration in International Studies*, Albany: State University of New York Press.

Simpson, B. (2005) 'Illegally and Beautifully': The United States, the Indonesian Invasion of East Timor and the International Community, 1974–76', *Cold War History*, 5(3): 281–315.

Smith, M. G. and Dee, M. (2003) *Peacekeeping in East Timor: The Path to Independence*, Boulder, CO and London: Lynne Rienner.

Smith, S. (1991) 'Mature Anarchy, Strong States and Security', *Arms Control*, 12(2): 325–39.

Smith, T. W. (2002) 'Moral Hazard and Humanitarian Law: The International Criminal Court and the Limits of Legalism', *International Politics*, 39: 175–92.

Snyder, C. A. (2006) 'Southeast Asian Perceptions of Australia's Foreign Policy', *Contemporary Southeast Asia*, 28(2): 322–40.

Snyder, J. and Vinjamuri, L. (2003/04) 'Trials and Errors: Principle and Pragmatism in Strategies of International Justice', *International Security*, 28: 5–44.

Song, Y. (2002) 'The Concepts of Human Security and Non-Traditional Security: A Comparison', paper presented at the Human Security Conference, Taipei, 16 December (unpublished).

Soros, G. (1998) *The Crisis of Global Capitalism: Open Society Endangered*, 1st edn, New York: Public Affairs.

Springer, S. (2008) 'The Nonillusory Effects of Neoliberalisation: Linking Geographies of Poverty, Inequality, and Violence', *Geoforum*.

—— (2009) 'Violence, Democracy, and the Neoliberal 'Order': The Contestation of Public Space in Post-transitional Cambodia', *Annals of the American Association of Geographers*, 98 (4).

St John, R. B. (1995) 'The Political Economy of the Royal Government of Cambodia', *Contemporary Southeast Asia*, 17: 265–81.

—— (1997) 'End of the Beginning: Economic Reform in Cambodia, Laos, and Vietnam', *Contemporary Southeast Asia*, 19: 172–89.

Stares, P. B. (ed.) (1998) *The New Security Agenda: A Global Survey*, Tokyo and New York: Japan Center for International Exchange.

Sucharithanarugse, W. (2000) 'The Concept of "Human Security" Extended: "Asianizing" the Paradigm', in W. T. Tow, R. Thakur and I. Hyun (eds) *Asia's Emerging Regional Order*, Tokyo: United Nations University.

Tadjbakhsh, S. (2005) 'Human Security: Concepts and Implications', *Les Etudes du CERI*, 117–18: 1–29.

Tadjbakhsh, S. and Chenoy, A (2007) *Human Security: Concepts and Implications*, London/New York: Routledge.

Tan, A. and Boutin, K. (eds) (2001) *Non-Traditional Security Issues in Southeast Asia*, Singapore: Select Publishing.

Tan, S. (2002) 'Is Public Space Suited to Co-Operative Inquiry?', *Innovation*, 15: 23–31.

Tayler, J. (1991) *Indonesia's Forgotten War: The Hidden History of East Timor*, London: Zed Books.

Terry, F. (2002) *Condemned to Repeat? The Paradox of Humanitarian Action*, Ithaca, NY: Cornell University Press.

Thakur, R. (1994) 'From Peacekeeping to Peace Enforcement: The UN Operation in Somalia', *Journal of Modern African Studies*, 32: 387–410.

—— (2003) 'Intervention Could Bring Safeguards to Asia', *Daily Yomiuri*, 14 May.

—— (2006) *The United Nations, Peace and Security: From Collective Security to the Responsibility to Protect*, New York: Cambridge University Press.

Thambipillai, P. (1985) 'ASEAN Negotiating Styles: asset or hindrance?' in P. Thambipillai and J. Saravanamuttu (eds) *ASEAN Negotiations: Two Insights*, Singapore: Institute of Southeast Asian Studies.

Thiparat, P. (ed) (2001) *The Quest for Human Security: The Next Phase of ASEAN?* Bangkok: Institute of Security and International Studies.

Thomas, C. (2000) *Global Governance, Development, and Human Security: The Challenge of Poverty and Inequality*, London: Pluto.

Thomas, C. and Wilkin, P. (1999) (eds) *Globalization, Human Security and the African Experience*, Boulder, CO: Lynne Rienner.

Thomas, N. and Tow, W. (2002a) 'The Utility of Human Security: Sovereignty and Humanitarian Intervention', *Security Dialogue*, 33(2): 177–92

—— (2002b) 'Gaining Security by Trashing the State? A Reply to Bellamy and McDonald', *Security Dialogue*, 33(3): 379–82.

Thomas, R. G. C. (ed.) (2003) *Yugoslavia Unravelled: Sovereignty, Self-Determination, and Intervention*, Lanham, MD: Lexington Books.

Tiffen, R. (2001) *Diplomatic Deceits: Government, Media and East Timor*, Sydney: University of New South Wales Press.

Toon, V. (2004) 'International Criminal Court: Reservations of Non-State Parties in Southeast Asia', *Contemporary Southeast Asia*, 26: 218–26.

Tostensen, A. and Bull, B. (2002) 'Are Smart Sanctions Feasible', *World Politics*, 54: 373–403.

Tow, W. T. (2000) 'Introduction', in W. T. Tow, R. Thakur and I. Hyun (eds) *Asia's Emerging Regional Order: Reconciling Traditional and Human Security*, Tokyo: United Nations Press.

Tow, W. T. and Trood, R. (2000) 'Linkages between Traditional Security and Human Security', in W. T. Tow, R. Thakur and I. Hyun (eds) *Asia's Emerging Regional Order: Reconciling Traditional and Human Security*, Tokyo: United Nations University Press.

Tow, W. T., Thakur, R. and Hyun, I. (eds) (2000) *Asia's Emerging Regional Order: Reconciling Traditional and Human Security*, Tokyo: United Nations University Press.

Tucker, R. (2001) 'The International Criminal Court Controversy', *World Policy Journal*, 18(2): 71–82.

Um, K. (1990) 'Cambodia in 1989: Still Talking but No Settlement', *Asian Survey*, 30: 96–104.

—— (1994) 'Cambodia in 1993: Year Zero Plus One', *Asian Survey*, 34 (1): 72–81.

UNDP (1994) *Human Development Report: New Dimensions of Human Security*, New York: Oxford University Press.

—— (1999) *Human Development Report: Globalization with a Human Face*, New York: Oxford University Press.

—— (2002) *Human Development Report 2002*, New York/Oxford: Oxford University Press.

United Nations (1999) *Report of the Group of Experts for Cambodia Pursuant to General Assembly Resolution 52/135*, www1.umn.edu/humanrts/cambodia-1999.html

—— (2004) *A More Secure World: Our Shared Responsibility*, Report of the Secretary-General's High-level Panel on Threats, Challenges and Change, New York: United Nations Foundation, www.un.org/secureworld

United Nations Department of Public Information (2002) *East Timor – UNTAET Background*, New York: United Nations, www.un.org/peace/etimor/UntaetB.htm

UN Secretary-General's High Level Panel on Threats, Challenges and Change (2004) *A More Secure World: Our Shared Responsibility*, United Nations Foundation, New York.

United States Census Bureau (2007) *International Data Base*. www.census.gov/ipc/www/idb

Urquhart, B. E. (1983) 'Peacekeeping: A View from the Operational Center', in H. Wiseman *Peacekeeping: Appraisals and Proposals*, New York: Pergamon.

Van Evera, S. (1998) 'Offense, Defense, and the Causes of War', in M. E. Brown, O. R. Coté Jr, S. M. Lynn-Jones and S. E. Miller (eds) *Theories of War and Peace: An International Security Reader*, Cambridge, MA and London: MIT Press.

Vickery, M. (2007) *Cambodia: A Political Survey*, Phnom Penh: Editions Funan.

Vincent, R. J. (1974) *Nonintervention and International Order*, Princeton, NJ: Princeton University Press.

—— (1987) *Human Rights and International Relations*, Cambridge: Cambridge University Press.

Walt, S. M. (1991) 'The Renaissance of Security Studies', *International Studies Quarterly*, 35: 211–39.

—— (2001/02) 'Beyond bin Laden: Reshaping US Foreign Policy', *International Security*, 26(3): 56–78.

Walton, D. (2004) 'Japan and East Timor: Implications for the Australia–Japan Relationship', *Japanese Studies*, 24(2): 233–46.

Waltz, K. N. (2000) 'Structural Realism after the Cold War', *International Security*, 25(1): 5–41.

Walzer, M. (1996) *Just and Unjust Wars, A Moral Argument with Historical Illustration*, New York: Basic Books.

Wang, Y. (2006) 'China Facing Non-Traditional Security: A Report on Capacity Building', in R. Emmers, M. C. Anthony and A. Acharya (eds) *Studying Non-Traditional Security in Asia: Trends and Issues*, Singapore: Marshall Cavendish Academic.

Washburn, J. L. (1996) 'United Nations Relations with the United States: The UN Must Look Out for Itself', *Global Governance*, 2(1): 81–96.

Watanabe, K. (2003) *Humanitarian Intervention: The Evolving Asian Debate*, Tokyo: Centre for International Exchange.

Watanabe, T. (1999) '*Higashi Timoru Dokuritsu to Indonesia Josei* [East Timor's Independence and the Situation in Indonesia]', *Ajia Jiho*.

Watt, F. (1998) *An Independent and Effective International Criminal Court*, Ottawa: World Federalists of Canada. www.worldfederalistscanada.org/icceffective.html

Wedgwood, R. (1999) 'The International Criminal Court: An American View', *European Journal of International Law*, 10(6): 93–107.

Weiss, T. G. (2004) 'The Sunset of Humanitarian Intervention? The Responsibility to Protect in a Unipolar Era', *Security Dialogue*, 35(2): 135–53.

Weiss, T. G., Cortright, D., Lopez, G. A. and Minear, L. (1997) *Political Gain and Civilian Pain: Humanitarian Impacts of Economic Sanctions*, Lanham, MD: Rowman & Littlefield.

Welsh, J. M. (2002) 'From Right to Responsibility: Humanitarian Intervention and International Society', *Global Governance*, 8: 503–21.

Wesley, M. (1995) 'The Cambodian Waltz: The Khmer Rouge and United Nations Intervention', *Terrorism and Political Violence*, London: Frank Cass.

Wheeler, N. J. (2000) *Saving Strangers: Humanitarian Intervention in International Society*, Oxford: Oxford University Press.

Wheeler, N. J. and Bellamy, A. J. (2001) 'Humanitarian Intervention and World Politics', in J. Baylis and S. Smith (eds) *The Globalization of World Politics: An Introduction to International Relations*, Oxford: Oxford University Press.

Wheeler, N. J. and Dunne, T. (2001) 'East Timor and the New Humanitarian Interventionism', *International Affairs*, 77(4): 805–27.

Wheeler, N. J. and Morris, J. (1996) 'Humanitarian Intervention and State Practices at the End of the Cold War', in R. Fawn and J. Larkins (eds) *International Society after the Cold War: Anarchy and Order Reconsidered*, Houndsmill: Macmillan.

White, N. D. (2002) *The United Nations System: Toward International Justice*, Boulder, CO and London: Lynne Rienner.

Willetts, P. (2000) 'From 'Consultative Arrangements' to 'Partnership': The Changing Status of NGOs in Diplomacy at the UN', *Global Governance*, 6: 191–212.

Williams, A. (1998) *Failed Imagination? New World Orders*, Manchester: Manchester University Press.

Williamson, J. (1999) 'What Should the Bank Think about the Washington Consensus?' paper prepared as a background to the World Bank's World Development Report 2000, Washington, DC: World Bank.

Wippman, D. (1999–2000) 'Atrocities, Deterrence, and the Limits of International Justice', *Fordham International Law Journal*, 23(473): 473–88.

Wolfers, A. (1962) *Discord and Collaboration: Essays on International Politics*, Baltimore, MD: Johns Hopkins University Press.

World Bank (2004) 'Steering a Steady Course: Strengthening the Investment Climate in East Asia', *East Asia Update*, November, Washington, DC: World Bank.

Yacoubian, G. (1999) 'The Efficacy of International Criminal Justice', *World Affairs*, 161(1): 186–92.

Young, N. (1987) 'Peace Movements in History', in S. Mendlovitz and R. B. J. Walker (eds) *Towards a Just World Peace*, London: Butterworths.

Zhang Y. (ed.) (2001) *Stability and Security of Socio-Economic Development in East Asia*, Beijing: China Social Sciences Press.

Ziauddin, A. (2001) 'A Continent in Need of the ICC – International Criminal Court Campaigns in Asia', *International Criminal Court Monitor* 19 (December): 6,15.

Zwanenburg, M. (1999) 'The Statute for an International Criminal Court and the United States: Peacekeepers under Fire?' *European Journal of International Law*, 10(1): 124–43.

Index

For Product Safety Concerns and Information please contact our EU
representative GPSR@taylorandfrancis.com
Taylor & Francis Verlag GmbH, Kaufingerstraße 24, 80331 München, Germany

www.ingramcontent.com/pod-product-compliance
Lightning Source LLC
Chambersburg PA
CBHW050438280326
41932CB00013BA/2165